TIME ZONES

JOE SCHLESINGER

TIME ZONES

A JOURNALIST IN THE WORLD

Random House
Toronto

Published in Canada in 1990 by Random House of Canada Limited, Toronto.

∞ This book is printed on acid–free paper.

Canadian Cataloguing in Publication Data

Schlesinger, Joe
Time zones

ISBN 0–394–22148–6

1. Schlesinger, Joe. 2. Foreign correspondents –
Canada – Biography. 3. Journalists – Canada –
Biography. 4. Czech Canadians – Biography.
I. Title.

PN4913.S34A3 1990   070.4'332'092   C90–094332–7

JACKET DESIGN: David Wyman
JACKET PHOTOGRAPH: Yuri Dojc

Printed and bound in the United States

The permissions notices which appear on page vi constitute an extension of this copyright page.

To the memory of my parents,
Lilli and Emmanuel Schlesinger,
who through their sacrifice and in agony
gave me life a second time

PREFACE

There is no escaping my time . . .
I am an imprint of these lands;
and one way or another they have absorbed my weathers.

Gabriel Preil
Sunset Possibilities

It was June 6, 1944. I got up as usual in time to catch the 6
A.M. BBC news that was broadcast at dictation speed to His
Majesty's ships at sea. Just as British ship radio operators
would transcribe the newscast and post it on mess bulletin
boards, so would I type it and pin it on the notice board of
the dining room of my boarding school in Wales in time for
the other students to read as they came down to breakfast.

That morning's news of the progress of World War II was
full of reports of action along the English Channel. British
torpedo boats had engaged German E-boats. There had been
air battles over France. After listening to the broadcast, I did
something I had never done before. I went beyond what I had
heard on the radio and started my report with a conclusion of
my own: "It seems the Second Front has started."

The Second Front was the long-awaited Allied invasion of
France that was to take the pressure off the First Front in

eastern Europe, where the Russians were battling the Germans.

As people started coming down to breakfast and read my bulletin, they scoffed that I must have been asleep and dreaming when I wrote it. The eight o'clock news and still no word of an invasion. In class, I took more razzing.

But then, sometime before ten, the word spread. The BBC broke in with a communiqué from General Dwight Eisenhower, the supreme commander of the Allied expeditionary forces: "Allied naval forces, supported by strong air forces, began landing Allied armies this morning on the northern coast of France."

It was D-Day on the beaches of Normandy. At age sixteen, I had my first scoop, a world scoop on history being made. Unfortunately, the only people who knew about it were some kids and teachers at a school in the remoteness of central Wales.

I didn't know then that D-Day would mark the start of a life career. I was editor of the school news bulletin not because I was endowed with literary talent or imbued with journalistic ambition, but precisely because I was not. My more talented classmates wrote poetry and scintillating articles for the school magazine, strummed romantic tunes on guitars, played on the school soccer team. I did not. Getting up in the morning before anyone else and laboriously pecking out the words of others on a typewriter seemed the only way open to me to achieve some distinction that might attract the attention of girls the way the accomplishments of the poets, the soccer players, the fancy dancers and the guitar players did. It did not.

Though I had no ambition to become a journalist, I was intensely interested in the news for personal reasons. The war had a direct impact on me. I was a refugee from Nazi-occupied Europe. And news, mostly threatening news that could not be ignored, had been with me since my earliest memories.

"In a dark time, the eye begins to see," says a poem by Theodore Roethke. My childhood was dominated by a dark time — the rise of Adolf Hitler — and that forced my eye to begin to see at an early age. Throughout my early years, I watched as the Germans kept coming closer and closer to my family home in Czechoslovakia until, in March 1939, they occupied the country. A few weeks before the war broke out, my parents managed to send my younger brother and me to relatives in Britain for safety while they stayed behind. So the end of the war meant returning home to rejoin my parents. Once Hitler was defeated and peace had returned, news would lose its life-and-death importance.

It wasn't to work out that way. By the time I returned to Czechoslovakia in the summer of 1945, it was clear that my parents had not survived the war. They had not been heard from since March 1942, when they were deported from Slovakia by the Germans and their puppet Slovak allies. Even now the best information available is only that they probably were shipped to Lublin in Poland and that the Jews from Slovakia who survived the hardships of the Lublin ghetto were then transferred to Auschwitz. Surviving in Auschwitz for a few weeks, a few months even, was barely possible; the chances of a middle-aged couple surviving there for nearly three years were nil.

But there was little time for mourning that first summer after the war. Millions had been killed, but the accounting at war crimes trials and the reflections on the meaning of what had happened were yet to come. All that seemed to matter those first few months after the war was that it was over, that peace was at hand.

War is so overpowering, so pervasive that it tends to sweep everything aside, problems as well as dreams and hopes. In wartime, the idea of peace attains magical qualities. It is seen not just as an end of war, an absence of fighting; it is embraced as a beginning of a new life better than anything that went before. During the war, it seemed to most people on the Allied side that once the fighting was over, once Hitler was dead, anything would become possible. And most of the young who, like me, knew little else but the war believed that having gone through the bloodletting, the winners would recognize the futility and dangers of petty nationalistic and ideological feuding; that a new sense of justice would be brought to the social and economic order; that having gone through the nightmare of the Nazis' Übermensch fantasies, the world would discard all traces of racism; that there would be no more of the economic folly that brought on the Great Depression. The hopes of peace, a real peace, shone brightly for many of us that summer of 1945. But only briefly.

Peace did not bring tranquillity to Europe. The initial euphoria of victory quickly evaporated into a new conflict, the Cold War between East and West. For most people in the West, the Cold War may have been vaguely threatening but it was a distant and abstract affair. In Czechoslovakia, the threat was palpable. News again became something that could not be ignored. As Hitler had done in the thirties, now Joseph Stalin was steadily coming closer. In 1948, the communists took over Czechoslovakia and the country was once more totally under foreign control. In the paranoid terror that was Stalinism, the news suddenly stopped.

In relatively sane and benign societies, news may be interesting, useful and even important. But in societies run by dictators — particularly mad ones like Stalin — news is more than just important. News as true reports of what is happening, as opposed to news as propaganda, is an essential tool for survival. One day, a thousand flowers of opinion may be allowed to bloom; the next, not a petal is left. You need to know what you can say and to whom without blighting your career or being arrested. It might also pay to know in time that the party line on, let's say, friendship with Yugoslavia is about to change before you are seen having lunch with that nice Yugoslav student you met at a party. In the shortages of goods endemic to such regimes you could also use consumer information to let you know, for example, when toilet paper might next become available in the stores. (A shortage of toilet paper raised the value of copies of the Communist Party's official newspaper.) You may even need to know what to wear, as they did in China during Mao Tse-tung's Great Cultural Revolution in the late sixties when all of a sudden the blue cotton Mao suits, along with badges displaying the moon-faced image of the Great Helmsman himself, became the mandatory uniform for every man, woman and child.

Wearing a business suit or a skirt would have been a dangerous political act of defiance.

Yet as this practical need for political information becomes indispensable for everyday living in totalitarian societies in much the same way we use weather reports to tell us whether to take a raincoat, the news dries up. Most of what passes for news in the regime's media — the panegyrics to the party and its leaders, the reports of industrial production targets exceeded, the boasts of bountiful harvests, much of which somehow never show up on the table — is irrelevant.

My need for information about what was going on was particularly pressing because I was among the damned of the Communist regime. I was damned because I came from a "bourgeois" background and I was even more seriously suspect because I had been educated in the West, because I had relatives in the West and none in Czechoslovakia to be used as hostages to my good behavior. As Stalin's paranoia got worse and the terror escalated, it also became evident that, even if these other strikes against me had not existed, I was irrevocably damned because I am a Jew. (As it turned out, even being a communist in good standing was not enough protection for Jews in Stalinist Czechoslovakia. Shortly after I left the country, the party arrested the Jews in its leadership, including its secretary-general, Rudolf Slanský, and hanged most of them.)

By the end of 1948 it was obvious that it was time to leave, time to become a refugee once more. But that required information, access to that scarcest of commodities: relevant and reliable news, information about how to get out of the country. To get it, I started cultivating journalists working for Western news agencies. That led to a job as a translator in one of the few places in Prague where information was still relatively freely available, the bureau of the American news agency, the Associated Press. Inevitably, it also led to reporting.

I came to journalism, then, somewhat in the same way as an alcoholic may turn to bartending or pub-keeping — it gets him close to a regular supply of what he needs most. It wasn't that I couldn't leave the news alone; it was the news that wouldn't leave me alone.

In the first two decades of my life, I was battered by history as a victim and a survivor. Since then, I have had the luxury of witnessing it from the privileged position of a foreign correspondent. For nearly thirty years, I have reported on the problems, crises, tragedies and wars of others.

The experiences of my youth were good training for my trade. They taught me to recognize the signs of political dissolution, to feel the fear and pain of the persecuted and the panic of the threatened, to decipher the bombast of demagogues, to understand the feeling of abandonment when your country is threatened and the outside world doesn't care, to realize that people fear change — even change for the better — because they are afraid of the unknown much as children are scared by darkness. There is also, I discovered, the obverse, the atavistic urge to carry on, to minimize and ignore misfortune, to behave as if nothing were happening as everything around you crumbles, as though things were normal even as the fabric of life is unravelling. Above all, though, I learned how the urge to survive sharpens all senses in the way the blind develop their senses of hearing and touch.

When I saw Vietnamese refugees fleeing bombarded towns, I knew what it felt like to be driven by the dread of the known into the fear of the unknown. When a crowd, angered by Argentina's defeat in its war with Britain over the Falkland Islands, chased me down the street in Buenos Aires because I spoke English, I understood their rage even though I did not sympathize with their cause and didn't like being chased. When I stood in St. Peter's Square in the Vatican and heard the announcement that Karol Cardinal Wojtyla had been chosen to be pope, I did not have to talk to a Pole to know the exultation of national vindication every Pole was feeling and what an epochal event it was for Poland.

When Mikhail Gorbachev came up with *glasnost* and his plans for economic reform, I could imagine what was going through the minds of the Soviet people: the first hesitant little skip of hope in the heart; the calculations of the cautious of how far to dare; the eagerness of the daring to test the limits, to extend them, and if not stopped, to breach them; the nervousness of the complacent elite that their cocoon of privileges might burst; the anxiety that comes to those used to closed doors when the door opens a crack and no one knows whether it will open further or snap shut, or what dangers lurk outside it. Similarly, I was not surprised how quickly the fires of freedom were doused in China, how even some of the most daring retreated from noisy exuberance to a silent sullenness once the door was violently slammed shut in Tiananmen Square. I had experienced that sudden onset of desperation when hopelessness, helplessness and fear grip the chest like a vise.

Luckily, it can work just as quickly the other way. It did in 1989 in Berlin and Budapest, in Warsaw and Bucharest. And in Prague. Forty years after I left Czechoslovakia, I was back to watch with amazement as the structures of repression that had driven me out, the mechanisms of intimidation that had been so carefully built up over the decades, unravelled in days. It was a joyful experience I thought I would never live to see. Here I was in my sixties, when I thought I had seen just about everything, filled once again with wonder about the resilience of the human spirit, still learning that the human condition never stands still.

Learning. That has been the greatest joy of being a journalist. Always learning, always discovering something new. The lesson that helped me most as a reporter — a lesson every journalist must learn, a lesson I was fortunate to learn when I was young — is that today's news is hardly ever just made today. Except for freak accidents, it always goes back to something that happened days, years or even centuries ago. History becomes news, and news becomes history.

History is time. History is people. History is place. History is not only then; it is also now. The powerful write history; the powerless suffer it. History hurts.

"In this world without quiet corners," Salman Rushdie wrote years before Ayatollah Khomeini put a price on his head, "there can be no easy escapes from history, from hullabaloo, from terrible, unquiet fuss."

I have suffered and survived some of the great hurts of that "terrible, unquiet fuss" of history and witnessed many others. The greatest hurts of this century — Hitler and Stalin — have to a great extent made me what I am. For most of my life in the many places I have lived and worked, I could say as King David sang in the Psalms: "I am a stranger with thee and a sojourner."

What has been most rewarding for me as a lifelong sojourner in many parts of the world has been to be able to compare people and places, how they are different and, even more, the difficult and often unanswerable question of why.

The difference between a Russian Marxist and a Chinese one has not much to do with anything Karl Marx would have recognized as part of his teachings; it is rooted in Russian and Chinese history.

If you want to know why the Japanese eat raw fish and the Chinese cut food into little bits and then quickly stir-fry it, look to their fuel supply. If they had had enough wood to burn, they, too, might have had the stews and baked bread of a heavily forested Europe.

If you want to go back to the roots of the conflicts in Central America, take a look at the mating habits of the conquistadors. If the Spaniards had brought women with them the way the French did to Canada or the Pilgrim Fathers to Plymouth Rock, El Salvador might still have had grave problems but they would have been vastly different problems. But then if Henry VIII had not been so intent on fathering a son, the England of today might also have been radically different.

To understand Iran, go back to the words of Mihyar al-Daylami, a Persian poet who 900 years ago wrote: "I base my pride on the majesty of the Persians and the religion of the Arabs." The last thousand years of Iranian history have been driven by the split in the Iranian psyche between Persian nationalism and Islamic fervor.

If you want to know how the Czechs coped with the dead hand of communism, read Jaroslav Hašek's *The Good Soldier Švejk*, a chronicle of surviving the idiocies of authoritarian government with *sancta simplicitas*, the holy simplicity of morons, by combining humor and cunning, guileless deference to force with a subtle defiance of obtuse petty bureaucrats.

What I learned as a reporter helped me to understand my

own past and come to terms with it. I came to see that although the scale and the means of the horror that killed my parents were unique, all horror is unique to those who suffer it and that nothing, not even the Final Solution, is final.

This book is written from the two contrasting and yet complementary perspectives of my life: of the child and youth wandering naïvely through some of the greatest tragedies of our time and surviving, and of the peripatetic reporter, armed though he was with professional scepticism and protective layers of dispassion, coming to learn that, despite all the miseries of our age, there is hope.

"A book," Franz Kafka wrote, "must be the axe for the frozen sea within us." For me, this book has been that axe.

CHAPTER I

Run rabbit, run rabbit, run, run, run.
Here comes the Hun with a gun, gun, gun.
If he catches you, he will make a stew.
So run rabbit, run rabbit, run, run, run.

British World War II song

The last time I saw my father we spent the night in the washroom of a small railway station in Nazi Germany. We sat
on a wooden bench next to the tar-coated urinal while my
younger brother, Ernie, slept beside us. We were waiting for
a train and had taken shelter in the toilet because, as Jews, we
weren't allowed into the waiting room.

Neither the smell of the urinal nor the indignity of having
been herded into the washroom bothered me. I was too excited. I was on my way to England, to a new country, a new
language, a new life and I was full of questions — about my
cousins in England, about the ship that would take us across
the English Channel, about how I could make sure that Ernie
and I ended up in Newcastle-on-Tyne, where our uncles lived,
and not in Newcastle-under-Lyme or any of the other half
dozen Newcastles I had found in the atlas at home.

1

My father was wide awake for a different reason. In a few hours he was going to send his children away, not knowing when or whether he would ever see them again. The pain he must have felt then, the pain my mother felt earlier that day as she said goodbye to her sons, the pain they must have felt for the three years of life left to them haunts me still. And so does my babbling incomprehension of that long ago night.

It was June 30, 1939. World War II was only two months away, and I was eleven years old.

Even at eleven, though, I couldn't help but be aware that the world around me was collapsing. I had heard Adolf Hitler's voice on the radio often enough. He was hard to understand, sometimes because of the crackling on the radio, at times because he used words I didn't know, but mostly because he would work himself up until he screamed so hard it all came out as just a roar of rage. But the words didn't really matter; there was no mistaking the hate whether it came wrapped in bellows of anger or in softly spoken sarcasm.

I had heard the hate first aimed at Austria, and Austria had disappeared, gobbled up by Hitler's Third Reich. I had heard it aimed at my country, Czechoslovakia, and Czechoslovakia had been dismembered. Now there were new threats, this time against Poland, and the Poles were about to suffer. But beyond this, I knew that above all Hitler's hate was aimed at Jews, at me and everyone I loved.

What I experienced as a child, I have witnessed again as an adult happening to others, in varied forms, under different circumstances, in many parts of the world.

I have come to recognize some of the signs of the madness that leads to tragedies on a grand scale. Old grievances are resurrected and refurbished with new intensity. Ancient injustices are insufferably aggravated. Politics are elevated to religion. Religion is mired in politics. Nationalism is degraded by ideologies of exclusivity, racial superiority and supremacy. There are always scoundrels — demagogues and megalomaniacs posing as prophets and saviors — ready to light the match. And behind them, an army of self-righteous fanatics, self-serving bureaucrats and opportunistic sycophants willing to feed the flames.

It is different every time. Yet it always starts the same way: with the loss of civility, reason and tolerance.

I still remember civility and tolerance in Bratislava, the home town of my childhood. The street signs were in three languages — Slovak, German and Hungarian. The city even had a different name in each of these languages: Bratislava in Slovak and Czech, Pressburg in German, Pozsony in Hungarian.

Bratislava was the capital of Slovakia and very much a border town. Austria and Hungary lay just beyond a sliver of land on the other side of the Danube from the city. Vienna was a short ride away.

Though my parents lived in Bratislava, I was born in Vienna, a fact that seemed neither here nor there. Bratislava was very much in Vienna's cultural orbit: the same coffee with whipped cream in its cafés, the same *fin de siècle* architecture of imperial pretensions and the same laid-back habits of Austrian *Gemütlichkeit*. Budapest was the counterbalance to Vienna's influence, a dash of paprika, of wine and gypsy music.

My father was educated in Budapest. My mother was born in Prague but was raised in Dresden, in Germany. It all seemed part of one world, Mitteleuropa, which meant more than just a geographic term for the centre of Europe. It was a term for a multicultural, polyglot society that crossed political borders, a world in which people changed from one language to another with ease. I spoke Slovak and German. I had picked up Czech from a Moravian maid my mother had. I could understand Hungarian, but my spoken Hungarian was confined to the fringes of the language. On the one hand, I had picked up swearwords on the street; on the other, I knew the basics of polite chit-chat, such as greeting my mother's Hungarian women friends with a proper "*kezet sokolom*" (I kiss your hand).

It was a pleasant world. We lived in the centre of town, beneath the castle that dominates Bratislava. The city has been there for 1,000 years. Long before that, in the first century, it had been a part of the "limes," the line of fortifications that marked the borders of the Roman Empire. For more than two centuries it had been the capital of Hungary. Hungarian kings were crowned in its cathedral and the Hungarian parliament sat there until 1848. In 1805, after Napoleon defeated the combined Austrian and Russian armies at Austerlitz, he sent his foreign minister, Talleyrand, the only man in his entourage more famous than his marshals, to nearby Bratislava to make peace. There, in the Hall of Mirrors, Talleyrand and the defeated Emperor Francis I of Austria signed the Peace Treaty of Pressbourg — the French name for Bratislava — under which the Hapsburg emperor gave up the last tatters of his family's claim to the once resplendent title of Holy Roman Emperor. Many of Bratislava's buildings were from the fourteenth and fifteenth centuries. The architecture stretched from Gothic and Renaissance through Baroque to the city's modernistic pride: a skyscraper all of twelve storeys high.

Life was slow and easy. My father would come home for lunch and afterwards he would take a siesta or go over to a café to play chess, read newspapers, or argue politics with friends.

My father was the owner of the Bratislava Petroleum Market, a store that sold cleaning products from floor-scrubbing soap to perfumed face lotions. The "petroleum" in the name of the store went back to his father, who had started the business in 1884 selling kerosene and lamp fuel. My grandfather recruited students and equipped them with harnesses with hooks on which they hung the cans of lamp oil they sold door-to-door. (Three-quarters of a century later, in an updated communist revision of the nineteenth-century history of the city, my grandfather would be excoriated as the "Petroleum King of Bratislava" who exploited student labor.)

With the arrival of coal gas and then electricity, the lamp oil business disappeared. But the automobile came along and my grandfather switched to selling gasoline. The hand-operated gasoline pump at the curb in front of the store is one of my earliest memories. As the oil companies built refineries in Bratislava and organized their own distribution system, the pump disappeared and my father concentrated on cleaning materials.

Some of the products he carried were marked with his own trademark. It showed two black men, wearing only grass hula skirts. One stood bent over while the other scrubbed his backside. With the arduous application of Schlesinger soap, the man's posterior had turned white. You couldn't see the color contrast in the rendition embossed on soap bars, of course, but it was there in color on the life-size mannequin cut-outs of the two in the store window. To make the point clear, an electric motor kept the scrubbing hand brushing back and forth all day long, weekends and holidays excepted.

Even though central Europe had always been race conscious and was at the time convulsed by racism and extremist nationalism, no one objected to my father's trademark as being offensive. The differences between Slav and German, between Magyar and gypsy, between Jew and gentile were sensitive matters. It would have been unpardonable to mistake a Hungarian fiddler for a gypsy, or to presume that a German name made one German or a Magyar one Hungarian.

But no such sensitivity was necessary in dealing with blacks because there were no blacks in Bratislava. Most people had seen blacks only in films. The blacks people did know about were admired. There was Jesse Owens, the American sprinter, who had embarrassed Hitler at the 1936 Olympics in Berlin by winning four gold medals. I remember the joy when heavyweight boxing champion Joe Louis defeated the German Max Schmeling in 1938. It kept my father, who didn't know or care anything about boxing, chuckling for days.

But by then civility was all but gone. Something that at first was happening only in Germany had come to our doorstep. Hitler had occupied Austria and had come home to Vienna in March of 1938, and his troops were now just across the river from Bratislava.

The threatening noises no longer came just from Germany. They could also be heard in Czechoslovakia, preparing to tear the country apart from inside. There was growing support for Hitler from the German minority of Czechoslovakia, the Sudeten Germans. They manoeuvred and plotted with Berlin, marched and chanted to be delivered from Prague's rule.

Lieber Führer/ Dear Führer
mach uns frei/ make us free
von der Tschechoslowakei/ from Czechoslovakia.

Over and over they would chant it at rallies, arms thrust stiffly into the air. And then the Nazi salute: "*Sieg Heil. Sieg Heil.*"

The Sudeten Germans were not alone in wanting Czechoslovakia and its democracy destroyed. There were Slovak nationalists who wanted to break up the country. They had armbands just like the Germans, except that theirs, instead of the swastika, carried the double cross of Slovakia, the top cross-arm shorter than the lower. They also had their own storm troopers in black uniforms, called the Hlinka Guard, after Andrej Hlinka, a Roman Catholic priest who founded the movement. Its main objective, at first, was autonomy from the central government in Prague. But as German pressure on the Czechs grew, the demands of Slovak nationalists changed to complete independence and a parroting of what the Germans were doing.

As if all that weren't enough, there were also Hungarians called irrendentists, who wanted Slovakia back as part of the Magyar kingdom as it had been for eight centuries before the Austro-Hungarian empire broke up at the end of World War I.

Hungarian irrendentists, Slovak separatists, German Nazis, and finally even the Poles wanted Czechoslovakia, the last bastion of democracy and tolerance in central Europe, torn apart. And, with the help at Munich of Britain's prime minister, Neville Chamberlain, and France's premier, Edouard Daladier, tear it apart they did.

The Munich crisis. September 1938. Munich has entered the

languages of the world as a term for short-sighted, futile appeasement and betrayal. And the furled umbrella Chamberlain used to carry became the symbol of Munich-style appeasement. Munich and its results have been used as justification for everything from the American participation in the Vietnam war to Soviet domination of eastern Europe.

It's all in the history books, and when I look back at it now, I am surprised how well what was apparent then even to a child's eyes has stood up to the test of time, hindsight and history.

That summer was a time of excitement and crisis. The Czech crisis, it was called. Hitler threatened to crush Czechoslovakia unless the Sudetenland, the border areas where the Sudeten Germans lived, were ceded to the Third Reich. The talk everywhere was about war. The Czechoslovak government appealed to Britain and France for help under treaties guaranteeing their support of Czechoslovakia in the face of an external threat. All summer the British and French pressured the Czechs to compromise with Hitler. They did not want to confront the Führer and, along with most of Europe, resented what they saw as the stubbornness of the Czechs, a stubbornness that could plunge the whole continent into war.

Memories of childhood are a fragile web that needs to be nourished by the recall of others and reinforced by familiar surroundings or mementoes. The toy of my childhood I remember best is a locomotive my father gave me. I remember it because for years I had a photograph of me holding it. That photo told me much more than it showed; it helped preserve in my memory how I got it. I can still see myself lying in bed sick and remember the joy of seeing my father coming in carrying a big, shiny dark green locomotive. Teenagers may groan or start rolling their eyes heavenward when their parents start intoning: "Do you remember when you were little how you used to . . ." But it is these banal recitations that are the glue that keeps memories whole in adulthood and give us the awareness of the continuity of life, of our lives, of the lives of those who came before us and of those who follow us.

In my mind, most of the memory traces of early childhood seem to have been severed. I can remember the school I went to — the entrance and schoolyard — but no teachers or schoolmates. If I had friends in school or even enemies — and I must have had — I cannot remember them. I remember best the family reunions attended by uncles, aunts and cousins who survived to remind me of them later in life. But I cannot remember the faces or even names of my father's sister, her husband and their two sons who disappeared in the Holocaust. Perhaps if I had had a snapshot of them I would have remembered their names and much more, because photographs stimulate memory even about things that are not in them.

I have a photograph of Ernie and me when he was two and I four. We are both in winter coats, wool caps on our heads, our legs encased in wool leggings. The background of the photo does not show much: only a bit of a balustrade and blurry buildings. But I know precisely where it was taken: near a statue of the Slovak poet Pavol Hviezdoslav in a park in front of the National Theatre in Bratislava. Neither the statue nor the theatre are in the picture, but I know they are there, just out of the frame of the photo. I was so sure of this that more than half a century later, sitting in a café looking out on the park, I knew with absolute certainty that the statue was out of place, that Hviezdoslav now sat further away from the theatre than he had when I was a child. Indeed, a surprised waiter confirmed that many years earlier the statue had been moved back about twenty metres to make room for car parking.

Reading Dr. Seuss books to my children many years ago brought back memories of the books my mother used to read to me. *Der Struwwelpeter*, the book I remember best, was made of much sterner stuff than Dr. Seuss's *The Cat in the Hat*. In *Struwwelpeter*, the kid who sucks his thumb has it cut off by a tailor with big shears, the boy who refuses to eat his soup dies of starvation, the girl who plays with matches while her parents are out is "burned through and through, the poor child, her skin and hair, too." There was also *Max und Moritz*, a book by the celebrated German storyteller and illustrator, Wilhelm Busch. Max and Moritz are boys whose idea of fun is to blow up their teacher by stuffing his pipe with gunpowder. They eventually get a comeuppance no less grisly than their pranks: they are stuffed into a flour mill and ground to bits that are devoured by pecking geese. There is in these German books none of the sweet innocence of Dr. Seuss's "I do not like green eggs and ham, I do not like them, Sam-I-am." In *Struwwelpeter* and *Max und Moritz*, the verse is light, the pictures bright, but the moralizing is driven home with the gruesome subtlety of a sledgehammer.

Of life at home, I remember the repeated events of routine: my father at prayer in the alcove every morning, wrapping phylacteries, the amulets of devout Jews, around his arm, and of going to the market with my mother on Fridays to buy a carp. We would bring the carp home live and wriggling and let it swim about in the bathtub in the stately fashion of fat, lazy carps and then, in the late afternoon, with a wince, she would hit the fish over the head with a wooden mallet to prepare it for our regular Sabbath eve dinner.

I can recall looking on as my father, a diabetic, injected his daily dose of insulin. I remember watching my mother swimming; she loved to swim. I can still see her white bathing cap forging through the water and the arms coming up in slow, strong strokes. Like most children, I used to watch my father shaving, but it was no ordinary shave. To comply with Orthodox Jewish custom, he made do without a razor. The ban on razors harks back to Samson — "If I be shaved, then my strength will leave me, and I shall become weak" — and his death after Delilah betrayed his secret. Instead of using a razor, my father would apply a vile-smelling depilatory to his face once a week, wait until it dissolved his beard and then scrape it off with a wooden tongue depressor.

I can recall these everyday details of life, but not the feelings that went with them, not love nor lack of it, not joy nor sorrow. I do not remember my parents either hugging me — and I am sure they did — or being angry and scolding me — as they surely must have. Did they love each other? Did they have fights? My children know these things about their parents; I do not know them about mine. Remembering life with my parents is like watching a movie with the sound turned off.

Memory, the psychologists tell us, is the restimulation in the central nervous system of tiny neurological traces of past experiences. My parents, my teachers, my schoolmates, my aunt, uncle and their sons did not survive to "restimulate" my nervous sytem. For me, not only they but a whole society imploded into a memory hole.

What is missing in me, what was taken from me besides my parents and the community from which I sprang are those fine-spun traces of emotional childhood remembrances that give later life its flavor. Instead, my remembrance of childhood has been shaped by the blows of history. Remembering becomes almost like watching two films: the first of flickering silent black and white images, plot unknown and unknowable; the other, a scary newsreel full of blaring fury and gory colors. The newsreel that is so clearly etched in my mind starts in the summer of 1938.

The names and faces from the headlines of that summer and what they did are more embedded in my mind than the fairy tales my mother told me.

There was Eduard Beneš, the president of Czechoslovakia, a frail and tragic figure who, after standing up to Germany, gave up when he was abandoned by his allies in the face of Hitler's threats of war. Twenty years later, ill and heart-broken, he was even less capable of standing up to Stalin's bullying, and Czechoslovakia once again lost its independence.

The Czech strong man of 1938, or so it seemed then, was General Jan Syrový, the inspector-general of the Czechoslovak army who became prime minister. He had a bullethead with a black eye patch that made him look reassuringly tough. He mobilized the Czechoslovak army that summer and we were all given gas masks.

The gas masks made great toys but we played with them

only when no one was looking. Adults seemed to think it was bad taste or bad luck to take the masks out of their tin canisters for anything other than air-raid drills.

Most of Europe looked at this war preparation in Czechoslovakia with irritation at being roused out of its summer vacation slumber.

The British and French used diplomatic subterfuges in 1938 that are still being used. They urged Prague to settle the crisis by dealing directly with Konrad Henlein, the leader of the Sudeten German Nazi party, even though they knew that he was a puppet of Berlin dependent on German money and Hitler's orders. I was reminded of Henlein in recent years when the Russians used to insist — until Mikhail Gorbachev came along — that anyone who wanted to negotiate an end to the war in Afghanistan and the withdrawal of the Soviet occupation forces from the country had to deal directly with Moscow's puppet regime in Kabul. Henlein also came to mind whenever the Americans rejected requests by the Sandinista regime of Nicaragua for direct talks with Washington about American concerns with Nicaragua's role as a military surrogate in Central America for Havana and Moscow. The Sandinistas were repeatedly told they must deal directly with the contra guerrilla forces that the U.S. financed and controlled. In the end, the Sandinista government did talk to the contras, but only after the U.S. had demoralized the guerrillas and undercut their bargaining position by cutting off their military supplies. Najibullah of Afghanistan and Adolofo Calero of Nicaragua, the Henleins of the eighties, ended up being cut loose by their sponsors because the struggles in Afghanistan and Nicaragua had become too long and costly for the superpowers. The Henlein gambit worked much better for Hitler because it suited the British and the French.

Chamberlain's determination to pacify Hitler by forcing Czechoslovakia to surrender to German demands was reinforced by another gimmick: the Runciman Mission. In August 1938, the British prime minister sent an emissary, Lord Runciman, to Prague ostensibly to mediate between the Czechoslovak government and the leaders of the Sudeten Germans. It was a cynical gesture because everyone knew

Henlein and his men had no authority to make a deal, and Chamberlain himself had let it be known publicly beforehand that as far as he was concerned the solution to the crisis was the ceding of the Sudetenland to Hitler.

I hadn't thought of Runciman's name for more than forty years until I was in Buenos Aires in April 1982. I was covering a mediation mission by the U.S. Secretary of State, Alexander Haig. General Haig was shuttling back and forth between Buenos Aires and London, trying unsuccessfully to avoid a war over the Falklands. Haig was acting as intermediary even though it was clear that if it came to war, the U.S. would side with Britain against Argentina. The Argentinian reaction to Haig reminded me of the reaction in Czechoslovakia to the Runciman Mission. In both cases, the mediation mission was seen as a cover-up of a sell-out and the mediators as reincarnations of Pontius Pilate.

By the end of September 1938, it was all but over for Czechoslovakia. Chamberlain met Hitler at Berchtesgaden, Bad Godesberg and finally Munich and each time he gave in to Hitler a little more. The British prime minister called the crisis "a quarrel in a faraway country between people of whom we know nothing." This though Czechoslovakia was no further from London than the Shetland Islands, certainly a lot closer than India or the Suez canal, and its position in the heart of Europe was the key to the control of central Europe.

Abandoned, Czechoslovakia caved in. The Germans got the Sudetenland, and the Hungarians and the Poles swooped in to get their slices. The Slovaks got autonomy. The Germans took Petržalka, the sliver of Czechoslovak territory across the Danube from Bratislava. From the river bank we could now see the Nazi flag flying just at the other end of the bridge. What was left of the country was called Czecho-Slovakia. Everyone knew that the newly inserted hyphen only masked a death sentence.

The war talk had now gone but so had the air of bravado and defiance of midsummer. Glumness and uncertainty prevailed. Even the joy of Slovak separatists at their newly gained autonomy was tempered by the uncertainty of what Hitler would do next and the prospect that the rule of Berlin would be much tighter than that of the Czech centralists in Prague.

The fall-out of Munich soon made itself felt in our house. My parents had planned to send me to a French second- ary school. France was Czechoslovakia's principal Western patron and role model, and French was considered the lin- gua franca of the middle class now that the Germans had subsided into barbarism. I had been enrolled in a French preparatory class for that fall, but after a few days I was sent home because I was Jewish and therefore no longer accept- able. The autonomous Slovak authorities had heard the voice of their German masters and applying the Nazi Nüremberg racial laws was one point on which they seemed more than willing to accede.

For me, the turning point that fall was Yom Kippur, the Jewish Day of Atonement. I was in the anteroom of the syna- gogue taking a break from the day-long services — playing hooky, really, with some of my friends from the tedium of seemingly endless prayer — when they half-carried my father out. He had collapsed during the service.

As a diabetic, my father had to watch his diet and limit his intake of starch. He even went as far as digging out the soft, doughy centre of the hard roll that is the staple of central European breakfasts and eating only the crisp crust. I still catch myself sometimes digging the centre out of rolls or French baguettes the way he did.

It had always been understood when my father fasted on Yom Kippur that he would break the fast if he felt faint to avoid going into insulin shock. He carried sugar cubes with him to boost his blood sugar level in an emergency. When he regained consciousness that day, he refused to take the sugar. His friends argued with him, telling him what he already knew, that Jewish law sanctioned the breaking of religious observances if they threatened life and that in fact he would be sinning if he persisted in fasting at the risk of his life.

My father never spoke about the incident. But somehow my childish mind sensed the despair behind his gesture and its cause. Until then the events around me had not greatly affected by life. I was used to people worrying about crises, people afraid of what Hitler might do next. I was used to Hitler. We made jokes about him and imitated his funny mustache and weird cowlick hairdo. I used to enjoy reciting the definition of the perfect Aryan: as blond as the dark-haired Hitler, as slim as the obese Goering, as fleet of foot as the clubfooted Goebbels, as eagle-eyed as the bespectacled Himmler.

Hitler had always been part of my life. I had heard about him ever since I could remember. Hitler, I knew, was bad. He was bad for Jews. He was bad for Czechs. He was bad for democrats, workers, writers, Slavs of all varieties. He had hurt people. He had killed people. He had affected the lives of many people I knew. But he had, so far, not hurt them. My aunts, uncles and cousins in Germany had managed to leave for England. Other relatives who had lived in the parts of Czechoslovakia the Germans had occupied as a result of the Munich settlement had left for Prague before the Nazis came. It was not until Yom Kippur, 1938, that I understood that our lives — the lives of my family, my life — were in danger.

Day by day, the Germans tightened the noose. In November, the most ominous development, Kristallnacht, The Night of Broken Glass. Nazi toughs roamed through Germany attacking Jewish homes, shops and synagogues. Twenty thousand Jews were arrested and several hundred murdered or raped.

The talk in the Jewish community in Bratislava that winter was no longer just about how best to cope with the new circumstances but how to leave, where to turn to get beyond Hitler's reach.

At a wedding of family friends that winter, a joyful affair on the surface, the talk between toasts and courses, between songs and dances was about the sombre business of emigrating. The bride and groom were heading for Palestine. Someone else had American relatives who had got him a U.S. visa. One family was heading for South America. For the first time, I heard my mother talk about sending her children to her brothers in England: "Only for a short time, you understand, until the situation calms down."

December 1979, Teheran. The day's demonstration at the
U.S. embassy ran late. Lots of yelling against the Shah and
the U.S. The usual circus, only later in the day than usual. By
the time I get back to the hotel they've stopped serving lunch.
After much argument, a waiter agrees to get me a sandwich.
As I wait, I become aware of familiar music drifting in. It's
the hora. An Israeli dance in Ayatollah Khomeini's Iran? I
tell myself I am getting tunes mixed up once again. I listen
again. It definitely is the hora.

There are not many Jews left in Iran. Most got out in the
waning days of the Shah's regime, when the El Al flights to Tel
Aviv were fully booked. (The flights were jokingly called the
Flying Carpet because so many people boarded with Persian
rugs, a portable form of wealth at a time when exporting
assets had become difficult.) But by now, almost a year after
the fall of the Shah's government, Jews are being constantly
denounced by the media and the mullahs as agents of Zionist
and American imperialism.

Singing the hora in Teheran seems risky. If a pazdar, one
of the ayatollah's militia of the faithful, or, more likely, one
of the militant students from the American embassy who
constantly come to the hotel to pass along information and
disinformation, hears it, there'll be trouble. Or will there?
Most pazdaran and students probably can't tell the hora from
"The Yellow Rose of Texas."

But perhaps there is a story in it. I abandon the chances of
getting my sandwich and follow the sound down the corridor. It's coming from behind a closed double door. I open
the door.

It's a wedding party of perhaps two dozen people. The men
wear yarmulkas. The bride is dancing. Everyone is looking at
me. But they go on singing and dancing, their eyes staying
focused on me as they turn. I smile. They don't smile back.

Three men come walking towards me, eyes serious. I keep
on smiling. I say I heard their music, that I'm Canadian and
Jewish. They don't seem reassured. They don't say a thing;

they just keep looking at me with anxious eyes. I would like to tell them about that other wedding that I attended as a boy far away and long ago. I would like to tell them: "Get out of Iran while you can." But all I say is "I'm sorry," and I turn and walk out, closing the door behind me. The sound of the hora follows me down the corridor.

On the Ides of March, 1939, Hitler finished off what he had started at Munich. The German army occupied what was left in Czechoslovakia so quickly that by nightfall Hitler was in Prague's Hradčany castle, the ancient seat of Bohemian kings.

The Czech lands — the provinces of Bohemia and Moravia — were put under "direct protection of the Third Reich," which meant they became German colonies. Slovakia was granted pro forma independence under Msgr. Jozef Tiso, a roly-poly priest who had succeeded to the leadership of the Hlinka party when its founder died.

By now it was settled: Ernie and I would be sent to England. We began to take English lessons. We didn't learn to speak English but we did learn to sing "My bonnie lies over the ocean, my bonnie lies over the sea."

But getting out was not going to be easy and it was getting more difficult by the day. By then there were hundreds of thousands who wanted to put the sea, or at least a border, between themselves and Hitler. But the ports of refuge were closed to all but a fortunate few. For more and more people in Europe, survival had become a desperately rare lottery prize.

Nicholas Winton was happy that Friday evening as he finished work at the London Stock Exchange. It was December 1938, and the thirty-year-old stockbroker was due to leave for Switzerland on Monday for a skiing holiday. But when he got to his flat in Hampstead, he had a phone call that changed his plans. And helped save my life.

The call was from Winton's friend, Martin Blake, who was to have gone to Switzerland with him but was now cancelling his vacation. "I'm off to Prague," Winton recalls Blake saying. "There's an awful lot of work to be done there and I need your help.

"I'm in a tearing rush," Blake continued, "and can't go into details on the phone. But my address will be the Hotel Šroubek. Come to Prague as soon as you can."

That was still all Winton knew when he arrived in Prague four days later. He went, he recalled half a century later, because "I felt certain that this mission of his was connected with the subject we had so often discussed — Hitler."

Winton knew what Hitler stood for because he had studied and travelled in Germany. "I had seen how families were being divided amongst themselves, how Jews were being beaten up and the ruthless aggressiveness of the S.A. [storm troopers]." He was appalled by the apathy of most of his countrymen towards the growing Nazi menace. He and Blake shared the conviction that it would lead to war.

There was another factor behind Winton's impulsive decision to go off to Prague and into the unknown: he was young, unfettered and adventurous. Even now he still recalls "how wonderful it was . . . to do exactly what one wanted on the spur of the moment."

In Prague, Winton found out Blake's mission: getting out of Hitler's clutches those whose lives were threatened by the advancing Nazi armies. When the Germans occupied the Sudetenland, thousands had fled to what remained of Czechoslovakia. There were Jews and Czechs, of course, but also many ethnic Germans threatened by the arrival of the Nazis: writers, socialists, academics, trade unionists. And there were also Germans from Germany itself and Austrians who had already fled from Hitler once before and thought they had found refuge in the Sudetenland. Many of these refugees lived impoverished in improvised camps around Prague. They had to be helped to survive the winter until places could be found for them abroad.

By the time Winton got to Prague, it was evident that before too long the Germans would take what was left of the country, and the number of those in need of saving would multiply many times over. Blake had called on Winton because the British Committee for Refugees from Czechoslovakia, for which he worked, had come across a new problem: helping organize an exodus of children of those who could not or would not leave the country, people like my parents who were desperate to send their children to safety abroad.

A new way out had opened up for these children as a result of British outrage over the barbarity of Kristallnacht in Germany. Within two weeks of the Nazi pogrom, public sentiment had forced a change in Britain's restrictive immigration laws. The new rules provided for the admission of an unspecified number of refugees under the age of eighteen as "transmigrants," that is people who were given shelter but were expected eventually to move on elsewhere.

The first "Kindertransporte" (children's transports) started rolling from Germany itself and from Austria in December 1938. Eventually, the lives of 10,000 children would be saved by the Kindertransporte.

In Prague, the refugee committee was unprepared for the mass movement of children without parents. It was geared to helping adults who were in danger and their families. That was difficult enough. Arranging an unprecedented exodus of children would require a separate organization. For one thing, hundreds of British families would have to be found to take in the youngsters. Blake thought Winton was just the man to handle the job.

Winton was dazed. In his new role as a Scarlet Pimpernel, he was besieged by parents and organizational problems. He did have help. Doreen Warriner, the head of the Prague office of the committee, showed him the ropes. But largely she left him alone because her main work was getting the endangered adults out.

Then Trevor Chadwick, an English prep school teacher, came along. His school had offered to take in two refugee boys from the Sudetenland. He and the school's games master had flown to Czechoslovakia in the fall of 1938 to choose them and successfully completed their mission.

What Chadwick had seen in Czechoslovakia had made a

deep impression on him. "We so often saw halls full of confused refugees and batches of lost children, mostly Jewish,"
he wrote after the war. "And we saw only the fringe of it all."
So he returned to Prague to help get more children out.

First, Winton had to make up a list, giving priority to
those most endangered. Everyone felt quite naturally that
his or her child's case was the most urgent. "There was no
need for an alarm clock," Winton recalled half a century
later, "as someone would surely knock at my door early to
plead the case of some child being put high on the priority list.

"Often it was heartbreaking. Some had plenty of money.
Others had not the price of a meal. Some of the mothers were
already on the streets to get money to buy food for themselves
and their children. I began to realize what suffering there is
when armies start to march."

The hard choices of whom to place at the top of the list and
whom to reject were agonizing enough for Winton. For the
parents, they were heart-rending. Many wept when he told
them he could not help them. When he said "Maybe," they
wept at the thought of the coming separation. Others reacted
to the imminence of separation by deciding they could not
part from their children.

Another problem was Nazi agents. They followed Winton
and spied on him and other committee workers. Many of the
adults they dealt with, after all, were either on the Nazis'
wanted list or suspected by them. Still, the Germans did
not block Winton's and Chadwick's efforts even after they
occupied Prague. They gave the children exit visas and even
visas for transit across Germany. At the time, the Nazis were
trying to reassure the British that Hitler was reasonable, that
he did not want war and that he had no further territorial
demands. They were willing to make a few minor concessions
to make sure the British were not overly angered.

Finally, Winton was ready to start exporting his children.
His first acceptance, though, came not from Britain but from
Sweden. He met a Swedish woman, the representative of the
Swedish Red Cross in Prague, who said she had the authority
to take twenty children to Sweden. Winton was jubilant. He

was on his way. He arranged to have lunch with her and took Doreen Warriner along. He was in for a shock.

"Doreen and the Swedish girl seemed to be carrying on a lively conversation," he remembers. "Just as I was starting to say something about work, I got a kick from Doreen, who then started off on various small-talk subjects until the meal was over.

"As we parted, she whispered, 'Go easy.' Doreen had heard something which had made her suspicious. She checked with the Swedish embassy and found out that the girl was working for the Germans."

Winton was told by the committee he was to have nothing more to do with the Swede. Having had a nibble, though, he was not about to give up. As a volunteer, rather than a staff official, he could defy the committee and get away with it. He checked with the Red Cross and found the woman's credentials were genuine. So he went ahead.

"A week later I was at the airport and the first transport of twenty children were embarked for Sweden."

Fifty years later, Winton still chortles with satisfaction that he got his first kids out by co-operating with "a beautiful German spy."

It soon became apparent there were more children in need of saving than there were takers in Britain. Winton's first priority became finding homes in Britain for the hundreds of children on his growing list. He put Chadwick in charge of the Prague end of the operation and returned to London to organize an appeal.

With the British Refugee Committee's capabilities stretched to the limit looking after adults, Winton set out on his own to find sponsors for his kids. He set up what was in fact a bootleg organization. Without authorization from the official refugee committee, he had notepaper printed with the letterhead "British Committee for Refugees from Czechoslovakia, Children's Section, Nicholas G. Winton, Honourary Secretary."

In the meantime, Chadwick, who was a quixotic and erratic character, grew impatient at the delays. He chartered a plane — apparently with his own money — packed twenty children into it and flew them to London. "They were all cheerfully sick," he reported afterwards. There was such a shortage of sponsors that Chadwick had to cajole his mother into taking several of "his" children.

But Winton was slowly getting his operation going. He sent out flyers making his case. He said he had a list of 500 chidlren in most urgent need of rescuing and offered to send photographs and particulars to anyone interested in taking them in. He had cards printed, each with the photos of six children, their names and ages.

"This sounds horribly commercial," Winton says, "but the selling power created when somebody could actually see a picture of a child was enormous. The result was astonishing.

"We were at last in business. Eventually we had to set up an office of four people to deal with the work. The British Committee (the official refugee organization) had now no option but to accept the situation, confirm me in my office as honorary secretary and give us a room at Bloomsbury House."

By the end of March, Chadwick was able to send off a whole railroad car full of children — seventy of them.

But there were still problems, mostly with the British Home Office, the government agency that controls immigration to Britain. Immigration — for refugees or anyone else — was unpopular everywhere during what was still the Great Depression and rules were tight even for that bureaucratic fiction, the "trans-migrants." The Home Office was displeased with Winton's unorthodox hard-sell methods and dragged its feet. "Why rush, old boy?" Winton was asked. "Nothing will happen in Europe anyway."

Infuriated by the delays and frustrated because they could see the flow of the children coming to an end soon, Winton and Chadwick looked for a way out. They found it in Prague, where a co-operative printer made up a batch of fake Home Office entry permits. They weren't good enough to pass the scrutiny of British immigration officers, but they were good enough to fool the Germans, who put their exit approval stamps on them. Having used the counterfeits, though, Winton had to make sure that he had genuine permits on hand by the time the children landed in England so that his people could substitute them for the Prague fakes.

The Germans in Prague were also proving to be progressively more difficult. It took days of lining up to get an exit permit, and the Germans threw every conceivable obstacle in the applicants' way.

"At one time," according to Winton, "one of their questions was: 'Have you paid your dog licence?' Answer: 'I have no dog.' Reply: 'Then go away and tomorrow bring me proof that you have no dog.' "

Chadwick did find one source of help among the Germans: a Gestapo officer. Winton was suspicious. But, according to Chadwick, the Gestapo man was useful in speeding up the emigration process. Then one day, the German proposed to Chadwick that the refugee committee send back to Prague some of the "politicals" among the adults it had brought to Britain. The Gestapo man assured Chadwick that he would personally guarantee the freedom and safety of all those who returned. Winton was appalled. To accept the Gestapo offer was, of course, impossible; the returnees were certain to be arrested. But to refuse was to endanger the whole rescue operation. Winton blamed Chadwick for allowing himself to be hoodwinked and used by the Gestapo. He recalled him to London.

Chadwick was heartbroken. He had helped save hundreds of children. But there were still several thousands on his list that he had been unable to help. "I shall always have a sense of shame," he wrote, "that I didn't get more out."

It was June now, and the end of their mission was clearly near. In the six months since Winton and Chadwick had gone to Prague, they had managed to help rescue several hundred children. They had brought out children individually, then by the small planeloads of the day, then a whole railroad car.

Now Winton was waiting for the climax of his efforts, his biggest coup. On June 30, 241 children were to leave Prague on a special train, the biggest single transport Winton had yet organized. That night, there was agony on the station platform in Prague. One little girl remembered later how her mother hesitated, how she put her on the train, then

changed her mind and pulled her out through the window.
Three times the mother took her child back. Finally, she left
her on the train. And saved her life.

When the train left Prague that evening, it was two children
short: my brother and me.

The train from Prague was running several hours late. That's
why my father, Ernie and I were in the washroom of the station just inside Germany.

We had travelled from Bratislava all day through Moravia
and Bohemia, and the train even stopped in Prague. But
we were not permitted to get off and change to the special
children's train there because we were now aliens, citizens
of the Slovak state, travelling on a no-stop-off transit visa
through the German Protectorate. It was only after we got
to Lobositz, the first station inside Hitler's Third Reich, that
we were allowed to get off.

It was by these circuitous arrangements that my father managed to get us on Nicholas Winton's train out of Prague. We
were not originally on the list Winton and Chadwick had been
compiling in Prague; Bratislava was beyond the net they had
cast. What secured us our seats, what made adding us to the list
at the last minute possible was that Winton's organization did
not have to find a place to put us up, that we had my mother's
brothers in England ready to take us in.

We were sitting on the platform in Lobositz, which until
Munich had been a part of Czechoslovakia, when we were
told that the special train from Prague had been delayed.
When it got to the German border, it was discovered that,
because of a mix-up, the case with the passports and all those
precious, hard-won exit and entry visas had been left behind
in Prague. After much phoning, the case was found and a car
dispatched from Prague to catch up with the train.

In the meantime, though, a station guard came and told
us we could not spend the night on the platform. Since we
could not use the waiting room, he said, the toilets were the

only place left. He wasn't rude about it; on the contrary, he suggested we might be more comfortable there. What sticks in my mind is that this man in a German uniform who was telling us we were not considered fit for anything better than the pissoir addressed us politely as *die Herrschaften*, the gentlemen. I remember even more vividly that my father accepted it calmly and that I myself felt neither surprise nor anger. We had already begun to accept Hitler's New Order.

There are smells we remember all our lives, odors that we associate with a place, a person, even a whole country. The most vivid of these are usually the extinct smells of our lost childhood. There was the smell of the lavender sachets in my mother's linen closet. I see such sachets sometimes in gift shops still; they sit there as relics of another — to me, certainly gentler — age. Then there was my Uncle Hugo's garden shed. They used scythes then and the cut grass smelled different than it does now when it's chopped into tight cuds by power mowers. And then there was the gas-works smell. When I had whooping cough, I was taken to the Bratislava coal-gas plant to inhale the odors to relieve my hacking cough. It is a smell that has all but disappeared with the conversion to natural gas, and doctors nowadays laugh at me when I ask them about the treatment. I can recall the smell; I sometimes think I still have traces of that gas somewhere in the back of my nostrils.

But the most evocative of all these smells for me is the odor of tar-coated urinals. It brings back the night at Lobositz. The feeling is not of humiliation but of warmth, of comfort and of drowsy contentment as my father quietly talked to me.

As I have grown older, older now than my father was then, as I have watched my children grow past the age I was then, my mind has gnawed at what must have been going through my father's head as he sat there waiting to send his children off on a journey that would take them to safety, to be sure, but also to a world where he could not follow and where his sons might remain lost to him forever.

I have caught myself at times looking at my own children, trying to capture some fraction of the dread and desperation my father must have felt that night.

March 1971, Dacca, East Pakistan. I am in Dacca to cover the crisis that is tearing apart the two widely separated wings of Pakistan. The Bengalis of East Pakistan want autonomy or independence. The Pakistani army, which runs the country and is largely composed of Sindhis, Punjabis and Pathans from West Pakistan, is determined not to surrender control.

There are demonstrations by supporters of Sheik Mujibur Rahman, the charismatic leader of the Bengali Awami league. Tensions are running high. There are daily confrontations between the army and civilians. And there are rumors, rumors that the army will crack down, rumors that Sheik Mujib will declare the secession of East Pakistan, rumors of the Biharis, the biggest minority in East Pakistan, being killed by their Bengali neighbors.

I set out for the airport to ship newsfilm we have shot of the negotiations between President Yahya Khan, the head of the military government, and Pakistan's two leading politicians: Sheik Mujib, whose Awami league has come out of recent elections as Pakistan's biggest party, and Zulfikar Ali Bhutto, the strongest politician of the country's western wing.

The taxi drivers outside the hotel refuse to take me to the airport. Too dangerous, they say. The Biharis are heading out that way, and everyone fears trouble. Anything — perhaps a stone thrown at a Bihari — could set off a bloodbath between Bengalis and Biharis, or the army and the Bengalis. Whatever the trouble, cars are always an attractive target; they are a symbol of affluence and authority and, besides, they are easy to overturn and burn.

I finally persuade a cycle rickshaw driver to take me. The rickshaw may be much slower than a car but it has the advantage of being inconspicuous and easier to manoeuvre through the throngs on the road.

When we get to the airport, the terminal building is surrounded by a shouting, pushing crowd of Biharis, desperate to leave or, at least, to be allowed to put their children and their women on a plane to Karachi in West Pakistan.

The Pakistani army and air force have taken control of the airport. It is their only link to West Pakistan. And a lengthy and tenuous one at that. The Pakistanis cannot use the direct route across India because the Indian government has closed its air space to them. They are forced, therefore, to fly all the way around India and rely on Ceylon (now Sri Lanka) for refuelling facilities. They say they have enough trouble keeping their forces supplied without being bothered by panicky civilians. Actually, they are bringing in more troops to enable them to crack down on the Bengalis. So they have closed the airport to most civilian traffic. They have taken out West Pakistanis trapped in the east wing, but they have no intention of adding to their problems by allowing in Bihari refugees.

The shut iron grille to the terminal building is guarded by soldiers. You can see the fear in the crowd outside. Some people yell; others push as if pushing a few inches forwards, a few feet ahead, would get them significantly closer to safety in Karachi, 2,500 kilometres away as the crow might fly but Air Pakistan cannot. But most faces show the patience and passivity of resignation. Many of the Biharis at the airport come from villages near Dacca where their homes and shops have been attacked and they know it could get much worse and quite quickly.

The Biharis know slaughter. They are Muslims from India who were driven to East Pakistan by the communal and religious massacres that accompanied the partition of British Imperial India in 1947 into two independent countries. They fled the murderous wrath of their Hindu neighbors in the Indian state of Bihar and sought refuge among their co-religionists in East Pakistan, the Muslim part of Bengal. More than twenty years later, they are still strangers regarded by the Bengalis as foreign competitors, as just so many more mouths to feed from an already strained larder, and, worst of all, as agents of the central power of Pakistan that carries the biased stamp of the country's west wing. The Biharis, in turn, do not try to hide their contempt for the Bengalis. Most of them insist on speaking Urdu or English rather than Bengali. It is precisely because they are such outsiders that the Pakistani officials from the west trust the Biharis and use them as part of the apparatus enforcing the authority of the central government.

I tap a man at the edge of the crowd on the shoulder. He looks around, sees my white face and taps the next person on the shoulder. The signal is passed on and slowly a corridor opens up for me. No one hesitates; no one balks. As I walk towards the gate, the crowd closes in behind me, unchanged by my passing. It is almost as if I were nothing more than a spirit armed with a white mask of untouchable power.

At the gate, two army guards in old British Tommy helmets, armed with ancient Lee-Enfield rifles with bayonets fixed, open the iron grille for me. I show them no papers — my face is my laissez-passer — and I walk through the gate.

The grille clangs shut behind me. I turn around and look outside. I can see the crowd in the brightness of the tropical sun, but I can't see the faces clearly. I know they are Biharis out there. But they could just as readily be Bengalis.

(Indeed, within a few days it was the Bengalis who fled for their lives. The Pakistani army cracked down on Sheik Mujib and the Bengali independence movement in a spree of violence made even more murderous by Biharis bent on vengeance. Within a year, with the victory of India over the Pakistani army in the war that created an independent Bangladesh, the circle would turn once again.)

Bengali or Bihari, those faces could also have been, as they have been all too often in this century, Chinese as well as Czech, Vietnamese and Cambodian, Arab or Jewish, Tamil and Sinhalese, Salvadoran or Nicaraguan, Azerbeijani and Armenian, French or Algerian, Ethiopian and Spanish, the faces of my parents, of my uncles, aunts and cousins.

It was still dark when the train from Prague finally came. My father embraced us, Ernie and I clambered aboard. A guard sealed the door behind us.

There we were, a trainload of children, being transported across Germany, under guard, in a sealed train as though we were some dangerous gang of terrorists or a highly contagious cargo, much like the occupants of the train that carried a Russian named Vladimir Ilyich Ulyanov — later to be known as Lenin — across Germany twenty-two years earlier on his way to the Finland Station and the Russian Revolution.

But we were kids. Some cried but most were irrepressible even though we had just been separated from our families, uninhibited even though we were now travelling through what all of us knew to be enemy territory, gregarious even though until now most of us had been strangers to each other. And curious, too. When the train stopped at a large train station, someone spotted a locomotive with a propeller. Immediately, clumps of small boys, train buffs all, rushed to the windows to inspect and argue. Did the prop really help pull the train or was it just decoration, another German propaganda show? Was it a diesel engine or electric? How fast could it go?

Finally, the Dutch border, and on the other side, a friendly welcome: cocoa, cheese and bread. But strange bread, not the dark rye we were used to but white and spongy, to many of us more cake than bread.

At the Hook of Holland, a Channel ferry, the largest ship I had ever seen. Compared to the ferries across the Danube, the tugs and barges at Bratislava, she was huge. So many decks, so many gangways, so many companionways, and young feet clattering about them exploring. Before I fell asleep in my bunk that night as the ferry headed across the sea, I remember hearing from somewhere in the bowels of the ship the sound of singing, the slow and doleful melody of the Czech national anthem. "*Kde domov můj, kde domov můj?*" Where is my home, where is my home?

Where indeed? It was a question that for us had no answer. There was certainly no going back and what lay ahead we did not know, least of all that for most of us the question would remain unanswered for many years and that for a few, whose hearts are not where their feet are mired, it has stayed unanswered to this day.

Behind us the doors had closed.

There was to be only one more train that would make it. The next, Winton's biggest, was to have left Prague on September 1, 1939. It never did. On that day, the Germans invaded Poland and World War II was on.

Nicky Winton helped save 664 lives. But what he remembers most and hurts him most are the children he didn't save.

Half a century later, Winton wears a ring given to him by some of those he saved. It is inscribed with a line from the Talmud: "Save one life, save the world."

Nicholas Winton did.

CHAPTER II

We were crowded around the radio. "I am speaking to you
from the cabinet room at 10 Downing Street," the voice on
the radio said. It was Neville Chamberlain, the man with the
furled umbrella who less than a year earlier had come back
from Munich saying that he had won "peace in our time."
Now he was saying that he had sent the German government
a message that "unless we heard from them by eleven o'clock
that they were prepared at once to withdraw their troops from
Poland, a state of war would exist between us." I not only
heard Chamberlain; I had also picked up enough English by
then to understand what he was saying. And what it meant.

It was 11:15 A.M. Sunday, September 3, 1939. We had been at war for fifteen minutes and that meant I would not be going home to my parents until it was over.

In the two months since I had left home, my world had changed. First came the separation from my brother. I stayed with one uncle in Gateshead-on-Tyne; Ernie went to live with the other uncle at the seaside. It was less than twenty kilometres away, but it was the first time we had been apart.

Within a month, it seemed to me as though Czechoslovakia was happening all over again. Once more, I was issued a gas mask, this time in a plain square cardboard box rather than the fancy, military-type, khaki metal canister we were given in Czechoslovakia. Then, three days before Britain declared war, just as I was getting used to my new home, I was shipped off again. I was evacuated with the children of my school in Gateshead-on-Tyne to a village in Yorkshire.

We were part of a huge exodus going on all over the country that day. The great cities of Britain and the large industrial areas around them — London and Birmingham, Merseyside and Clydeside, as well as Tyneside — were being all but emptied of their children. Hundreds of thousands of youngsters were moved into the countryside to get them away from the air raids the Germans were expected to launch once the war got going. For the parents and the children, for the teachers who moved with their pupils, for the families in the countryside that had volunteered to take in the evacuees, for the people who ran the hundreds of special trains and thousands of buses, it was a dramatic and traumatic day, a day of tears washed away by large dollops of English jollity, a day of confusion saved by the stolid British talent for muddling through.

Living away from my German-speaking relatives in completely English surroundings, my English improved rapidly. I quickly learned that there was more than one English language. I could hear now the difference between the way the squire at the Hall and the vicar of Ormesby spoke what was considered "proper" English and the way the rest of the village spoke it with a Yorkshire burr. Their English, in turn, was different from that of the children who had come to

Yorkshire with me from Gateshead. The Geordies of the Tyneside spoke a language almost incomprehensible to many other Englishmen. It didn't take long for me to realize that you could tell a lot about an Englishman by the way he spoke.

I learned about garden fêtes and whist drives; what was tea and what was high tea; to detest boiled mutton, which smelled, and cucumber sandwiches sliced so thinly they always left you hungry; and, since there was a war on and lots of soldiers around, about the differences in British regiments. It seemed at times as though there was no British army, only British regiments and competing, unequal regiments at that. The Northumberland Fusiliers stood higher in the pecking order than, let's say, the Durham Light Infantry, but had nowhere near the cachet of the Green Howards or Gordon Highlanders, to say nothing of the Guards regiments.

I learned to sing "Knick-knack, paddy-whack, give the dog a bone," along with new favorites such as "We'll be hanging our washing on the Siegfried line," and to belt out lusty Anglican hymns at school assembly. I joined the Boy Scouts, which inevitably meant more hymn singing because on Sundays, when we were not out camping, the Scouts were expected to attend church parade.

English churches were certainly different not only from the synagogue I was used to in Bratislava but also from the darkly intimidating Catholic churches I had diffidently peered into but never entered. From the outside, the Catholic churches smelled as though something were rotting inside (I had never heard of incense). And where the sound that drifted out of Catholic churches seemed sombre and powerful and the one emanating from the synagogue mostly a supplicatory mumbling, the singing that drifted out of Anglican churches struck me as cheerful. All things bright and beautiful, the English sang. They seemed indeed to regard God with a different eye than Jews or even, from what little I knew about them, Catholics did. To the English, God apparently was someone who was invariably on their side, someone who was up there to help them and who did what was expected of him, whether it was saving their king or leading them to victory in battle.

To Jews, God was made of much sterner, unforgiving stuff. And so were rabbis. All I remember of the most important rabbi in my life, the one who taught us religion in school in Bratislava, is his beard, his frequent anger and the two fat fingers he would bunch together, lift high and then slam down into my outheld palm to mark his displeasure. In contrast, the Anglican vicars I met always seemed to be smiling, patting children on the head, even unbelieving children such as me. And they seemed to spend a lot of time outside the church, taking tea with old ladies or presiding over one social church event or another. I certainly couldn't imagine a rabbi at home taking part in a sack race with kids the way the curates would. The English, it seemed, saw God's house as just another club.

I also learned some of the essentials of being an English schoolboy; how to play conkers, for instance; how to choose a strong conker, a horse chestnut; how to drill a hole into it and thread a string through it; how best to hold the string to give your opponent's conker a strong enough blow to smash it while leaving yours intact. And I learned to play cricket and got hooked on Charles Dickens and the humorous adventures of William, the hero of a series of books about the pranks and pratfalls of a schoolboy.

But before I could get used to my new life, it changed again. I was moved from Ormesby, which was near Middlesbrough, to another Yorkshire village, Sowerby, near Thirsk. In Ormesby, I had lived with a truck driver and his wife. I had just begun forming a friendship with him by accompanying him on his shorter rides in his Bedford lorry when I was moved to Sowerby into the home of an elderly spinster. She had as hard a time getting used to a child as I to her. As a result, she spoiled me.

Once more I tried to settle in, trying to get used to her fussing over me and her unvaried menu of alternating rhubarb pie and date tarts for tea, both of which I hated but out of plain cowardice never failed to praise, thereby prolonging my gastronomic misery.

But within a few months, I was moved once again; this time, back to my uncle's house in Gateshead. But not for long.

In the autumn of 1941, I was sent off to a boarding school in Shropshire, near the Welsh border. The school was not English, however; it was Czech. It was run by the Czechoslovak government-in-exile for refugee children. My uncle said he was sending me there because he had decided that I had better be prepared for the return to Czechoslovakia once the war ended. But I sensed then — and know now — that it was mostly just an appropriate way for my aunt and uncle to get rid of the problems of looking after another child besides their own. I understand it now, but it hurt then.

For me, the new move was a shock. It was as if I had been suddenly returned to Czechoslovakia. The school at Whitchurch was a total surprise, a sliver of Czechoslovakia ensconced incongruously in a Victorian brick and sandstone manor house, called Hinton Hall, in the middle of that, oh so English, gentle Salopian landscape.

People spoke Czech to me and I understood. But after only a little more than two years of not speaking Slovak — the two languages are not all that different; they are closer to being two distinct dialects than different languages — I found that the words I wanted were stuck somewhere in my head and I could not get them out to my tongue. In a way, I was once again having to learn a language.

I know now that as readily as children can learn languages, they also easily forget them. I know also that once a language is embedded in you, particularly a language you learned as a child, it can be pried out again. At the time, though, I was disoriented and discouraged.

Fortunately, the language came back quickly; Czech this time, rather than Slovak, because this was definitely a school run by Czechs. The students all spoke English, too, and many of them had picked up various other languages during the odyssey that brought them to Britain. Some had sought refuge in Poland with their families only to be forced to flee again by the onslaught of the German invasion. After the fall of Poland, many of them had wandered from country to country seeking safety. Others came after fleeing before the German advance through France to Spain, or escaping at the last minute from Bordeaux on freighters carrying what would become the nucleus of Charles de Gaulle's Free French army. Quite a few had come to Britain the way I had: on one of Nicky Winton's transports. We were a cosmopolitan, polyglot and, I suppose, somewhat traumatized bunch of kids.

I was to spend nearly four years at the Czechoslovak State School in Britain, as it was officially called, first in Shropshire and later in new quarters, a hotel at a tiny spa town in the centre of Wales called Llanwrtyd Wells. These years remain in my memory among the happiest, most carefree times of my youth.

I realized soon enough that I had really arrived among my own. Here were youngsters who had experienced what I had gone through. Most of them were here without their parents. These were people who knew what it was like to be among strangers. And, a few months after I came to the school, Ernie joined me there. Another attraction: the school was co-educational, to the great envy and bewilderment of visiting soccer teams from English boys' schools.

Before too long, the school had become my home. This was where I first kissed a girl; where I had my first beer in a pub, as opposed to having a sip of one at home, which didn't count; where I learned to swim and to dance. But above all, it was at the Czech school that I formed lasting friendships, some of which have endured to this day despite years and even decades of separation.

It also turned out to be a good school. It had to be because it had so much to do. The student body was a disparate one. Not only did some of the children not even speak the language when they came, some had never done so. Although they all came from Czechoslovakia, some had grown up speaking only German, Hungarian or even Ruthenian, the language of the tiny easternmost province of Czechoslovakia, which the Soviet Union annexed after the war.

The teachers, too, were a varied lot, many of them seconded from the Czechoslovak army in Britain. Some had more impressive academic credentials than teachers normally had but very little or no teaching experience. There were almost no textbooks, so teachers more or less had to make up their courses. Because there was no strictly laid-down curriculum, the courses sometimes took on a free-form quality that made them more memorable than a more orthodox education might have been.

The music teacher was an opera singer. So we sang. We sang at school; the school choir sang on BBC radio; it even gave a concert at London's Wigmore Hall.

The history I learned had very few names and dates of great battles that children are normally subjected to. That was because the history teacher was all but blind and could read only with the greatest effort by putting books right up to his nose. So he preferred to talk about what he remembered from before the time his eyesight failed him. And what he remembered best were fabulous tales of skulduggery and intrigue behind the battles and other famous events that made history come alive for me.

The maths teacher was an engineer by trade who made us aware of the practical applications of the trigonometry and logarithms we were learning. Because just about everything about the school was improvised, it made for a freer atmosphere in which teachers could challenge the students and children challenged the teachers.

Though Czech was the main language of instruction, there were also daily English classes. On top of that, French and Latin were compulsory. It was by the standard of most present-day schools a rigorous program and not just academically. The headmaster was an army officer who believed in lots of physical exercise for children and discipline. From English boarding schools, he borrowed the idea of not spoiling children with the comforts of home. In Shropshire, there was no heat in the bedrooms in winter. Sometimes, there was no hot water either. And classrooms were heated by coal fires set by students every winter morning. Kids washed the dishes, kids, usually boys, did stints at potato peeling as punishment for rule infractions. The dentist who periodically visited the school also provided some unusual training in stoicism. His drill was powered by a foot treadle. When the drill was not run at its proper speed, which happened often since the treadle was operated by students awaiting their turn in the chair, it turned into an instrument of slow-grinding torture.

Like English boarding schools, this one was run with prefects supervising younger children. I can still remember the daunting experience of being a prefect at fifteen and having a half-dozen hungry twelve-year-old boys watching my every move intently as I divided the food into individual portions. Give one of them — or, even worse, God forbid, yourself — a half ounce more than the rest and you were treated with contempt.

For the provisional Czechoslovak government-in-exile, the school was more than what it started out as: a place where its officials and service personnel could send their kids for a Czech education. It also became more than what it could have ended up as: a mere dumping place for refugee children rejected by their foster parents. It became, in a way, a showplace for the Czech cause.

When there was some celebration or commemoration of things Czech anywhere in Britain — a concert perhaps, a fund-raising drive — a group of children from the school would be in attendance in folk costume. Or perhaps the school folk dance group. Or the choir. If there was an international youth meeting somewhere, we would send a delegation. We could be depended on to say the right things about international friendship and the need for co-operation in a democratic postwar Europe.

There was a certain irony in what the school had become. The political, religious and ethnic minorities of Czechoslovakia — Sudeten German Social Democrats, Jews, Slovak Protestants, the kids of Czech communists, Ruthenians — were overrepresented among its students because of the simple fact that these were the people, more than the mainstream of Catholic Czechs and Slovaks, who were being forced to flee by Nazi persecution. Yet the school managed to build out of this motley student body a practical symbol of Czech nationalism. The BBC needed Czech Christmas carols? We supplied them. A picture magazine wanted a layout on children from one of the captive nations of Europe? We had them. Young Czechs in uniform? There was a flow of young soldiers who

were detached temporarily to the school to sit for their high
school graduation exams. Then there were the Boy Scouts.
In Hitler's Europe, the Boy Scout movement was banned.
So the troop at our school served not only to teach us how
to tie knots and apply a tourniquet but also as a symbol that
the Czech Boy Scout movement was still alive.

We also had one other role: warriors-to-be. The older boys,
I among them, were cadets in 2142 Squadron, a Czech unit of
Britain's Air Training Corps. In fact, the war would be over
for a year before we would be old enough to serve in the RAF.
But in the summer of 1944, when the Allied armies were still
struggling in Normandy, that was by no means certain. So we
were sent off for training at a Royal Air Force base. (As it
turned out, though not one of us served in the RAF, two of
our cadets ended up four years later as fighter pilots in the
fledgling Israeli air force and another went on to become a
flight test engineer for a French aerospace company.)

Apart from being marched endlessly around the parade
ground, our main training was in aircraft navigation, apparently on the theory that the only potential use we might one
day have for the armed services, apart from serving as cannon
fodder, was that some of us had above average math skills.

In the meantime, though, the only immediate use the RAF
had for ATC cadets was as choirboys at Sunday church services. The usual practice was to order all Catholic cadets to
fall out after the parade before the base commander and
march them off to the Catholic chapel. Those who were left
were then presumed to be either Anglican or Non-Conformist
— the English term for all Protestants who did not adhere
to the established Church of England. In our case, though,
once the Catholics had left the parade ground, we were, with
only a few exceptions, Jewish. We knew enough about military life not to volunteer to the officer in charge that he was
about to commit a mistake. So off we marched to the Protes-
tant chapel as ordered, pulled on the choristers' surplices we
were handed and gave a spirited rendition of "Onward Christian Soldiers."

We pulled it off. We missed not a hymn, not a verse. No
one noticed anything amiss, and we were well pleased with

ourselves. But what was to us a lark was also, even though we did not realize it, a sign of a problem most of us were about to face soon: Who were we? Or, more important, what were we going to be: refugees who would stay on to become His Majesty's subjects or exiles returning to a country we barely knew?

We were, in a sense, hybrids with roots shooting out in every direction but no earth in which to plant them. Most of us could sing Christian hymns, recite a few Jewish prayers (the school had a rabbi as well as a Catholic priest in residence), spout chunks of Shakespeare, dance Slovak folk dances, sing a Welsh song or two, declaim Czech poetry, as well as imitate various British regional dialects.

Though we were isolated at our Czech school and immersed in Czech culture, we did keep up with the Britain around us. Many of us had travelled extensively around the country. I would spend some of my holidays in Gateshead and later in London. I had vacationed in the Lake Country of Westmoreland and spent time in Kirkcudbright in Scotland. I had visited Manchester and Birmingham and knew Cardiff and Swansea, too. The last two summers of the war I worked, first in the Midlands as a farm laborer and the following summer in Somerset at a munitions factory. I had probably seen more of Britain than most British boys my age.

At school, we were engrossed with the war. Britain's heroes were our heroes. Her defeats were our defeats. And her victories, ours, too.

Most of the older students followed the course of the war by listening to the BBC news regularly. Of the newspapers that we got, I remember most vividly the war maps in the *Daily Telegraph* and the constant exhortations to greater effort in the defence of the British Empire in Lord Beaverbrook's *Daily Express.*

We knew the calibre of the guns on the German pocket battleship *Graf Spee*, the difference not only between a British Hurricane fighter and a Spitfire but also between the basic Messerschmidt 109 and the E and F versions of the German fighter. We could talk about the failure of the British at Singapore — the heavy artillery all faced the wrong way.

But, of course, the war was not all. There were movies and music, though both, despite the valiant talents of Noel Coward, Gracie Fields, George Formby, Laurence Olivier, Vivien Leigh and Leslie Howard, were being increasingly dominated by Americans.

There was one unchallenged British "cultural" institution: the Sunday *News of the World*, whose titillating tales of sexual shenanigans made it the most eagerly awaited newspaper of the week at the school, as in the rest of the British Isles. The newspaper, which boasted it had the world's largest circulation, delighted in recounting in the reticent language of Victorian prudery the rambunctious Edwardian behavior of the upper classes. There could hardly have been anything more British than the national fascination with accounts of the goings-on in English vicarages between a seemingly endless parade of randy curates and willing choir mistresses or vicars' wives.

We also got caught up in the winds of change that were sweeping Britain to the left. While Winston Churchill was enjoying the deserved plaudits of his people and the world as a successful war leader, the excitement was to the left of him. There was the Beveridge plan, the "cradle to grave" program drawn up by Sir William Beveridge that was to provide the universal unemployment and health insurance that shaped postwar Britain under the Tories as well as Labour.

What first got me interested in politics was not the politicians but a writer: J. B. Priestley, a famous novelist, playwright and journalist of the period. I heard Priestley speak at a Labour meeting at Gateshead Town Hall. What I remember about the speech now — and indeed all I remembered about the speech the next morning — was that it had nothing to do with the wider political aims of the Labour Party to nationalize the Tyneside shipyards or the Durham coal pits, or the even grander debate about the merits or failings of Karl Marx's teachings. What has stuck with me is what he said about things I knew about, things I had seen with my own eyes but had never much thought about.

Priestley spoke that day of the people of Tyneside. As a Yorkshireman, he was speaking of neighbors he knew well.

He talked about their children, how they were smaller and skinnier than other children. That was something I knew from my own experience. Among the children I went to school with in Gateshead, I was tall, but I also knew that I was not tall standing next to boys my age in Shropshire, the Czech school or the areas of London that I knew. I knew, too, that many of the children I had gone to school with in Gateshead had been raised on a diet heavy on bread fried in suet. And I knew of people who, before the war brought jobs back to the Tyneside, had been reduced to heating their homes, in an area that was full of coal mines, with coal scavenged from the pit slag heaps. But people used to excuse this by saying that it was all because of the Great Depression.

Yes, said Priestley, the Depression had made things worse. But the cause of their condition, he told the Tynesiders, went far beyond the Depression. Did they not remember, he asked them, people ridiculing the idea of giving them better housing because if they were given bathrooms they would waste them by using the bathtubs as coal scuttles? Did they not realize that their children were small because they themselves were small and their parents were small and that this was so because, after 600 years of coal digging in Durham, they had been bred small to be able to work in the narrow mine shafts just as surely as had the pit ponies that hauled the coal? He warned them that unless they stopped letting the pit owners and shipyard managers tell them how to vote, unless they stopped voting for Liberal solicitors and Tory squires, unless they voted for Labour, their lives after the war would return to where they had been before it.

But although I was fired up by this vision of England as a "New Jerusalem," I knew that I was not part of it. Most of us at the Czech school were comfortable with things British, with the language, the country, the people and their mores. But however easily many of us could pass as British schoolchildren, we all knew we were not British. Most of us were also aware that Britain was at the time an all but homogeneous country and not the steaming pot of immigrants it has since become. There was no guarantee that the British, who had treated refugees from the Nazi-occupied continent so generously, would be equally hospitable when we failed to return to the countries that Britain had at such great cost to itself helped liberate.

By contrast, at school our return to Czechoslovakia was taken for granted. But while we were being indoctrinated with a vision of a country that, once liberated, would fulfill the ideals of democracy and multicultural tolerance of its founding father, Tomáš Masaryk, the philosopher-king, it did occur to many of us that the reality might not live up to the promise.

Finally, the war was over. Great celebrations everywhere. At the school, too. But what was a time of great joy for everyone around us was, for those of us whose parents had stayed behind in Czechoslovakia, also a time of great anxiety and sorrow.

From the time that the concentration camps were being liberated towards the end of the war, it became clear that our chances of seeing our families alive again were slim. But although there were millions dead, there were also thousands saved. And that was grounds for hope.

But from my parents, of my parents, not a word.

At first, there had been lots of letters from my parents, cheery ones, saying the kind of things parents say to their children: make sure you eat well and dress warmly, do your homework, write home more often, make your bed, help your aunt with the dishwashing. There were even packages with clothing, shoes and sweaters my mother had knitted.

As the war wore on, the letters became more infrequent and the packages stopped. But my father managed to find ways of keeping the letters coming through his network of friends and relatives abroad. They came to us from Hungary, Romania, Switzerland, Italy and, towards the end, through Portugal. It often took months for their letters and ours to reach their destinations. The mail was also censored. In one letter, my mother complained that the censors had lifted photographs of Ernie and me out of one of our letters. Sometimes, after months in which they got no mail and worried about us, several letters would arrive all at once in a batch. Obviously, too, all the letters did not make it.

In their letters to their children, everything was always fine with my parents, even after they were deported from Bratislava to a small town where they must have known that their next stop would be a concentration camp or a ghetto in Poland. But there were also quite a few other letters from them that I did not get to see until long after the war. They were letters they had been sending to the adults of the family. These were quite different from the cheerful ones they sent their sons.

"We live a secluded life," my father wrote to his in-laws in England in November 1939, "and, except for work, don't go out. Our only enjoyment is radio music. At 6:30 in the morning I am already sitting by the radio and in the evenings we listen to music till 11:45. Hugo misses his radio very much."

There were hidden messages in these sentences. Since my parents worked and lived in the same building, it meant they never went out, presumably not by choice. The statement that Hugo — an uncle who lived in Prague — missed his radio meant that his radio had been confiscated and that he could no longer keep up with what was going on in the world. My father, on the other hand, could still enjoy his radio. And that meant not just music but also news of the outside world.

There were other such between-the-lines messages in the letters. "We often have guests nowadays," my father wrote in 1940. From other letters, it became clear that the guests were people who had been expelled from their homes. Sometimes the letters spoke about people having a new address, which meant they had been deported.

All this time, of course, they would have known that their turn would come too. As it was for all those who knew they were condemned, that it was only a matter of time before they started their journey to the gates of hell, it must have been a terrible wait. My parents would have been treated by most gentiles around them as if they no longer existed. Some perhaps would have drawn closer, a few out of sympathy perhaps but others only to circle like vultures waiting for their taste of carrion. In *Life with a Star*, a largely autobiographical novel, Jiří Weil wrote about a Jewish family in Prague watching a German couple, who would take over their apartment once they were deported, inspect their home:

"They didn't say a word. They didn't look at us; they pretended not to see us at all. I remained sitting at the table, and in my embarrassment I began to stir the tea I had drunk long before. They only looked at the objects in the room. They caressed the furniture, took the pewter mugs in their hands, felt the upholstery of the sofas. They calculated loudly between them the quality and sturdiness of various objects; they discussed how they would move the furniture around. We were already dead. They had come to claim their inheritance."

In the autumn of 1941, my parents were deported from Bratislava. But not to Poland. Not yet. They were moved to the small Slovak town of Hlohovec. But not to a camp. They were allowed to rent a room.

By now they had no work, no means of income; they were living on whatever money they had been able to bring with them. They also had nothing to do and nowhere to go. In December, my father would have lost his typewriter. There is a record of the order given to Slovak police to confiscate all typewriters owned by Jews and, indeed, the few letters my father was still to write were hand-written. They would have also lost their last lifeline to the outside world, the radio. The order to confiscate radios is also on the books. And so is the confiscation of all fur coats; the furs were collected to be sent to Russia to warm the Slovak troops fighting alongside the Germans. My mother would have lost the black Persian lamb coat she had had ever since I could remember. She also had one of those fox furs — the entire skin, the head equipped with staring glass eyes, tail, feet, claws and all — that women, for reasons that I still can't fathom, used to wear draped around their necks. These fox furs were more for parade than warmth, of course, and my mother, being a sensible woman, probably would have left it behind. She certainly would not have much use for it in Hlohovec.

My parents knew that for them Hlohovec was only a way station. That much is clear from their letters. All they could do now was to sit and wait, wait for "resettlement," the euphemism the Nazis used for deportation to the death camps of Poland.

My mother's letters to her brothers were full of anguish. "Each letter from our children and you is our greatest joy," she wrote in February 1942. "The sun then shines again for a few days. The longing for our dear ones is all but unbearable."

Then, in a letter dated March 17, 1942, this news from my father: "We have begun to pack even though we do not yet know for sure when and where we shall be resettled."

On the same day, he wrote his last letter to his sons:

"There are days when we regret that you are so far from us. Then come days like today when it makes us glad and happy. . . .

"May the Almighty give you further good health and may he let you grow up into just and decent men. Do not forget the precepts you were taught and the upbringing you enjoyed in your parental home."

Then silence.

Nine days after my father wrote his goodbye to us, the deportation of Slovak Jews to Poland and the death camps began.

We know that now because both the Slovaks and the Germans kept precise records of the "resettlement." For the organizers, it was a business transaction, pure and simple. The Germans charged the Slovaks $200 for providing "shelter, food, clothing and retraining" for each Jew they took. In addition, the Slovaks agreed to provide the trains. To the Germans, who were hard-pressed for rolling stock to supply their armies in Russia, this was an important concession. They also demanded payment for use of tracks in Germany and Poland. When the Slovaks balked at that, the Germans agreed to a fifty percent "group-fare" reduction.

On March 9, 1942, after weeks of rumors, the Jews of Slovakia got their first firm indication that the deportations were about to begin. A new regulation increased the size of the Star

of David Jews in Slovakia had to wear from six centime-
tres to ten. A similar order preceded the deportation of Jews
from Germany itself. That, presumably, was why my parents
started to pack.

On March 26, 1942, the deportation trains started rolling.
At first, they went to Lublin. Later, they dispensed with the
Lublin stopover; they went directly to Auschwitz. Altogether,
70,000 Jews from Slovakia were sent to Poland. Only 5,000
came back.

When we got to Auschwitz, they gave us a picnic lunch. Right
there where the rails that used to bring the trains that carried
the people to feed the furnaces entered the Birkenau killing
centre, they served us sausage, bread and beer.

It was hot that June day of 1979. I was thirsty. I took a
deep gulp straight from the beer bottle and I choked. I felt
sick. I felt anger. Mostly I was angry at myself for the pro-
fanity of having succumbed to my thirst in such a place. But
I was also mad at the people who had had the insensitivity to
serve lunch there and I was resentful of the situation in which
I found myself.

I was at Auschwitz-Birkenau not because my parents and
other relatives probably died there, nor because of the nearly three million people who certainly did. I was there because of the death at Auschwitz of one man. Ninety percent
of those who had been killed at Auschwitz had been Jews.
But no one in the crowd around me had come to remember them. They had come for ceremonies to commemorate
the death of a gentile, a Polish priest named Maximilian
Kolbe.

Father Kolbe richly deserved to be remembered and hon-
ored. He died having voluntarily taken the place of a man
condemned to death by the Nazis. The old Judaic dictum of
"save a life, save the world" certainly applied to Maximilian
Kolbe. But what went on that day at Oswiecim, the Polish name for the place the Germans had called Auschwitz,
was not so much a commemoration of a dead Polish priest

as a celebration of a living one. The Pope was coming to Oswiecim. The Polish Pope was visiting Auschwitz.

Karol Wojtyla had come back to Poland for the first time since he had left his archbishopric in Cracow eight months earlier for the Vatican conclave that had elected him pope. A storm of pride and piety engulfed the country on his return. After decades, even centuries, of being downtrodden as a land and a people, Poles were lifted out of their national despondency by the Catholic world's recognition of one of their own and his elevation to the throne of thrones, the see of St. Peter.

Their exhilaration was gentled by devoutness, a piety not so much of sinners seeking personal salvation as of a people yearning for national redemption, for a rebirth of its long-lost freedom. For Poles, the Roman Church had for a long time not been all that Roman or the universal church that Rome prided itself on being. It was a Polish church, a Polish national treasure that for centuries had protected the nation from the scourges of foreign occupiers and the ravages of alien faiths. Often, of course, the peril came from within, as it did now from Polish communists. Since the communists had taken over all institutions except the Church, religion had become even more important as an instrument of national salvation. But even the Church was besieged, even the Church was not free in Poland. Karol Wojtyla's improbable elevation to the papacy had eased the pressure by creating a Polish interlocutor who was beyond the reach of Poland's politburo and secret police. Karol Wojtyla's elevation was therefore taken by many Poles as a sign of divine intervention, a sign that God had answered the Polish nation's anguished prayers.

To most people in other countries, John Paul II is a charismatic figure. But in Poland that spring he was an elemental force. Everywhere he went, in Warsaw, in Gniezno, in Częstochowa, in Cracow, his diocese as archbishop, the crowds were transfixed by awe and adulation. Even the atheistic communist rulers of the country were forced to pay homage to him. You did not have to be a Pole or a Catholic to be caught up in the emotions of the crowds and feel the strength of the communion between them and their Pope. Down to the last Pole at the furthest fringes of the crowds at the open-air pontifical masses, not an eye ever seemed to leave that dot in white at the distant altar. John Paul infused his long-suffering people with hope, pride and confidence. And devotion.

The seeds he sowed then would ripen a year later with the rise of Solidarity and help lead, within a decade, to the breaking of Poland's chains. That spring, John Paul II was the uncrowned King of Poland. These were his people, and this was his land.

But now he had come to Oswiecim, a place different from the rest of Poland. True, Oswiecim is Polish. But Oswiecim is also Auschwitz and as Auschwitz it belongs to all whose blood was shed there and to those they left behind to remember them, Jews as well as Poles, Greeks and Frenchmen, gypsies and even Germans who in one way or another displeased Hitler enough to be sent there. Auschwitz, in fact, belongs to the world as a warning of the horrors to which hate can lead. But above all, Auschwitz belongs to the Jews because in this place and a few others like it the centuries-old rich civilization of Europe's Ashkenazi Jewry was all but destroyed.

Primo Levi, an Auschwitz survivor who wrote movingly about his experiences there, used to say that "you never escape from Auschwitz." I realized that day that though I had never even seen this accursed piece of ground before — and hope never to see it again — I, too, could not escape Auschwitz, that willy-nilly it would always be a part of me.

But while we waited for the Pope to arrive, I could see that, for that day at least, Auschwitz would not belong to its victims, certainly not to the Jews, nor, for that matter, even all that much to Father Kolbe. While John Paul prayed in private mourning in what had been the priest's cell, the crowds that had gathered at the other end of the Auschwitz complex were in a mood of joyful anticipation of his presence.

The Pope celebrated mass before a huge altar erected inside the Birkenau camp gate at the railhead where once the trains discharged their human cargo from overstuffed cattle cars, where SS men with a wave of a finger picked those who would go directly to the gas chambers and those who would be allowed to live for a while longer. Above the altar, a huge cross with a crown of barbed wire thorns. Below it in the crowd, more crosses and Polish flags and a few people in striped concentration camp uniforms. Nowhere, though, not at the altar, not in the crowd, not on the uniforms of the concentration camp survivors was there any reminder of the Star of David, the symbol worn by the vast majority of those who had passed through this gate of hell.

John Paul himself did pay tribute to the Jewish victims of Auschwitz. On his way from Father Kolbe's cell block to the mass, he laid a wreath at the Death Wall, a stark monument of rough stone inscribed in Hebrew to the memory of the more than two million Jewish victims of Auschwitz. But the furthest he would go in his homily towards dealing with the gaping anti-Semitic fault line in Poland's moral landscape was that "it is not permissible for anyone to pass by this inscription with indifference." It was, for a man given to strong, unambiguous moral stands, a statement of uncharacteristic reticence. But considering the strength of anti-Semitism in Poland, that it continued throughout the war though the Germans were slaughtering Poles as well as Jews, that it kept on after the war with the persecution of the tiny surviving remnant of Polish Jewry, and that it exists still although there are almost no Jews left in the country, it was not surprising that the Polish Pope held back from his strong views on anti-Semitism. He had, after all, come home to inspire the Poles, not to chastise them.

Seven years later, John Paul stood in Rome's main synagogue taking turns with the Chief Rabbi of Rome in reading from the Psalms. He thus became the first of the 264 successors of St. Peter to attend a synagogue service. "You are our dearly beloved brothers," the Pope told the congregation, "and in a way you are our elder brothers."

It was an historic and generous gesture, even if it was centuries overdue. But it would have been more historic, more generous, more courageous and certainly more effective if John Paul had said these words of reconciliation between the Church and Jewry not in Italy, where Jew and Christian live amicably side by side, but in Poland, where it was needed, either at that mass at Auschwitz in 1979 or at Warsaw's Umschlagplatz whence the Jews of the Warsaw ghetto started their journey to their Calvary. Not for the sake of Jews. For the sake of Poles.

The Royal Air Force Halifax bomber dipped low over Cologne. From my seat in the rear gun turret I could see the spire of Cologne cathedral. The cathedral was clearly visible — it stood alone. Just about everything around it had been levelled by bombs. Nearby, a bridge across the Rhine lay shattered in the water.

It was July 31, 1945, exactly six years and a month since I had crossed Nazi Germany as, more or less, a reprieved death-row prisoner. I was now heading the other way, flying home over a prostrate, conquered Germany.

I was all but bursting with elation. Sitting there in the gun turret, looking down on the ruins of Cologne, I felt almost as though I had fought and won the war. I remember singing; I don't remember what. If there had been any ammunition in the gun before me, I probably would have fired off a few rounds just to celebrate. But there wasn't. The Halifax carried no bombs, no ammunition. It was being used to ferry the first group of children from the Czech school to Prague.

The school had closed; it had done its work. Most of the students who had parents in Britain stayed there. A few, whose parents felt they had a role to play in the new Czechoslovakia, returned despite the growing evidence of chaos on the continent. For the rest of us, there was really no choice. There certainly was none for Ernie and me. Our relatives made no move to keep us in Britain, and we would have had nowhere else to go if we had wanted to stay. But the problem never arose. We had both convinced ourselves that, whatever lay ahead, we should go back, that we owed it to our parents and ourselves at least to take a look to find out what had happened to them.

We were flown over in RAF planes because there was no other quick way across Europe. There were no civilian flights. Most of the European railroad system lay shattered. On the roads there were few civilian vehicles and gas only for those who had military authorization or enough money to buy it on the black market.

Millions of people displaced by the war were crisscrossing the continent trying to find their way home. It was slow, painful going. Finding transport was difficult enough. Even when they did find transportation, the displaced wanderers were often stopped short of their destination — detained at processing camps; hassled at the military roadblocks of the various victorious armies for identity papers they did not have; stopped and harassed at borders.

Flying comfortably high above the misery of Europe that summer made us almost as privileged as I had been when I crossed Germany by train six years earlier. In fact, just as Nicky Winton had to resort to tricks to get us out, it took a subterfuge to get the RAF to take us back. My papers, endorsed by the British Foreign Office, stated that I was a "child of Czechosl. Govt. Official" and that I was travelling "on an Official Mission."

But once we landed in Prague and got off the RAF plane, we lost our "official" status and with it the cosseted protection we had taken for granted during our six years in Britain. The teachers and other people who had looked after us at the school in Wales left us; they were busy trying to put their own lives back together again. We were back to the realities of Europe.

We may have had dreams of being welcomed back home with open arms. A few of our group indeed had relatives who took them in. There were even a few cases where parents had survived by being able to hide out from the Gestapo. But for most of us, there was no one left. We were on our own. We had become a part of Europe's vast army of the displaced and dispossessed.

Our first new home in Prague was a quarantine station and reception camp in a school. An inspection for lice. A dusting of DDT, just to make sure. A blanket, a palliasse and a spot on a classroom floor. A field kitchen in the courtyard dispensed thin soup and sour bread.

All around us were the victimized flotsam of the Third Reich — liberated concentration camp prisoners, inmates of forced labor camps. By late July, apart from latecomers like us, the people at the reception camp were the hard cases. Some were still emaciated. More were puffed up, apparently by too much food taken too suddenly for their long-deprived bodies to absorb.

Among these suffering survivors, our small group of schoolchildren, well-fed, well-dressed and healthy, must have looked very much out of place. We certainly felt it. We were full of energy, impatient to get on with our new lives. But to the people who ran the reception centre, we were just another group of returnees who had to be processed. And being there was, in a way, good for us. It was a cold-shower reminder that we could not hold ourselves above the misery around us, that like all the other people in the centre, we, too, had nowhere to go.

When people started coming back in the first days after the war from Germany, from Poland and other reaches of Hitler's collapsed empire, they were welcomed as lost brothers and sisters. There were celebrations of their safe return, there was sympathy and help. But as the Czechs tried to put the war behind them, they became inured to the plight of the former concentration camp inmates and those who had been pressed into forced labor in Germany. There were so many of them and they all wanted help. What aroused the greatest antipathy towards them was that they wanted their lives back. They wanted the homes they had lived in, homes that were now occupied by others. They wanted their jobs and businesses back and found those jobs and businesses taken. Many of Hitler's victims came home only to find themselves unwanted and resented as intruders. They were home at last, but it was no longer the home they had dreamed about in captivity.

Indifference was now widespread. So was insensitivity and sometimes outright hostility. Some returnees were shunned because they were sick and looked terrible, or simply because their experiences had made them too different in some other way. Many were avoided because they were too wrapped up in their hurts and would not talk; even more were considered a nuisance because they could not seem to talk about much else than the pain of what had happened to them.

Filip was one of the talkers. Filip had his straw sack next to mine. He talked, and I sat there listening, riveted by the horror of his tale.

Filip had been at Auschwitz. But he was no ordinary inmate. Filip had been a stoker at the furnaces at Auschwitz, a member of the Sonderkommando, the Special Detail, the handmaiden of the death machine, the corps of the damned and the doomed. To the assigned to the crematorium meant life for awhile, if life it could be called, a life of watching hundreds of thousands, two or three thousand at a time, die, screaming, praying, singing; of undressing, brutalizing and robbing bodies, stacking them; of stirring corpses in the furnace with long pokers as if they were nothing more than logs; and then certain death.

The Germans routinely rotated the furnace work squads by exterminating them to make sure no one would stay alive to bear witness. Five times they liquidated the Sonderkommando that Filip was serving on, and five times he survived. He was spared in part because even the most efficient killing machine in history had its inefficiencies, and partly because, in their attempt at maximizing efficiency, those in charge of the machine became so subservient to its needs that they often ignored the larger aims of Hitler and Heinrich Himmler of keeping the extermination of the Jews secret and became loath to get rid of their best trained cogs lest it keep them from attaining the death quotas set for them by Berlin.

Only a few members of the Sonderkommandos survived and one of these rare survivors (I did not know then how rare) was now sitting on his palliasse next to me recounting what it had been like — the gas chamber disguised as a shower room, the people who had gone in trusting German assurances that it was only a disinfecting shower, the people who knew better but for whom by then death was a welcome liberation from their agony, the people who had resisted and were shot, beaten to death or thrown live into the fire of the crematorium, the tearing out of the teeth of the dead to retrieve the gold in their mouths, and the stench of death and smoke that always hung over Auschwitz.

Filip couldn't stop talking. And I couldn't stop listening. I had heard of the multitudes that had been killed by the Germans in the concentration camps before I met Filip. But the news accounts were of the dead, and for all the horrible pictures of the stacks and stacks of bodies, they were at least still, lifeless and beyond hurt. What Filip spoke of was the torments of the living, of mothers whose babies were torn out of their arms and smashed headfirst against walls, of people who were dead long before their lungs breathed the Zyklon-B gas and knew it, an agony of living more unbearable than the throes of death.

As Filip talked, his face torn by grimaces of pain, his fists pounded the floor, mostly in anger, but also, it seemed to me, in remorse at having survived. Usually, I was Filip's only audience. Most of the others around us didn't listen because they already knew; most of them were only too aware of the closeness of their escape from death's clutches. But for me, a seventeen-year-old schoolboy who had spent the Auschwitz years picking hazelnuts and blackberries in the peaceful backwaters of Britain and knew no greater danger than the risk of being caught stealing an apple from a farmer's orchard, Filip's revelations were shattering.

By then, of course, I knew that there was no hope of still finding my parents alive. If either of them had survived, there would have been word by now. A letter to the family addresses they knew in England. A note. A card. They would have somehow contacted their children if it were the last thing they ever did in their lives. After all, we had heard from my cousin Hanna promptly after the British army liberated Bergen-Belsen, the concentration camp in which she had been detained. Of all my relatives in Czechoslovakia who had not managed to flee, Hanna was the only one to survive. But only briefly. Shortly after her liberation, she died of typhoid.

Because I did not know when my parents died, how they died, where they died, their death was for me in a way only an abstraction. They had been alive six years earlier and now they were not. In between, I had grown up without them, independent, inured to the absence of love. I had not really missed my parents at school because so many around me were parentless. I grew up in what was essentially a community of orphans who didn't know yet that they had been orphaned. I could not even say when it was that the realization dawned on me that my parents were not just absent but dead. The change from being aware in 1943, when the first reports of the death camps reached us, that I might never see them again to the certainty that they were no longer alive was so gradual that there was no single moment of shocked awareness. In a way, my mother and father had not so much died as faded out of my life.

It was Filip who brought home to me the fact that my parents had not just died and disappeared, but that they had been murdered in ways heretofore unimaginable. It did not matter whether they made it all the way to those gas chambers in Auschwitz or managed to escape from this life on the way. Stuffed into cattle cars, suffocated, starved, abused, beaten, whipped, shot, snarled at by dogs and guards, people do not die; they are torn from life. And even then, they were not left alone. There was still soap to be made from the little fat they had left, lamp shades from their skin and gold to be mined from their teeth.

Listening to Filip turned what had been my sorrow into anguish, anger at the Germans, anger at the world that had allowed it to happen, and guilt and shame, guilt at having survived while so many others died and shame at having lived a normal, happy life through all the time that they had suffered. It was the violation of the dead that haunted me most. For years after the war, I had nightmares in which my father's gold-crowned teeth were being pulled out of his head. And even now, nearly a half century later, I find it easier to say that my parents "died in the war" than to talk about what really happened to them.

More than forty years later I saw Filip again. In a movie. He was interviewed at length in Claude Lanzmann's *Shoa*, the nine-hour recounting of the Holocaust. There was no mistaking Filip Muller. His hair had gone sparse and grey but the twist of the mouth and the intensity of the eyes were still the same. So was the story, if not the telling.

Where in 1945 he had been angry and overwrought, in '85 he is calm, almost clinical. He recounts that the four crematoria of Auschwitz-Birkenau were numbered Two, Three, Four and Five. Crematoria Two and Three, he tells us, were identical and were served by an underground "undressing" room of 180 square metres and a gas chamber with a capacity of killing 3,000 people at a time and fifteen ovens to dispose of them. Four and Five, by contrast, had no underground room for undressing and its three gas chambers and eight ovens could accommodate only 1,800 to 2,000 people at most.

He talks of the most terrible of all the horrors he saw, the scene in the gas chamber after the shrieking and screaming had stopped and the door had been opened, of finding the corpses of the weaker lying battered at the bottom of a heap as the stronger in the last seconds of their lives clambered over them to get to the door they could never hope to open or towards the ceiling for a last desperate breath before the gas rose to reach them.

Only once does Filip break down in the film interview. He stops, unable for a moment to speak, and the tears start running down his cheeks as he recounts the fate of the first group of Czech Jews to come to the gas chambers. These are people who speak his language, many of them people he knows, not the strangers whose dying he has witnessed over and over. Most of the Czechs are aware, as so many thousands of others before and after them were not, what is about to happen to them. As they go into the gas chamber, they start singing. They are singing the Czech national anthem and then the Zionist Hatikvah, later to become the national anthem of Israel.

The two songs fit the moment. They are not, as so many other national anthems, a call to battle, a summons to stand on guard, or a celebration of great victories and of the glories of kings and flags. The Czech anthem and the Hatikvah share a lyrical wistfulness. "Where is my home?" the Czechs sing, "Where is my home?" And the Hatikvah proclaims that "Our hope is not yet lost . . . so long as within his heart the soul of the Jew yearns."

Hearing his countrymen singing of home and hope when they no longer had either, Filip decided he wanted to die with them. He realized then, he says, that his life was no longer worth living. He went into the gas chamber with the others. There, while the preparations for death went on around them, a group of women he knew came up to him to talk him out of dying, to convince him that his death would be senseless. "Your death will not bring us life," he recalls one of them saying. "You must get out of here alive. You must bear witness to our suffering."

And so Filip Muller chose life and lived to bear witness for history of what happened at the epicentre of the hell we now call the Holocaust.

In 1945, there was no talk yet of a Jewish Holocaust. If comparatively far more Jews were killed than gentiles, if European Jewry had been all but exterminated, it seemed then, given what Hitler had stood for, not all that surprising. After all, he had made it clear right from the beginning that the Jews were his primary enemies and that he was determined to exterminate them. Yet the killing of the Jews, even if it was a greater calamity than all the many disasters that have befallen Jewry since the disappearance of ten of Israel's twelve tribes into the maw of Assyria, still seemed in 1945 to have been an integral part of the war.

The realization that the Holocaust was something apart from the war — not only for Hitler but for the Allied leadership, too — did not come till much later. It grew out of the revelations of war crimes trials at Nüremberg, from the first writings of Ely Wiesel and Primo Levi, the poets of Auschwitz, and swelled to its present acceptance as a concept of ultimate horror after Simon Wiesenthal hunted down Adolf Eichmann, after Eichmann's trial and its stunning revelation that this chief architect of the killing machine was not some raving fanatic obsessed by anti-Semitic hate but only a bland, boring bureaucrat preoccupied with his paper-shuffling duties, a man for whom mass killing was mainly only a problem of logistics, the embodiment of a phenomenon Hannah Arendt came to call the "banality of evil."

Yet even now, all after the trials, the hundreds of books and studies, we are still left with all too many questions with no answers. How, for instance, could men, normal men, not pathologically twisted killers, go on killing defenceless men, women and children day after day as just another day's work? And can such people be called normal because they still love their families, are kind to their dogs and civil to their neighbors? Or, what was it that made the German war machine persist in the Holocaust killings even at the cost of any chance of victory and at the peril of Germany's own survival? There have been many attempts to explain such questions but there are no sure answers that might explain the past as well as safeguard the future.

Questions that have no answers haunt us. We cannot dispose of them, write finis, wrap them up, tie a ribbon around them and put them away to gather dust. Unanswerable questions can only lie there festering, ready to burst forth with new virulence. The bitter eruption more than forty years after the war of the Waldheim affair — the evasions of Austrian President Kurt Waldheim's answers to questions about his dubious Nazi past — is but one example of the potency of this particular brand of poison.

In the summer of 1945, I was first faced with the pain of questions for which there were no answers then, nor since. They were the most basic questions about what happened: where, when and how? When did my parents die, where and how?

In Prague alone, there were tens of thousands of others asking similar questions — of officialdom, which was swamped
with them and, for the most part, stumped for an answer, and
of each other.

The Old Customs House in Prague was the place to go for
the answers. You stood in long lines and filled out long ques-
tionnaires. Then you waited. And left. And came back and
waited again.

But there was another way. Something you could do while
you waited for an official answer. The long corridors of the
Customs House were filled with notices pasted to the walls
as high as the eye could see. The notices all had different
names on them but the same message: "Anyone who knows
anything about the whereabouts of ——— please contact
———." There were old, pre-deportation home addresses,
ages, perhaps additional details such as "last heard from in
such and such a place," and often even pictures.

There was also a more optimistic version. These notices
didn't just presume the possibility of survival as the ambigu-
ous "whereabouts" did. They asserted survival and defiantly
denied death its due by addressing themselves peremptorily
to the missing person directly: " ———, get in touch with
your brother ———."

I walked the corridors, scanning the walls, looking for my
parents' names, for a clue, any clue, the word Bratislava, or a
name I knew, or the name of some distant relative or family
acquaintance, a name that I perhaps no longer remembered
but one that might jog my memory when I saw it.

There was nothing on the wall. Nothing from the authorities. Not in Prague. Not in Bratislava. No trace of my parents
once they left Hlohovec.

El Salvador, March 1982. Estela Escobar comes to the Catholic Legal Office of the San Salvador archbishopric every few
days just as I used to go to the Prague Customs House. She
is looking for her son, Ricardo, who was taken away from her
house by a group of men in a National Guard truck and never
seen again.

At the Customs House, they had names, but not the people. Here at the Legal Office, they have bodies, but not their names. The bodies are found every morning dumped by the sides of roads or tossed onto garbage dumps. It's the night's harvest of the killers of the Salvadoran army, the police, the rightist death squads and, occasionally, of the leftist guerrillas. According to the Legal Office, there have been 13,000 such killings in the past year and the number is rising fast. What passes for investigations of these deaths — they are at best mere inquiries — lead nowhere.

All the Legal Office can do is to keep count, call the world's attention to what is going on in El Salvador and try to find names and graves for the dead. They have stacks of photos, album after album full of pictures showing men who were shot in the head, or were garrotted, or had their skulls bashed in. Many show signs of torture; some have had their eyes gouged out.

Estela Escobar goes patiently through the lastest grotesque pictures without showing a flicker of emotion. Ricardo is not among them. She is relieved. As long as she does not find him in one of the photos she can still hope that perhaps Ricardo is in jail somewhere or that he managed to escape and joined the guerrillas in the hills. She probably no longer believes that, but she says she does. She has nothing else.

I watch her leave, an old lady, much older than her age, with no one to go to and no one to look after her. Tomorrow, or the day after, she'll be back to look at a new batch of dead faces.

Estela Escobar has probably never heard of the Holocaust in Europe. She doesn't need to. She knows what it is.

CHAPTER III

In the end one can get used to anything.

Václav Havel

The major was a war hero; he became one after the war was over. The major prided himself on being a family man; yet for years he also had a secret mistress. The major was a patriot who preached sacrifice for the sake of the country; he also dealt on the black market. The major was the manager of a capitalist enterprise and an anti-communist. Then one fine day, he joined the Communist Party.

Major Antonín Rakouš was my guardian and foster father. If you have concluded by now that I did not like him very much, you are right. I will admit that some of the things I have just said about him are not quite fair — as I will explain in a moment — but they are all true. And because they are true, I was disabused as a teenager of the belief that all heroes are heroic, patriots patriotic and that upstanding citizens of impeccable reputation are necessarily honest and honorable.

It has occurred to me in later years that perhaps I should have thanked the major for having taught me that lesson. Indeed, more than forty years later I can look back on him with a chuckle. He was quite the card. And I do acknowledge that I owe him a debt of gratitude. After all, he took me in and gave me a home. But at the time, I felt betrayed. My benefactor, my hero was a fraud.

It was bitterness that made me think of the spiteful crack about the major being a postwar hero. What made him a hero happened in Prague between May 5 and May 9, 1945. By May 5, the Germans had all but stopped fighting. Those who hadn't surrendered or been captured were busy fleeing westward to avoid falling into Soviet hands. Grand Admiral Karl Dönitz, Hitler's successor, stalled on surrendering to give his troops more time to reach the lines of the Western Allied armies, where German prisoners were treated more humanely than in Soviet captivity. It was only after Gen. Eisenhower threatened to close his lines to refugees and fleeing soldiers that the German High Command signed the unconditional surrender of all German forces on May 7. The next day was VE-day, the official end of World War II in Europe.

Among the troops trying to reach Allied lines was a pocket of German forces in Czechoslovakia. The Russians, having captured Berlin, were turning south towards Bohemia to mop them up. The nearest American forces, Gen. George Patton's Third Army, were only 60 kilometres southwest of Prague, near Pilsen.

The Czech underground resistance decided that the situation offered it an opportunity to liberate Prague on its own before the Allies got there, as the Parisians had fought to liberate their city the previous summer. It would be a politically and historically powerful symbol to be able to say that Czech forces, rather than foreigners, had liberated the capital of Czechoslovakia.

The trouble was that the Germans were not about to surrender to irregular forces. They knew what had happened elsewhere to Germans who had surrendered to local partisans. At best, they were humiliated and paraded before the people they had conquered and controlled to be spat at. Given the mood for revenge among the victims of the Nazis and the sudden need of those who had collaborated with them to demonstrate how they had really hated them all along, the

Germans also ran the risk of being massacred. So they resisted, and what became known as the battle of the Prague Uprising was on.

That's where the major came in. He lived across the street from the Prague radio station, a prime target of the insurrectionists. They needed the radio station to induce more people to join the uprising, to give orders to their fighters and also to give history a little propaganda shove to launch it in the right direction.

The major went out and, as an experienced military man (even if only a retired signals officer), led the assault on Radio Prague. He and his men took the station.

It was one of the few successful actions of the uprising. As the weight of German superiority in weapons began to grind down the lightly armed resistance forces in the city, they broadcast an appeal to the Allies to come and rescue Prague.

In response, Soviet Marshal Ivan Konev sent an armored column racing south to Prague. The Americans could have easily got there first, and Patton was itching to have his tanks beat the Russians to Prague. But his superior, General Omar Bradley, much to Patton's annoyance, ordered him to stay put because Prague was on the Soviet side of the line that Roosevelt, Churchill and Stalin had drawn across the map of Europe at the Yalta conference. Having once handed over Czechoslovakia to Hitler, the Western powers this time were making a present of it to Stalin.

On May 9, the Russians reached Prague. The last skirmish of the war was over. Soviet troops were lionized as heroes. So was the major. He also became my hero by saving me from an orphanage. He had contacted the welfare authorities and offered to take in a war orphan. And though he was a Catholic, he specifically asked for a Jewish child. But not a small child that needed a lot of looking after, he said. His wife had been injured when their home had been hit by a bomb in an American air raid and was an invalid. Besides, his two children were in their early twenties.

I was picked to fill the bill. The social worker who looked after my case told me I was very lucky that a man of such high reputation was willing to take me in. I was not quite so sure about my luck. I had originally had a vague idea that Ernie and I would set up housekeeping along with some of our friends from the school in Wales who found themselves in the same fix we were in. But the welfare people scotched that thought; they insisted that as minors we would either have to live with a family or be placed in an institution. In the end, the idea of moving in with strangers was less abhorrent than staying in the barren surroundings and impersonal ambience of the youth hostel where I had been staying since I was released from the returnee reception centre.

After a few weeks' wait, the Rakouš family moved out of their bomb-damaged apartment into a new and more spacious place, and I moved in with them. The major's wife, a wraith of a woman, welcomed me with a cake that, she announced triumphantly, had real eggs in it. The cake was indeed a handsome welcome since fresh eggs were almost as rare in food-short Prague as those of the Caspian sturgeon.

Still, I was wary of these strangers. I had passed through the hands of too many of them by now. But my wariness was soon overcome by the Rakouš children, Dalibor, the son, and his sister, Darča. They treated me with the friendly familiarity of the young and the tolerance of amused superiority that those who have just graduated from teenagehood reserve for teenagers.

The uncertainty and unease that had been gnawing at me since I had left Wales receded, especially after Ernie, who came to Prague several weeks after I did, found a home, too. He had moved in with an older cousin and her husband, who had also both returned from Britain. Our separate arrangements were not ideal but we had both managed to avoid having to spend the next few years in institutions.

All I had in the Rakouš household was a folding cot that was set up in whatever space was available. Sometimes I slept in the living room, sometimes in the dining room, but most often in a tiny space next to the furnace. In a way, I was only camping out there. But I didn't mind. I now had a family, not my own family to be sure, but still a family to come home to and a sense of belonging somewhere. I began to like the fact that my foster father was a man of substance — apart from being a hero, he also ran a factory that made buttons, snaps and other fasteners. He was a general director, no less, a title that in Europe, be it France, Germany or Czechoslovakia, brings nods of deference. And I was proud of him when he appeared on official occasions in his prewar uniform decked out with medals.

The major knew how to please a seventeen-year-old boy. He was always bluff with me, jolly and jocular. He placed few limits on my freedom. I could come and go as I wished at night. When I came in late, he would joke about it the next day and even sign an excuse slip for coming late to school. To me, his permissiveness was a mark of trust, an acknowledgment that I was being accepted as a grown-up. And he never made me feel, as had my aunt in Gateshead, as though, whatever I did, I could never be grateful enough for what had been done for me.

So once again I began putting together a new life. I was actually well off, not just because I had a home, but because for the first time in my life I had money, my own money, money I had earned.

I earned the money teaching English. I had two students whose spoken English was all but non-existent. Both were high school teachers who made their living teaching, of all things, English. I suspected — but never had the courage to ask them about it — that they had both taught German during the war and had found themselves with nothing to teach when it ended. German, the lingua franca of most of Europe during the war, became a non-language once the Nazis were defeated. It was replaced by Russian, which, for political reasons, was made mandatory in Czech schools, and, by public demand, by English.

My teacher students usually seemed to be only one lesson ahead of their students. And sometimes barely that. My job was to prepare them for the next day's classes. I often had a hard time keeping myself from laughing at the wonderful ways they found of mangling the English tongue. They, in turn, were frequently irritated with me because of my ignorance of the structure of English grammar. They wanted rules for everything; I knew none. I had been drilled at school in Latin and French grammar, but when it came to English, all I knew was how to speak it. I knew what a gerund was in Latin but not in English. I knew what the rules for the use of the subjunctive were in French but didn't even know that there was a subjunctive in English. Needless to say, I spoke neither Latin nor French. But then, I am almost certain, neither did my students ever learn to speak English, to say nothing of the poor students of my students.

I spent most of the money I earned exploring the night life of Prague. Much of it — from jazz and dancing to plays and operas — had been suppressed under Hitler. It now flourished, propelled it seemed by a need to purge the pain of long deprivation. Anything the Germans had proscribed — Smetana's opera *Libuše*, the boogie-woogie — was now a hit. Above all, Prague was dance mad. Glen Miller, whose plane was presumed to have been shot down when it disappeared over the English Channel towards the end of the war, was alive in the dance halls of Prague. But while the Miller sound was all around town, the dancing had been adapted to local conditions. Dance floors were so packed that there was no room for the space-consuming gyrations of the jitterbug. Instead, the Czechs developed a dance called the *třesák*, the shaker, which transformed the horizontal whirling and twirling of jitterbugging to vertical shaking. In the *třesák*, the dancers more or less stayed in place and bobbed up and down to the rhythm of the music. It was not a patch on the original. It was, as were so many things in Europe in those days, *ersatz*, a substitute, a poor substitute perhaps, but the best available.

Tobacco was *ersatz*; cigarettes were made mostly of weedy cousins of the tobacco plant. Stockings were thick and ugly rayon instead of either the old prewar silk or the new American nylon.

Much of the food was certainly *ersatz*. The so-called coffee was made of acorns, malt or barley, in fact anything but coffee beans. Bread was said to contain sawdust and sausages definitely were mostly bread. The beer was watery, eggs came powdered, and meat was almost non-existent and, when available, stringy and tasteless. And also strictly rationed.

The system was a good deal more restrictive than the one in Britain. In London, meat was rationed at the butcher's and eggs at the poulterer's but they were not if you bought them cooked in a restaurant. In Prague, on the other hand, to order a salami sandwich in a restaurant, you had to surrender a ration coupon for one hundred grams of bread, one for fifty grams of meat and another for butter.

No one starved, however, because there were two additional sources of food. The first was American aid. But unless they had nothing else to eat, people would frequently turn up their noses at it because so much of it came in cans containing tomatoes in one form or another. There was spaghetti in tomato sauce, tomato soup, ravioli in tomato sauce, tomato juice, beans in tomato sauce, even sardines in tomato sauce. It seemed to many Czechs as if the Americans never ate anything that was not smothered in tomatoes.

The other source was the black market. You could get anything illegally if you had enough money: the pork Czechs love so much, fresh eggs, chocolate and butter.

Some of these extras used to show up at the table in the Rakouš household. There was the occasional cake made with fresh eggs or sausages that tasted like sausages. Or there would be a pork roast on Sunday and once in awhile even a whole roast goose. The goose would come to the table swimming in fat. "Lean meat," the major would say, "is for women; men need fat." If he were still alive, the major would certainly be no quiche eater.

Whenever we had one of these feasts, the major would let it be known that the food had not come from the black market, that it had come from relatives in the country. The major and his wife both came from farming families, and their relatives, it seemed, always had a little to spare. The food would usually be brought into town by Pepík, a nephew who often stayed at the apartment but spent many of his weekends with his family in the country. Family helping out family, the major would say.

To me, it always seemed that the Rakouš household, me included, was lucky to have such a good source of extra food. But I wasn't certain whether getting unrationed food as a gift from relatives was morally superior to buying it on the black market. Not that I let it deter me from eating it with relish. It did bother me, however, to listen to the major denouncing others who were not as lucky as we were for patronizing the black market. During the war, he would argue, the black market had been needed because it not only helped people survive, it also sabotaged the German war effort. It was also dangerous; if you were caught by the Germans, it could mean death. And he told stories of his own exploits of bringing home contraband food by outwitting the Nazis. But now in peacetime, he would say, the black marketeers were only undermining the recovery of the country.

If it had not been for the major's homily about the evils of the black market, I don't suppose I would have thought much of it when a policeman in uniform arrived at the door one day while I was at home alone; he pulled a salami out of his briefcase and said, "For the major. Tell him I'll be back for my money." The policeman acted as though he were on his regular delivery rounds.

The salami incident struck me as a contradiction between what the major preached and what he ate. It got me wondering whether perhaps I had missed something about the geese and all the other goodies that came supposedly as gifts from relatives. So I asked Pepík about the food he brought to the house. He just laughed. "My uncle pays just like anyone else."

I was bothered but certainly not shocked to find out that the major was a regular black-market customer. The black market was everywhere, and the judgments about it were similar to the varied moral distinctions being made these days between smoking an occasional joint and snorting coke regularly or peddling it. It depended what you did and who was passing judgment. But for me, the main aspect of the major's black-market dealings was his hyprocrisy.

Pepík, amused by the fact that I had believed the food from his family had been a gift, had even more unsettling news for me.

"If you are that naive," he said, "you probably also believe that my uncle took you in just out of the goodness of his heart." And he explained how my arrival at the Rakouš household had been part of the plan to solve the major's apartment-hunting problems.

The housing market was extremely tight in Prague when the major started looking. Even though war damage in the capital was minimal compared to most other European cities, no new housing had been built since 1939. Now, apart from the long-suppressed demand of people who had married and had children in the intervening years, there was also the sudden pressure of people who had come back from exile, from German jails and concentration camps.

In most cases, the returnees could not get their homes back because someone was living in them. Possession was more than nine-tenths of the law at a time when the law was only slowly recovering from the damage done to it by the Nazis. One of my friends from school in Britain, for instance, found that she and an aunt, a concentration camp survivor, could not get the family apartment back because there were only two of them and the apartment was now occupied by the family of a butcher. The housing authority, which had the final say in these matters, was not swayed by the fact that the apartment belonged to my friend's family and that there were not more than the two of them only because the rest of the family had been butchered by the Germans.

There was only one large category of housing that was available when the war ended: the apartments vacated by recently fled Germans or those confiscated from their collaborators. These, naturally, included some of the best housing in town and were now the main battleground of the house hunters.

The major had a better claim than most to an apartment. His own apartment, after all, had been damaged by a bomb and he did play a significant part in the Prague Uprising. If he had a problem despite his good connections, Pepík explained, it was that the apartment he wanted, the one we were now living in, had been categorized by the housing authority as housing for six persons. And there were only four Rakoušes. So the major needed two more people and that, said Pepík, was how he and I had become part of the Rakouš household. What's more, he said, that wasn't the only way in which I had been useful to the major. He was also using the fact that I was a Jew to ingratiate himself with the Jewish owners of the factory he managed.

At first, I didn't believe Pepík. I knew he didn't like his uncle because he believed the major treated him condescendingly as a country bumpkin. I thought what Pepík told me sounded like just so much spite. But the more I thought about it, the more it made sense. I remembered the temporary disappearance of the major's favorite picture from the wall. It was a painting by Joža Úprka, who had enjoyed a measure of fame in Czechoslovakia before the war. It was an impressionistic paean to Czech village life, a celebration of peasants in folk costume. The painting's disappearance, it turned out, coincided with a visit to Prague by the widow of the owner of the button factory; she had come from New York to try to reclaim the family's property. After a few days, the painting reappeared.

I wanted to think it was a coincidence. But the pattern was too familiar. It had happened to too many of my friends; indeed it happened to me in Slovakia.

By the time Ernie and I went to Slovakia, I was more or less prepared for what we were about to encounter. I had heard quite a few tales by then of people who had experienced the shock of coming back and finding strangers in their homes, strangers who received them with blank stares of hostility because the returnees represented a threat that their home might be taken from them. And although there were warm welcomes from many family friends, some of those who were closest to the deported family cooled the moment any mention was made of the money, furniture, or a painting that had been left in their safekeeping. There always seemed to be an explanation; either the money had supposedly been repaid or the fur coat had been confiscated by the Germans for their troops in Russia. As for businesses, confiscations that were disguised with bills of sale that were either fictitious or represented a ludicrously low extortionist price were now being passed off as valid, bona fide contracts.

Not all people behaved this way, of course. Nor was it a problem only Jews encountered, just as it was not exclusively a European phenomenon. Many of the Japanese deported from British Columbia and the west coast of the U.S. during the war undoubtedly had similar experiences when they returned. But in the case of Jews, there was another dimension to the reception they received, symbolized by a question that was never asked aloud but that all too frequently seemed to hang over such encounters. The question: "With all the millions of Jews who were gassed, why is it that my particular Jew had to come back?"

Some of my friends from Wales who came back to find that their parents were dead at least found adult relatives who had returned or neighbors who had stayed throughout the war who could help them orient themselves by jogging their memories and recalling family friends.

If Ernie and I had had someone to turn to who was older, who knew our past, who was around in those final months before our parents were deported, it would have helped us reach out mentally to find whatever little there was left of the recognizable roots of our childhood. But there was no such person in Bratislava.

The town itself was familiar. We had no trouble finding our way from the railway station to the main square, over the old moat, through the Michael Gate, down to the Corso, on to the building that housed both the apartment in which we had lived and the store. Nothing seemed to have changed. Only the people. There was no one we knew. It was almost as though we were in a replica of Bratislava where they had copied every stone of the original but had decided to change the people.

The store looked the same, too, except that I noticed that my name, really my grandfather's name, had been taken down. Two strange men were behind the counter. They were friendly enough but said they were only running the store as temporary managers and there wasn't much they could do to help us. The matter was in the

hands of lawyers. As for the apartment, the strangers
there did not even invite us in to take a look.

The child welfare authorities had retained a lawyer to look
after our parents' estate. He assured us all was under control. He would get the store back for us and the house, too.
But not just yet because our claim was being contested. The
man who was laying claim to the property was the original
arizator, a term for the "Aryan," i.e. gentile, partner Jews had
to take on under a law passed by the Slovak government. To
ensure Aryan control of the economy, the law gave the "partner" fifty-one percent of the business. My father's "partner"
now claimed that he had bought the shop from my father.
But don't worry, said the lawyer, he won't get it back; he was
a member of the fascist Hlinka Guard and he is lucky not to
be in jail. I asked the lawyer what was holding up the process.
Oh, these things take time, he said, but I'll keep in touch. (It
took three years for us to get ownership of the family store.
By then, though, the communists were in power and the shop
was promptly nationalized.)

The few surviving Jews who said they knew my parents
knew them only vaguely and knew nothing of what happened
to them after they left Bratislava. In fact, they themselves
were still alive only because they had managed to evade the
Gestapo and the Slovak police or were sent to the camps
much later. I tried to find one of my father's gentile friends.
I couldn't remember his name, but I knew where he lived because we used to go visiting there at Christmas and played
with his extensive toy train collection under the Christmas
tree. But the people living there now were strangers to me
and I to them.

Ernie and I followed the trail to Hlohovec, the small market
town where our parents spent five months awaiting "resettlement." All we had was an address. There, at last, we found
someone who had had contact with our parents. But the woman at No. 73 Hviezdoslav Street didn't have much to say.
Yes, they had stayed at her house for five months, but she
didn't know much about them. Quiet people, she said. No,
they didn't give her any idea where they were going next.
Did they leave anything behind, a letter perhaps? No, she

said. Was there anyone else in town who might know something about them? Well, she said, there was the man in the store down the street. He was pretty friendly with your parents; they say your father set him up in business, gave him money.

The man at the store was friendly and full of sympathy. Such a tragedy, he said. Such nice people. Of course, things were rough for us, too, you know. Oh yes, he said, your father did lend me some money. But I paid him back just before they left.

If I had not heard so many similar stories before, if it hadn't been for the temporary disappearance of the major's painting, I might even have come to believe him.

I tried to put the painting out of mind. After all, I could not very well write to a woman in New York whom I didn't even know and whose address I didn't have to ask her whether, by any chance, her family had entrusted a picture by Joža Úprka to the major's care when they left Prague. And I didn't dare broach my suspicions to the major. I was afraid of being wrong. But I was even more afraid of being right. Once I opened that door, there was no telling what I might find.

I was just beginning to realize the extent of the major's talents as a survivor. It was a tribute to his skills that he had managed to hang on to his job through all the turmoil and changes in Prague. He was appointed to it before the war by the factory's owner. Yet, though he was the appointee of Jews, he managed to stay on all through the German occupation. And now he was still hanging on after the war.

Either of these changes of regimes might have bowled over a lesser man. The Germans doubtlessly would have known that the major owed his position to Jews; he would have had to have convinced them somehow that he was not a Jewish protégé. After the war, he would again have been vulnerable, this time, as was anyone who had managed an enterprise under the Germans, to charges of having been a

Nazi collaborator. He presumably survived that hurdle because, as a hero of the Prague Uprising, he was a certifiable patriot.

Now the major was caught up in yet another threat to his position. It was not personal but rather part of the political power struggle going on all over the country. On one side were the communists and some socialists who wanted to nationalize everything in sight. They were helped by the fact that so many businesses were without owners. Either they had been removed by the Germans, perhaps because they were Jews or because they had not co-operated sufficiently with the Nazis. Or the owners had worked with the Germans and had left or been ousted and condemned as traitorous collaborators once Hitler was defeated.

The businesses owned by collaborators were the easiest targets. They were subject to outright takeovers and nationalization. (That was happening even in western Europe. It was how Charles de Gaulle, who was prime minister of France right after the war, nationalized the Renault car company and quite a few of France's largest banks.)

Companies in Czechoslovakia whose owners had been ousted by the Germans were put in the hands of "national managers." These managers ran them under state supervision, ostensibly only temporarily until their proper ownership could be determined. My father's shop in Bratislava was under national management. So was the much larger enterprise the major ran.

The major was under pressure. The owners were trying to get their plant back, or, failing that, were prepared to claim compensation. At the same time, the plant works committee was pushing for nationalization. Moreover, his status as a hero of the Uprising was no longer the protection it once was. The communists had started berating the leaders of the Uprising for having negotiated with the Germans for the surrender of their forces in Prague. The communists denounced the negotiations as an attempt by bourgeois elements to deprive Soviet forces of the glory of liberating the city.

So the major not only did not know which side was going to win; he also could not be sure of retaining his job no matter which side won control of the factory.

The communists were steadily strengthening their political power. The Soviet army had withdrawn its troops by December 1945. But it left behind a government apparatus in which, from the national government to local councils, communists were in the driver's seat. The government was a coalition of four parties. But communists were in charge of key departments such as the ministry of the interior, which ran the police, and the ministry of information, which controlled the press, broadcasting and film production. A communist headed the central labor federation and controlled an armed workers' militia in the factories.

The communists were also in charge of the grandest patronage machine of all: the ministry of agriculture. It not only gave farmers easy credit; it was also in charge of distributing the confiscated land and property of Sudeten Germans. These Germans, having opted in 1938 to be part of Germany, were now being deported to join their own in Germany. More than 1.5 million Czechs were resettled in the border areas where only months before 2.5 million Germans had lived, and the communists took credit for giving them their farms, their homes, their businesses. But they held these new "capitalists" hostage as their clientele by delaying giving them title to their properties. (Once the communists came to power, of course, they took back most of what they had "given.")

But in the spring of 1946, there still seemed a chance to stop the communists' march to power. President Beneš called parliamentary elections for the end of May.

May Day, 1945. The four Czech parties of the coalition — the Communists, the Social Democrats, the National Socialists and the Catholic People's party — were using the holiday for their biggest election rallies of the campaign. Curiosity took me all over town that day, flitting from one rally to the next, comparing crowds, comparing speeches, comparing moods.

It was an uneven match. The non-communist parties had limited manoeuvring room. For one thing, they would have a hard time trying to outdo the communists in their sudden devotion to freedom and democracy. The communists argued that they had demonstrated that they were good democrats by participating in a coalition for the past year and observing the niceties of parliamentary government. They said not a word about revolution or class war in the campaign. Instead, there were soothing promises that "small and middle-sized enterprises, particularly the property of farmers, remains and will remain untouched and will receive support, and that the middle classes in the city will be guaranteed the security of their existence."

In any normal election campaign, this communist line would have been quickly exposed as a sham. There was, after all, no lack of evidence that where the communists were in power, be it the Soviet Union or Yugoslavia, there was dictatorship, or that the Czechoslovak Communist Party was a creature of Stalin, a tyrant, and would jump to obey his every whim. But the communists' opponents could not use these arguments. Under the limited sovereignty Czechoslovakia was allowed by Moscow, criticizing Stalin and the Soviet Union was simply off limits. Any overt criticism of Moscow would have opened the critics to attacks as a remnant of fascism that had to be rooted out. The Red Army had left Czechoslovakia at the end of 1945, but it was not far away. Indeed, as a reminder of this, the Russians announced just before the elections that they were planning to move some of their units from Austria and Hungary across Czechoslovakia to East Germany. They didn't, but the threatening psychological message got through.

With the anti-communists campaigning under restraints, the communists' propaganda machine pretty well had a free ride. They hammered away at the Czechs' sensibilities about having been sold out by the Western democracies at Munich. They kept reminding the Czechs and Slovaks that it was the Russians who freed them from Nazi occupation. They spread scare stories of German "revanchists" plotting to take back the Sudeten region with the help of the West. And they tagged the "bourgeois" parties as the architects of the Depression of the thirties. Only socialism and the Soviet Union could protect Czechoslovakia from all these dangers.

Millions agreed with them. Sure, the Soviet Union is no democracy, they argued, but then the Russians never had a democracy. Certainly Stalin is a dictator, but then the Russians have always been used to autocratic rulers. Stalin is nothing but a modernized version of their *Batyushka Czar*, Father Czar. Our communists, so the argument went, are different because we are different. Look, didn't they even have a picture of Bethlehem on the front page of *Rudé Právo*, the party newspaper, at Christmas; you won't see that in *Pravda*. Our communists, people would say, don't believe that Leninist nonsense about religion being the opiate of the people. Why, they go to church just like anyone else.

From the start, the Czechs were more kindly disposed towards the Russians than their neighbors, the Poles, because, unlike the Poles, they had never before had to deal with the sting of Russian imperialism. So many Czechs and Slovaks were pan-Slavist, believing that the Slavs must stick together against the Germans.

On Election Day, the results surprised even the communists and shocked their opponents: the Communist Party got thirty-eight percent of the vote. With its allies, it had a six-vote majority in the National Assembly. What enabled the communists to break out beyond their core constituency of industrial workers was their successful wooing of the hitherto conservative peasantry. The land grants and the cheap loans for farm machinery had paid off.

The coalition government continued. Though their opponents did not see it yet, the communists now had a stranglehold on democracy in Czechoslovakia. It would take them only twenty-one months to choke it to death.

But no one was going to outflank the major. He got on the band-wagon before it got rolling. He joined the Communist Party.

By Election Day, politics was the last thing on my mind. My

life had once again taken an unexpected turn. I was flat on my back in a hospital. I couldn't walk.

The morning after the May Day rallies, I had woken up with a pain in my right leg. I tried to get out of bed, but my leg buckled under me. The pain was excruciating. Too much walking yesterday, I thought, and got back into bed. But the pain only got worse.

Karel, a doctor who was the fiancé of the major's daughter, took a look at me and ordered bed rest. The next day, he brought me crutches. But hobbling on the crutches just increased my pain. It became so fierce I collapsed and fainted. They took me to a hospital, took blood samples and X-rays of my leg and chest. When I asked what was wrong with me, they just shrugged their shoulders.

On May 11, my eighteenth birthday, they told me. I had tuberculosis, they said. Don't be silly, I said, there is nothing wrong with my lungs; it's my leg that hurts. So they explained that TB was not just a lung disease, that it could strike anywhere and that I had a tubercular hip joint. What's the treatment, I wanted to know, and how long will it take? The answer: more shoulder shrugging.

But the pain did go away and after more than a month of bed rest, much to my joy, I was released from hospital. But not for long. The pain came back in the fall and for the next two years I was shuffled from one hospital to the next. I spent time in a lung disease sanatorium in northern Bohemia, at a specialized bone disease hospital in western Bohemia, another one in Silesia at the Polish border and yet another in eastern Bohemia, which, under Hitler, had been a euthanasia institution to rid the Reich of the insane. Sometimes I was just confined to bed; at one place, my hip was in a cast for six months; at another, I lay for months with my right leg sticking up, suspended in traction.

I lived among people whose bones were rotting away through carbuncles oozing pus, people whose legs just seemed to shrink upwards into the body as their hip joint disintegrated. There were people with amputated limbs and patients whose TB had spread to other organs. In others, the TB had receded, leaving a limb locked frozen where there had been a joint. There seemed to be a daily recitation of the litany of suffering that TB could inflict.

There was always talk of a cure somewhere around the corner. Someone heard of a new American antibiotic that you could get only on the black market. Or some other medicine that was being reserved for a favored few. Or a revolutionary surgical technique. Or a faith healer perhaps. But there was no cure, only treatment. The prescription: time, rest, clean bandages, crutches, hope of the disease just running its course, sometimes surgery, always dreams of miracles. For many, there was only resignation to a blighted life.

Once again, looking at the misery around me, I felt lucky. I had no festering sores, no twisted limbs, nothing, in fact, but a painful hip. When I was not pinned down by pain, I was healthy, full of energy and itching to get out. I resented being a prisoner of my hip; not letting it get the better of me became an obsession. I would race around on my crutches to prove to myself that my hip could not hold me back. I started a library at one hospital where there had been nothing to read. At another, I organized a hospital newspaper. Encased in a cast from the right knee to the hip, I played volleyball. And when I was in traction, I would have one of the walking patients untie me from the traction pulley at night after the lights were out, pull on a pair of pants I had hidden under my pillow and a shirt and shoes, and climb out the window to go dating and dancing. A victory of hormones over brains, no doubt, but also much-needed therapy for the spirit if not the hip.

If being confined in a hospital was depressing, the news from outside was no better. The communists were tightening their hold on the police and factories. Their propaganda against the "reactionary bourgeois" parties became more threatening. The non-communists in the coalition government were being accused of being hostile towards the Soviet Union, of trying to turn the clock back by aligning the country with the West. If proof were needed about who held the ultimate power over Czechoslovakia, it came when the government, the communists included, agreed to join the Marshall Plan, which offered American aid for the rebuilding of Europe. Stalin called the

Czechs to the Kremlin and ordered them to reverse their decision because the Marshall Plan was directed against the Soviet Union. If they did not, he told them, it would be considered a hostile act. On July 10, 1947, the Czech leaders backed down. Stalin had ended any illusions they may have had of independence and freedom.

When Czechoslovakia's foreign minister, Jan Masaryk, the son of the country's first president, returned to Prague, he told friends, "I left for Moscow as minister of foreign affairs of a sovereign state. I return as Stalin's stooge."

With political conditions deteriorating, many of my friends were leaving the country. So did the cousin my brother had been living with. Ernie moved in with some friends, but they left, too. Finally, my brother was forced to move into an orphanage. He was so miserable there, so despairing of his future and that of the country that, when he was offered an opportunity to go to Canada under a program to get Jewish war orphans out of Europe, he jumped at it.

As for the major and his family, I hardly ever heard from them despite the fact that they had profited considerably from my illness. I had become their meal ticket. Tuberculosis was considered such a threat that the food rations of those infected and their families were raised substantially to make sure that the bacillus did not thrive and spread because of poor nutrition.

Unlike pulmonary tuberculosis, the bone version of the disease wasn't really contagious, but the rationing regulations did not take that into account. The rations were so generous that for basic foodstuffs — bread, meat, eggs, butter and milk — the Rakouš family no longer had any need for the black market.

I had rendered the major my last and greatest service.

Prague, December 1989. I am in the lobby café of the Alcron Hotel waiting for the major's son, Dalibor, and his wife. The hotel is still as I remember it, all polished stone, dark wood, chrome, mirrors, heavy curtains, crystal chandeliers, high ceilings, straight out of the thirties. The Alcron used to be the grand hotel of Prague, more modern than the *fin de siècle* places on and off Wenceslas Square. I now find the frippery of the old art nouveau hotels more attractive and interesting than the modern drabness of the Alcron. But for years the Alcron was what I imagined all luxury hotels to be, sumptuous palaces of glamorous intrigue. Sexual intrigue. Political plotting. Illicit money deals. Spies, diplomats, cops, black marketeers, wayward lovers and pricey call girls, they all met in the Alcron lobby. Even journalists.

This is where in my imagination Ilsa, sometimes also known as Ingrid Bergman, made the deal that got her out of Nazi-occupied Prague to Casablanca and into the arms of Rick, known to some as Humphrey Bogart; where Nicholas Winton must have met his beautiful Swedish spy (please, Nicky, don't tell me it wasn't so!); where I pictured Trevor Chadwick negotiating with the Gestapo officer for the lives of his endangered children. This is where a decade later I myself was introduced to the world of intrigue (peewee league division). It was a convenient place for meeting news tipsters, hustlers who claimed they had safe, sure-fire ways of getting out of the country and visiting foreign journalists trying to figure out the lay of the land. We would talk about the weather or perhaps the latest film hit while we had a drink and then we'd leave to discuss what we had come to talk about outside in the street where the cops couldn't eavesdrop. No one ever talked business in the Alcron lobby. The walls had ears.

Now, as I looked around, I saw that in the intervening decades the walls had also sprouted eyes. I counted eight TV cameras looking down on the lounge. Outside, the Communist regime was falling before the onslaught of huge demonstrations just down the block in Wenceslas Square. But here in the Alcron lobby, the police peepers were all but surely still prying, not because anyone was still interested in what they had to report, or could act on it any longer, but because a job is a job and even spies have to eat. Poor things, I thought, they must be worried; if things continue going well for Czechoslovakia, they'll be losing their jobs soon. I raised my glass to the nearest camera and gave it a little wave of my hand. Toodle-oo! And good riddance!

If the hidden microphones were still turned on, the eaves-droppers must have had blisters on their ears. With the communist system crumbling, people were letting all their resentments and hate spill out. Someone was probably tell-ing a tale of communist iniquity and incompetence at just about every table in the place. At our table, Dalibor's wife, Manuela, was denouncing the communists as swine. Her bit-terness sounded odd at first, considering that when I left Prague both her husband and father-in-law had been party members. But then, being a communist was never a guarantee of a life of peace and harmony. For Manuela and her family, communism turned out to be their misfortune.

Not for her father-in-law, of course. The major, who died in 1975 at eighty, was a survivor to the end. He survived his wife. He survived his mistress, the secretary in his office with whom he had carried on an affair in the years his wife was slowly dying of the effects of her war wounds and whom he then married after his wife's death. He was to go on and marry a third time. Despite his conversion to communism, though, he did finally lose his job as the boss of the button factory and leave the party. But it no longer mattered because by then he was old enough to live out his life safely as a pen-sioner who had done well enough while the going was good.

The major's talent for survival, it turned out, did not pass to his son. At first, Dalibor did well as a communist. Manuela, who had been against him joining the party and at one time even tore up his party card in anger, admitted that for twenty years having a husband who was a party member was good for the family. Dalibor rose in the government bureaucracy as a foreign trade expert. He travelled abroad frequently. That meant they had access to goods most people in Czechoslovakia could only dream about. They were members of the elite and during the brutal fifties survived all the twists and turns in the party line.

Then, during the Prague Spring of 1968, Dalibor made a mistake. He openly sided with the reformers. When the Soviet invasion toppled the reformist regime of Alexander

Dubček, Dalibor and Manuela were in Britain on vacation. They thought of staying abroad; Dalibor had an attractive job offer in Italy. But their son, also named Dalibor, was in Prague in medical school. They couldn't just leave him. If they defected, Dalibor Jr. would certainly have been expelled from the university. (If his father had not been a communist, young Rakouš probably would never have made it into medical school in the first place.)

Dalibor and Manuela returned home. And immediately regretted it. Dalibor was kicked out of the party and lost his job and ended up as a taxi driver. Purging him was not enough for the communists. They were firm believers in Machiavelli's doctrine that a dictator who kills Brutus to stay in power must also make sure to kill the sons of Brutus. Dalibor's political sin was visited upon his son. Young Dalibor, who was in his last year of school, was kicked out as politically unreliable. For years, he tried to get back into the good graces of the authorities. They suggested he could earn a place back in school if he were to prove his loyalty to the socialist system by working as a medical orderly. The young man did menial work in hospitals for several years. It did him no good; the aparatchiks never relented. The major's grandson was never able to become a doctor.

In the Alcron lobby, as she picked at her *vánočka* — Czech Christmas cake — Manuela was almost in tears. "What's happening is wonderful," she said. "We've been out in the square every night at the demonstrations. But for us, all this is too late. Little Dalibor ["little" Dalibor was over forty by now] is too old to ever become a doctor, and his father is too old to get his job back. Those swine, they ruined our lives."

What happened to the major's son and grandson explains, perhaps better than anything else, why the major, living where he did and when he did, honed his skills at survival and used them at every turn. If he had been faced with the Prague Spring in his prime, there is no doubt in my mind that he would have managed to place bets on both sides. And survived. By 1990, of course, he would have once again been a good democrat.

CHAPTER IV

Only he merits freedom, merits life
Who daily has to conquer them anew.

Johann Wolfgang von Goethe

They were burying Eduard Beneš the day I returned to Prague from my two years in hospital. The city was in mourning, black everywhere, flags at half-mast, people crying in the streets.

The country was mourning more than just its former president; it was in mourning for itself. The Beneš funeral in September 1948 was a mass demonstration of the nation's grief over the loss of its freedom. It was the last such demonstration the communists were to permit for the next twenty years.

It had all happened quickly. At the beginning of the year, there had still been hope that the communists would get their comeuppance at the next election. Although they had expected to improve on their good showing of the 1946 election, they were actually slipping. They were caught in a paradox: as they used their increased hold on the police and propaganda machinery to try to assure themselves of a majority in the coming election, their high-handed exercise of that power was losing them the popular support they would need to win. There was only one solution left to the communists as they saw it: grab total power and prevent the election.

For the non-communists, the reverse seemed their only course. They had to force a quick election before the communists could consolidate their hold enough to control the outcome of the vote. So the non-communist ministers created a cabinet crisis in February by resigning. They believed their action would force the fall of the government and that President Beneš would then call a new election.

It didn't work out that way. The communists launched a virulent campaign, accusing their opponents of having shown their true colors as anti-Soviet reactionaries and lackeys of Western imperialism. There were huge communist rallies demanding that Beneš entrust the party with forming a new government without the "traitorous" ministers. Arms and ammunition were distributed to factory militias, and special police reserves under communist command were brought into Prague. Newspapers hostile to the communists were shut down and anti-communist student demonstrations were broken up. In effect, the communists threatened civil war.

On February 25, Beneš, sick and dispirited, caved in. For the second time, he surrendered his country's freedom without a fight. Once the communists got his go-ahead, they did not just form a new cabinet; they took the resignations of twelve ministers as an excuse to eliminate their parties. Non-communist politicians were arrested; officials of their parties down to the lowest levels were fired and party offices closed. There were purges in every branch of the government, in universities, unions, newspapers, broadcasting, factories. All opposition was crushed.

The communists had managed to use the political manoeuvring of democratic cabinet-making to stage a putsch. They were now ready to begin imposing the terror of the Stalinist one-party state on the people of Czechoslovakia. And, eventually, in show trials and purges, on each other.

All around me, everything was crumbling. But I was happy. I

was free. I was free of hospitals; I was free of the major. My hip was no longer bothering me: I didn't even have a limp. But best of all, I was in love and I was loved. For awhile, nothing else mattered.

But reality inevitably intruded. It became apparent that what had happened was only a beginning of something larger and more ominous. And it was not confined to Czechoslovakia. In Poland, Hungary and Romania, the sham coalition governments the communists had maintained to placate the Western powers were being replaced with outright communist dictatorships. Stalin was dispensing with the last vestiges of the pretence that the east Europeans would be free to choose their own form of government, as he had promised Roosevelt and Churchill at Yalta. The countries of eastern and central Europe were to be nothing more than satrapies of the Russian empire.

Even being a loyal communist was no protection. In Poland, the communist leader, Wladyslav Gomulka, was ousted as a deviationist; he at least lived long enough to make a comeback. In Hungary, Laszlo Rajk, the communist interior minister, was not so lucky; he was hanged. It was a process that was to continue in the Soviet empire with growing savagery till Stalin's death.

This renewal of the communist revolution's appetite for devouring its favorite children spread fear at all levels throughout eastern Europe. For the communists, it was not enough that people not be against them; they had to be demonstrably with them. Political reliability was the measure of all things, the opening to any job other than the most menial, the key to an apartment, the ticket to travel, the test for university admission.

But political reliability meant more than just adhering to the party line. That would have been difficult enough since the party line changed shape as quickly as Silly Putty in the hands of a four-year-old. Anything — the wrong friends, the wrong remark, the wrong love, the wrong birth — could bring upon the sinner the party's anathema. The criteria of reliability had about them an aura of quasi-religious redemption. To be born of bourgeois parents was to be born in ideo-

logical sin, which only abject repentance and dutiful worship of the party could wash away; to be the child of workers, on the other hand, was to be brought into the world
in a state of grace, at least until the party decided otherwise.

Reliability was enforced by an army of snoops and snitches,
by major show trials and minor harassments. People were
cowed. Worse even than the fear of the new rulers was that
people ceased to trust each other. Informers were everywhere;
in their hands, the most innocent of remarks could lead to
dangerous consequences. So people were close-mouthed with
strangers and cautious even with friends. They were careful
with friends not necessarily because they believed they might
be betrayed by them; some things were just better left unsaid
to friends to avoid endangering them.

Fear, suspicion, bitterness and despondency, those were
the hallmarks of the new society the communists had unleashed. Despite my absorption in my new-found love and
liberty, I knew that I could not go on living in such a society. I also knew that it had no room for me. People with my
background were automatically politically suspect. I did not
have the slightest chance of ever going to university nor much
of a prospect of anything better than a job on a production
line or mine, or, at best, translating boring technical texts or
dreary communist propaganda. But I was not worried about
my future. I knew that one way or another I would leave the
country.

In a curious way, my illness helped me. My papers said I
was disabled by tuberculosis. That gave me immunity both
from two years of compulsory military service and the drive
to recruit labor for the country's undermanned factories and
mines. I did not have to get a regular job if I didn't want to
and could afford not to have one, an unusual privilege in a
society where having a job was obligatory even if work and
decent pay were not. Since I was by then getting some money out of the family store, I had the luxury of looking around,
of trying to decide what to do next.

I felt I had to stay in Prague to try to get a passport, or, if I
could not, to try to arrange an escape across the border. Ernie,

who had started his emigration process before the communists took over, managed to get a passport and left for Canada. In the early days after the communist takeover, quite a few of my friends departed. Some were allowed to join close relatives in the West. Others were allowed to leave for the new state of Israel.

Then one night, I found myself dancing with my love, singing "Only five minutes more, only five minutes more, only five minutes more in your arms." She, too, had received permission to leave. The next day, she was gone. I never saw her again.

By then I had realized that there would be no passport for me. I was too late. The communists had firmly shut the door. If I was going to get out, I would have to do it the hard way and find my own hole in the Iron Curtain.

Abe, the American chief of the Prague bureau of the Associated Press, took a look at my copy and said, "Not a bad lead." Then, before I could even muster a smile of satisfaction, he took his pencil and slashed apart what I had written. "You'll get the hang of it someday," he said as he handed the mutilated copy back to me.

If I didn't quite have the hang of the news business yet, I had certainly acquired a taste for it. I had been hired in December 1948 by the AP as a translator and interpreter. My main job was reading and translating interesting articles from the newspapers and the news wire of ČTK, the Czechoslovak news agency, for the Americans in the bureau. Several other local employees and I also took in reports over the phone on anything from soccer results to the day's proceedings from the AP's Budapest stringer of the espionage trial of Jozsef Cardinal Mindszenty, the primate of Hungary. I wasn't exactly going out and covering the news. The closest I got to that was going occasionally to Sunday mass to check whether the priest was going to say anything politically interesting and covering tennis, or, to be more precise, just phoning in the score after each set.

But I did eventually learn how to organize what I had translated into a semblance of a news story, punch it out on a tape
and send it over the teletype to the AP's Frankfurt bureau. I
wanted to do more. I was caught up in the excitement of news,
in the conspiratorial atmosphere of a bureau watched by the
secret police, riddled by informers and, all but certainly, by
hidden microphones.

The biggest story in Czechoslovakia in the spring of 1949
was the battle between the government and the Roman
Catholic church. The communists challenged the power of
the church by putting its own overseers into every episcopal
office. When the primate of Czechoslovakia, Archbishop Josef
Beran of Prague, protested this state intrusion into church
affairs, he was put under house arrest. In a pastoral letter a
week later, the bishops challenged the communists' efforts to
curb religious freedom. The police tried to prevent the letter
being published but we managed to get a copy and got the
story out.

It was taken for granted at the bureau that almost everything said there would eventually find its way to the state
security police. I remember one of the local staffers warning me in couched terms that she had no choice but to report
everything she knew to the police. She was, in effect, pleading
with me to watch my tongue. If I didn't know about the others, neither could they be sure about me. Looking back, I can
only guess that the security police did not try to rope me in because I was alone. They preferred people with families; they
could enforce their co-operation by treating their families as
hostages to their good behavior. Besides, as a greenhorn, I
probably knew too little for their purposes and was there too
briefly.

Even taking the job had been a risk. It was inevitable that
it would bring me to the attention of the security police. But I
had no idea then, nor did anyone else in the bureau, how dangerous it would really turn out to be. (In the purges of the early
fifties — after I had left Prague — most of the bureau personnel, including the American bureau chief, William Oatis,
were arrested. They were convicted of espionage and given

sentences ranging up to sixteen years. Oatis was released after a couple of years, but some of the Czech staffers stayed in prison until the political thaw of the sixties.)

I took the AP job mostly because I was afraid that if I went to work for a Czech organization I might get stuck in Czechoslovakia. I could see myself giving up, being overcome by the inertia of a dreary existence and allowing myself to be engulfed by the pessimism of powerlessness and passivity that had gripped so much of the country. Besides, working in a Czech office or factory would also have meant cutting myself off from the information and the contacts I had to have to find a way out of the country. At the AP, I would at least be better informed about where and when to cross the border and, most important, with whom. Finding a reliable local guide or smuggler was difficult. It now seems clear to me that what I actually was doing was burning my bridges to a normal life within the communist system. Joining the AP was, in effect, my first step into exile.

Indeed, the bureau was an outpost of the outside world. It was one of the very few places left in Prague where you could still read what was happening without having most of the truth bleached out by the censors and mangled by the propagandists. We talked to people in Frankfurt and Vienna on the phone every day and exchanged messsages on the teletype with people in London and New York. That alone helped lift the spirit. It was good to know that the non-communist world was still out there and that it wasn't in its death throes or threatening to blow up the world as Stalin and his henchmen would have had us believe.

The people in the bureau, too, the people who came to the office for one reason or another as well as the people who worked there, were more interesting, perhaps even more alive than those outside it, because being there involved a certain risk, a conscious decision not to conform. Some of them were kooks, of course, some rogues and tattletales. After all, normal law-abiding, Stalin-fearing citizens knew better by then than to go through doors marked with subversive signs in foreign languages such as "The Associated Press."

And then there were the American correspondents. There was Dick, who had a shelf built above his typewriter to hold a water carafe, a glass and his bottle of whisky, the better to cope with the impenetrable language, the unpronounceable names and the indigestible food of Czechoslovakia. There was Harvey, who, in the hours of interminable waiting for some bit of important news that was expected to happen actually to happen, would hold forth on the pleasures of life in Paris, the wonders of California, the marvels of New York, the finer points of tennis and the practicality of Oxford cloth shirts with button-down collars. I don't remember what the important news was the night Harvey lectured me on the differences between Bordeaux and Burgundy wines, but I do remember that it was the first time I had heard of the 1855 classification of the great wines of Bordeaux.

Abe, the bureau chief who hired me, was older than the rest. He had his wife and two children with him and was frequently preoccupied with the difficulties of family life in a land of shortages and the problems of arranging food supplies from abroad. It struck me as an astonishing indulgence that he even brought Coca-Cola for his kids through the Iron Curtain. This seemed to me, in the priggishness of my youth, a conspicuous waste and an abuse of the privileges of Westerners. (Many years later, when I was buying my own children corn flakes in Hong Kong or popcorn in Paris, which surely is not much different from bringing dried camel dung to Newcastle, I would remember my puerile disapproval of Abe's pop shipments with a smile.)

Abe used to wonder why he was in Prague facing all these problems when by now he should have had a posting in Paris or London. He envied the "specials," the correspondents of newspapers and magazines, the star reporters who came floating through for a few days. They would pump us for information, skim the cream off the story and then wander off again while Abe had to stay around to slog through the muddy trenches of wire-service journalism.

I found these men fascinating because they were the first Americans I had got to know. They were the new Romans from a confident new world looking with condescension at what was left of exhausted Athens and defeated Sparta. They dealt daily with Europe's current problems, but they seemed unaware or uninterested in the old causes of these new problems. The mechanics of situations fascinated them, but not the philosophies behind them. They walked and talked, it seemed to me, with the certainty of power, the confidence of wealth, the assurance of immunity from the debilities that afflicted Europeans.

I know now that as wire-service reporters they were the badly paid cannon fodder of journalism whose work had very little influence; the "specials" from *Time* magazine, the *New York Herald Tribune*, the *New Yorker* were the influential ones. But at the time, having one's written words flash around the world, not having to worry about the police, any police, to be able to cross frontiers almost at will, to belong to a free and rich society, seemed to me a life as remote, inaccessible and desirable as that of the gods on Mount Olympus. I hungered to share that freedom and that confidence. And I knew I would. But first I had to get out.

Getting out, however, was becoming harder all the time. The Iron Curtain was constantly being strengthened. More barbed wire, more machine-gun towers, mine fields and booby traps. Even getting near the border was no longer easy; special passes were required for travel to border areas. Since it was harder, since more people were getting caught, fewer of the people who knew the border were willing to act as guides. And those who still were wanted more money, and some, according to rumors, stayed in business by co-operating with the police by handing over some of their customers.

I had also realized by then that working for the AP was a hindrance rather than a help. It did help me make contacts, but it also created problems in following them up. One such contact refused to have anything to do with me after he noticed that I was being followed to a rendezvous with him by a man in a leather coat. He had enough problems, he told me later, without dealing with people who were on the police watch list.

But the interest of the security police now went further than just keeping track of us. In the fall of 1949, they arrested the first AP staffer. The word was that Lydia's arrest had nothing to do with the AP, that it was the result of her association with a Yugoslav diplomat; Yugoslavs had become prime targets once Tito had broken with Stalin. But this was hardly reassuring and it seemed only a matter of time before others would be pulled in.

So I quit the AP and decided to concentrate full-time on the problem of getting out of the country. I was able to afford to do this because of my inheritance. When my father's store was nationalized, I was paid a lump sum as partial payment for "goods in stock." That gave me enough money to live on for a few months and, even more important, enough to pay someone to help me across the border.

And so once again, my parents came to my rescue. From beyond the grave, they gave me my freedom. A second time.

December 21, 1949, was Joseph Stalin's seventieth birthday. For weeks, even months, before the big day, Stalin's empire was in a frenzy of adulation. It was no longer enough to have the great man's picture on every wall, to have his name sprinkled all over the front page of every newspaper every day. It was no longer enough to hang huge red banners with slogans praising his leadership from every public building. It was time for action. From Vladivostok to Carlsbad, Stalin's subjects worked extra shifts for his glory, rushed building projects to completion so that even more roads and buildings and factories could be named after him on his birthday, painted portraits of the great generalissimo, made movies of his victories, composed music and poetry celebrating his achievements and attended endless rallies to show their devotion.

I, too, decided to celebrate the great holiday. My own way. My celebration would be more restrained, private, even solitary. I wanted to mark Stalin's birthday by escaping from his clutches.

The timing had not been my idea; it came from a contact I had made in Bratislava, a man who knew the area across the river from the city where the Czechoslovak, Hungarian and Austrian borders met. He said he could get me into Austria and suggested the night of Stalin's birthday would be ideal because the border guards would be busy with the official celebrations. In fact, he said he had heard that in the sector where we would be crossing, the usual patrols had been suspended for that night.

The border with eastern Austria was easier to cross than further west. That's because the eastern part of the country was put into Soviet hands when at the end of the war Austria was split up by the Allies into four occupation zones, in much the same way as Germany.

Crossing the border into the Soviet zone only confronted refugees with a new set of dangers. They were routinely picked up inside Austria by Soviet patrols and sent back. Because of this, the border guards on the Czechoslovak side were more relaxed about the Soviet sector of their border than they were further west, where they faced the Americans. Those who made it across the border into the American zone were home free, which is why the Czechs made it much tougher to cross the border into the U.S. zones of Austria and Germany.

So those trying to flee Czechoslovakia had a choice, a trade-off between trying to break past mine fields, electrified fences and booby traps to freedom directly, or taking the easier route across the border into the Soviet zone and then taking a chance on evading capture by the Russians and making it to Vienna. The Austrian capital was then in much the same position as Berlin was for decades: a large part of it was controlled by the western Allies but it was surrounded by Soviet-occupied territory. The western sectors of the city were the magnet that attracted prospective refugees like me.

On Stalin's birthday, when the whole of Bratislava seemed to be on the move from one celebration to another, my guide and I took a bus across the Danube to Petržalka, the little sliver of Czechoslovak territory on the south bank. No one challenged us, no one checked our papers when we got off. That was the first hurdle. We walked along some back roads and then hid in a shed till darkness. Once it was dark, we crossed some fields and were, according to the guide, only

300 metres from the border when we heard some voices. We dropped to the ground and hardly dared breathe as the voices came closer. There were two men, obviously guards. And, worse, a dog.

I dug my face into the ground, waiting for the dog to discover us. Would he come sniffing? Would he come running and snarling and attack us? I tried to lie still, but I could feel my pulse pounding.

There was no barking, no snarling, not even a dog sniff, just voices fading into the distance. When we raised ourselves from the ground, I felt elated. Now, I thought, we are in the clear. No, said the guide, we have to go back. If we go forward, he said, they are bound to cross our path on their way back and the dog will pick up our scent. Even if we were across the border by then, the Russians would help them catch us.

I went back reluctantly. The guide tried to console me by saying that we could try again in a day or two. But I couldn't wait; I had to return to Prague. If I didn't get back quickly, I might find the police waiting for me when I finally did get there.

My problem was my room-mate, Asaf. We were friends who had been thrown together by the housing shortage. It would have been better for our friendship if we had not lived together, because Asaf was a problem for me and I for him. He was a university student who came from a communist family. Consorting with someone like me who had worked for an American organization and who, he suspected, was likely to leave the country one way or another could compromise his position. If I did leave illegally, he would have to report me missing pretty quickly to avoid being accused of having covered up for me or even helped me.

I knew that my absence for two nights running would have made him nervous, that he would be asking himself whether he could afford to wait another night to report me. That is why I rushed back from Slovakia.

When I got back, Asaf was overjoyed to see me. He had been steeling himself to go to the police. He had told his aunt about his suspicions about me the day before and she had told his brother. The brother, who was an ardent communist working his way up the ladder of party aparatchiks, told Asaf that if I were still missing by noon the next day he would have to report me. I showed up shortly after breakfast time.

I knew that I did not have much time left, that the next time I disappeared from Prague, I had better disappear for good.

On the morning of February 6, 1950, I got up before dawn. It was cold outside so I wore my warmest suit and my winter coat, a coat that I had a tailor make from the warmest material I could find, a khaki U.S. Army blanket that I had dyed brown. I put on shoes in which I had hidden several hundred Austrian schillings I had bought on the black market. I put on a hat that had $40 U.S. tucked behind the sweatband. The hidden money was my fortune, my start to a new life. I carried nothing else with me, not a toothbrush, not even an extra handkerchief. If Asaf had woken up, I would have told him that I would be back in the evening. He didn't.

At the railway station, I met Helena, my new girlfriend. Helena had also worked at the AP and she, too, had decided that getting out was the only solution. Ours was more an affair of convenience than of the heart. We were brought together by a shared determination, even desperation, to break out, an emotion that can bind two people together closely but one that broke down once our shared goal was achieved.

It was Helena who found Pavel the Smuggler. Pavel said that, for a price, he could get us papers that would allow us to enter the border area at České Velenice, a town in southern Bohemia right on the Austrian border. All that separates it from the Austrian town of Gmünd is a small river. Because Gmünd was in the Soviet zone and the two towns were so intertwined, Pavel said, the Czech authorities there relied more on stringent travel restrictions and screening than the usual barbed wire and mine fields.

Pavel travelled with us; he was carrying some small Czech

cameras to sell to American GIs in Vienna. When we got to České Velenice, there were several policemen on the station platform checking papers. Seeing them before we got off the train, I was all but certain they would not be fooled by our papers or the cock-and-bull reason for being there that Pavel had drummed into us. But they were, and we were waved through.

It wasn't till we were in the street that I realized that, in my nervousness, I had forgotten my hat and its $40 on the train. I certainly was not going to go back to face the police once more. So I wrote off half of my stake. I have had an aversion to wearing hats ever since.

Once in town, Pavel announced that we were on our own; he would go his way, we should look for our own way across. He assured us that the ice on the river was solid enough to hold us and warned us to watch out for machine-gun towers.

Helena and I walked arm in arm along a street that parallelled the river. We knew we did not have long to make our move; the likelihood of someone becoming suspicious was just too great. Once in awhile, we would embrace, to give the semblance of casually strolling lovers.

Then we found our break, our hole through the Iron Curtain. There was a slope towards the river and, on it, children sledding. Arms around each other, we watched them sliding down the slope. We stood at the bottom of the slope, looking up, shouting encouragement to the kids. Now, it seemed to us, we had time to look around. We put our arms around each other, kissed, looked up and down the river over each other's shoulders. And then, on a count of three, we separated, turned and ran across the river.

On the other side, we ran up the bank and flopped into the snow beyond it. When I lifted my head, I saw on the other side of the river, perhaps fifty metres from where we had crossed, a machine-gun tower. I could see no movement, no people, and the children on the other bank were still playing as if nothing had happened.

We just lay there, rolling in the snow with happiness. We had necked our way through the Iron Curtain.

We still had the Soviet lines to cross. We knew we couldn't go into the centre of Gmünd to catch the bus to Vienna. The Russians, we had been told, routinely checked the papers of passengers boarding buses there. We had to skirt the town and catch the bus in one of the outlying villages. But we didn't know the roads, so we found ourselves wading through fields and deep snowdrifts. My shoes were soaked. We were freezing, city people in city clothes caught in a situation in which we should have worn ski clothes, but couldn't, of course, because when we had left home in the morning we had been pretending to be setting out for just another normal day in the city. Luckily, I had enough sense to take my Austrian money out of my shoes before they got too soggy.

By nightfall, we had reached the road we thought we wanted. We found the bus stop but stayed away from it till the last moment lest we attracted the attention of the wrong people. When we saw a bus coming, we ran, signalling frantically to have the driver stop. It was the bus to Vienna.

But the moment we got aboard, we ran into a problem when I pulled out my Austrian money to pay for the tickets. The driver looked at my dearly bought schillings and said they were no good. There had been a currency reform and the bank notes I had were no longer valid. Then he smiled and assured me that I could still exchange them for the new currency at any bank. In the middle of the night in the middle of nowhere? By then, of course, the driver and the passengers sitting near him knew where we were from. If my no longer valid money had not given me away, my German would have; it certainly was not Austrian German.

I struck a deal with the driver: I would pay him for the tickets twice what he could get for my old money at the bank in Vienna. We were, once again, on our way. Because the seats at the front of the bus were filled, we had to sit at the back. That turned out to be a piece of luck that saved us.

Just before we got to Vienna, the bus was stopped at a Soviet roadblock. A Russian soldier got aboard to check papers.

He came up the aisle, checking documents. Helena and I sat frozen at the back; there was no way out. Neither the driver nor any of the passengers, who knew we were the kind of people the Russian was looking for, said anything to betray us. They didn't even look at us. Then, when he was a few rows in front of us, the soldier apparently got tired of looking at ID cards. He got off and waved the driver on.

Then Vienna. We get off the bus in a square dominated by a huge monument. At the top of it, a statue of a Soviet soldier. We are clearly still in the Soviet sector. We walk around to get our bearings, acting casual, trying hard not to attract the attention of anyone who might ask to check our papers. Suddenly, we realize that freedom is only a few hundred steps away. Out of the square, past a building guarded by Soviet soldiers, across the street, not too quickly, and there we see a hotel, and, going in and out of it, American soldiers. We turn a corner. A sign tells us we are in the international sector of the city. We have made it. We are safe.

I am free.

Summer of 1988. I am back in Prague. It's only the second time I have been here since I left in 1950. I made the first trip last summer with my wife and children to show them my roots. It was a sentimental journey, more melancholy than nostalgic, during which I largely blotted out Czechoslovakia's grey and unpleasant present. This time, I have returned as a reporter to explore how the country has changed and where it stands.

I am at the headquarters of the Czechoslovak Communist Party interviewing the party boss of Prague. When I last lived here, I would have been, to say the least, uncomfortable to be sitting where I am now. People, even loyal communists, were so scared of party headquarters then that they would cross the street rather than use the sidewalk in front of it. There were too many cases of people who had gone inside and not come out again except for a last short ride to Pankrác, the Prague courthouse and prison the Nazis and the communists used for their similarly grisly purposes.

Yet here I am, four decades later, sitting at ease, relishing my immunity as a Canadian and a journalist. I feel myself smiling inside with impish glee and yet keep my face serious as I ask Miroslav Štěpán, a member of the party's powerful secretariat and a comer who is being touted as the party's next leader, why, since he has admitted that the party made grave mistakes in the Stalinist fifties, and in the Brezhnevian sixties, to say nothing of the deadeningly repressive seventies, and, come to think of it, in much of the eighties too, why anyone should believe that the Czech communists are serious now about their promises to reform the system.

In earlier days, the reaction to such a question would have been, at best, a rote answer from lips wrapped into a tight scowl. But now I get a showing of pearly teeth, a gleaming smile signalling sincerity. With the sigh of a patient man trying to pierce what he obviously considers to be my dimwitted and outdated scepticism, Štěpán starts explaining how sincerely the party leadership is committed to implementing the democratic reforms of the Prague Spring of 1968.

The leadership he is talking about, of course, is the same group — slightly reshuffled — the Russians installed in power after they invaded Czechoslovakia in '68, and the reforms he speaks of are the very same ones the Soviet tanks crushed. But that doesn't bother Štěpán. What went wrong in '68, according to him, was not the content of the reforms but the runaway pace of change. The reformist leader Alexander Dubček, he says, was toppled not by Soviet tanks but by his own inability to control the country. "In the U.S.," Štěpán argues, "they would never have left a president who made as many mistakes and was as incompetent [as Dubček] in office as long we did."

Besides underestimating the capacity of Americans and of their system to tolerate and deal with inept presidents, Štěpán's argument does not explain why the new leadership threw out reforms it claims to have favored along with the reformers, or why, besides Dubček and his presumably equally "incompetent" close collaborators, it felt compelled to purge hundreds of thousands of other people who had done nothing more than voice their approval of the reforms that he and the party also endorse. The closest he comes to it is to argue that the process of democratization needs time, tolerance and prudence and did not get it from Dubček and his people. This time, he insists, the party will make sure it controls the pace of reform. As an example of the party's steady progress towards democratization, he cites an art exhibition in Prague that he, as chief of the Prague party apparatus, has sponsored. It is the first time in twenty years, he says with pride, that an art salon has been put together in Prague without regard for ideological criteria.

Indeed, there is not a trace of socialist realism at the exhibition in the Park of Culture, once the showplace of the stultifying Stalinist version of art. But neither is there a cohesive artistic message. It is rather an hodgepodge, a medley not of styles aborning but largely a compendium of Western vogues past. A glimpse of cubism here, great derivative blobs of abstraction everywhere, relieved by dollops of tired expressionism and even — would you believe it? — dots here and there of pointillism. There is a bow to *perestroika* — Mikhail Gorbachev, complete with livid birthmark, floating above the Kremlin — but it is only a Chagallesque pastiche. As a show, the Prague '88 salon is all *arrière-garde*.

If there is a message here, it is of a mood of apathy and negativism. That mood is most provocatively expressed by a statue of a potbellied man, nude but for a sun hat, sunglasses, a camera slung across his chest and a sneer of cynical disillusionment. Unlike almost everything else in the show, this is a work that tries to speak of its time and place. Czechs stopping by the statue snicker in recognition because they see in it their neighbor (never themselves, of course), the Ugly Czech of the eighties, who cares only for his beer and smoked meat, for the suntan brought back from a Bulgarian beach, about his access to Tuzex, the chain of stores the government maintains to soak up dollars from foreign tourists and attract German Marks hidden under domestic mattresses, the place where he gets his American cigarettes and Scotch whisky (to hoard rather than smoke or drink so he can pay off the doctor or the plumber when he really needs them) and the ultimate indulgence of a VCR so he can watch Western programs.

Homo Bohemicus, circa Anno Domini 1988, is paid little for his work and makes sure he works even less than he is paid for. But he manages to get by because he is always on the lookout for a fiddle, a bit of black marketeering now and then, or filching something at work and swapping it for some other article he may need but can't find in the stores — tiles for the bathroom he is refinishing perhaps. He does not like the system, but he is aware that he could be much worse off. Like the Russians or the Poles, for instance. For the Czech communists, the poverty and the shortages of food in neighboring Poland are propaganda fodder. What is happening in Poland, they argue, is not the result of forty years of socialism as Western propaganda has it; it is rather the result of continuous strikes, anti-state agitation and protest rallies by malcontents egged on by the West and the Catholic church. In private, they often cap their argument with a bit of anti-Polish chauvinism such as, "Surely, we Czechs are more organized, disciplined and sensible than those pigheaded Poles."

By Polish or Russian standards, the Czechs have a consumer society. By Western standards, it may be a shabby, ersatz kind of consumerism. But the Czechs lack neither essential foodstuffs as the Poles do nor do they suffer from a chronic lack of basic goods such as toilet paper, as in the Soviet Union. Where the despair of hunger drove Polish workers to rebellion, full bellies made most Czechs complacent. Apathy was so pervasive in Czechoslovakia that it allowed the communists to relax the big stick of intimidation. It also all but isolated the activists of Charter 77, the most prestigious and persistent human rights group in the country. The activists were not only up against the party's apparatus of repression; they were also bashing their heads against the wall of popular indifference. People sympathized with them. They even appreciated them as the conscience of the nation, as a goad to pierce the smugness of the communist apparatus. But in the same breath, they would dismiss them as being peripheral and quixotic.

The cynical Czech went along with the regime's deal, a social compact expressed disdainfully in typically Czech earthy fashion as "neserte na nás a nevysereme se na Vás," or "don't shit on us and we won't shit on you." For his mess of roast pork with dumplings, he gave up on politics or any hope of real freedom. Not for him the turbulence of Poland, nor the travails of Czech human rights activists nor even the comfort provided by the newly resurgent but still besieged Roman Catholic church. His faith, if he had one, was in his family; his temple was his *chata*, his cottage.

The *chata* represented the opposite of its Russian counterpart, the *dacha*. In the Soviet Union, the country cottage was a symbol of privilege, a reward from the system to its chosen: politicians, bureaucrats, artists, sports stars. The *chata*, by contrast, was a bribe for the masses, the Czech regime's means of defusing political frustration, of buying peace by providing a measure of popular contentment. The countryside around Prague and the other large cities is inundated with cottages.

If a *chata* is not like a *dacha*, neither does it have much in common with a Canadian cottage. It does not sit in the wilderness, nor even the approximation of the wilderness that Canadian cottagers still try to maintain by keeping a stand of trees or bushes to shield them from encroaching neighbors. In Czechoslovakia, after all, there really is no wilderness; even nature is controlled here. New cottages are for the most part crowded along with other cottages on marginal farm land, perhaps an unproductive potato field the state subdivided and sold.

The Czechs didn't go to their cottages on weekends so much to relax and play as to work on them. They lavished on them and the tiny plots that came with them all the energy, ingenuity and devotion they did not invest in their workaday jobs. There were flowers in abundance, luscious vegetables never seen in stores, cottages meticulously maintained by people trying to make up for the painfully uncomfortable years they had spent living in apartment buildings that crumbled around them because of the state's indifference and neglect. People co-operated in the cottage colonies as they never did in town. They helped their neighbors build, paint and repair.

The idea of having a *chata* was not so much getting back to nature, or, for that matter, even getting away from other people. It was getting away from the system, from the state. The most important part about a *chata* to a Czech family was that, in a country where everything belonged to the state, this was theirs to have and to own. Watching people working on their plots, it struck me as though they were preparing shelters from the dismal realities of life.

For all the complaining — Czechs groused freely about the system if not about the leaders of the regime that imposed it — there was also an awareness here of improvements, of hope. Not that there was any faith that the party reformers actually wanted reforms, but there was a growing conviction that, given what was happening in Moscow and elsewhere in eastern Europe, it was no longer possible for the communist autocrats to turn back to the total repression of old.

The fear of the regime and the paralyzing fright of the knock on the door in the middle of the night were gone. But there was still a certain nervousness, concern that the screws of repression might be tightened again, the knowledge that the apparatus was still in place. Police informers were still everywhere and the security police still maintained their black dossiers. Dissidents were still harassed and imprisoned, if no longer tortured and executed. They and foreigners were followed everywhere they went. My crew and I had a translator-guide baby-sitter assigned to us by Czech TV. When he was not with us, we were constantly tailed by other people. Still, it was far from the terror of old.

The regime was at that dangerous moment that, as Alexis de Tocqueville noted, comes to bad governments when they start trying to reform. But the greatest danger appeared to come from inside the party, from its foot-dragging, internal splits and rudderless drift. By contrast, there seemed no great threat to the regime from the opposition of a few people such as Jiří Hájek, Dubček's foreign minister, an old man of sweet, almost saintly reasonableness, ready to risk more police persecution by expounding to any visiting foreign journalist on the crimes of the regime; of Dubček himself, consigned to obscurity in Bratislava to harbor his dreams of a rebirth of his "socialism with a human face"; of Karel Srp, the founder of the Jazz Section, a cultural organization that was constantly being hounded by the regime; or of Václav Malý, a priest whose preaching was so bold that the government suspended him from his priestly functions — governments that finance the church and pay the priests can do that — and consigned him to cleaning toilets in the subway. Yet Malý dodged police surveillance to preach in secret and to celebrate mass in people's apartments.

When I interviewed Malý in the garden of his father's house just under the flight path of the planes landing at Prague airport, he reminded me of portraits I had seen of Martin Luther. He had the same fire of conviction about him. Even his head seemed much like Luther's: the round, open face, the intense eyes, the fringe of hair across his forehead.

Malý was almost as hard on his people as he was on the communists. They were too passive, he said, too willing to compromise their beliefs in exchange for tranquillity and comfort. But he saw the situation changing. "A part of our society knows we must do something and . . . is getting up from this passivity." But it was still a long way from mass activism or any kind of organized opposition. The very concept of Charter 77 was that of a declaration of principles rather than of an organization. Organizationally, the dissidents were a small, loosely connected and lonely band.

If they had a leader, it was not the sequestered politicians of the Prague Spring — Dubček and Hájek — nor any of the many prominent exiles. It was Václav Havel, playwright and *homme extraordinaire*. If Dubček was the martyr and symbol of Paradise Lost, Havel was the troubadour of Paradise Regained. In his plays — plays that were performed abroad but never at home — he explored the ambiguities of morality even as in life he unambiguously pursued a stout-hearted stand that repeatedly landed him in jail.

Where Malý cleaned toilets and Jiří Dientsbier, once the country's top foreign correspondent, stoked furnaces, Havel was put to work by the authorities manhandling beer barrels in a brewery. The Sisyphean work of rolling out the barrels was not fun but Havel managed to transform it into an auto-biographical play, called *Audience*.

In it, a boozy brewmaster offers to reassign Havel's alter ego, Ferdinand Vaněk, to lighter work. The price of getting the cushy job: doing a little informing — on himself. The brewmaster explains that he has had to supply "them," the secret police, with reports on Vaněk — innocuous ones, he says — but is running out of things to tell them. He wants Vaněk to write the reports himself. Nothing that would incriminate him, of course. "I'm on your side," he keeps insisting as he gets tipsier.

When Vaněk refuses the deal as being against his principles, the brewmaster rails: "Principles! Principles! You're making a killing on them, you're living off them, but what about me? All I'm good for is to be the manure that your damn principles grow out of." The cops, he says, are keeping tabs on Vaněk because they are afraid of writers. But people like him — "just a brewery hick," he calls himself — "they just squash."

The play belittles the idea that the dissidence of intellectuals was heroic. Writers, Havel argues, just have better intellectual weapons to resist with than most other people do. The play in effect gives absolution to ordinary people like the brewmaster who cope by co-operating with "them." At the same time, by inference, it is an indictment of intellectual hacks who behave like brewery hicks.

Yet the very qualities of intellectual integrity that made Havel and company strong were also their weakness. They were preachers, not organizers; moralists, not bread-and-butter politicians. They were more keepers of the flame, guardians of the nation's conscience than revolutionaries.

I was at a dinner given in early August by the Canadian ambassador to Prague, Barry Mawhinney, at his residence, a small palace along the lines of Toronto's Casa Loma. The guest list was a *Who's Who* of the leadership of the dissident movement: Havel, who happened to be between jail terms, Malý, Srp, Hájek, Rita Klímová, a purged economist eking out a living as a translator while she moonlighted editing underground economic journals, and a few others. Drinks in the garden, candle-lit dinner inside. All very proper, polite and stimulating. But I couldn't help thinking bad Mao thoughts: A revolution is not a dinner party. Real revolutionaries would be out drinking beer with the proles rather than sipping sherry with foreign dips (diplomats). The dissidents were all admirable people who had paid dearly for their independence of mind, but they were an elite whose voices were being heard mostly only by their peers, who took vicarious pleasure from their courage. For all the time the dissidents had been forced to spend on the lowest rungs of life pushing barrels, feeding furnaces and washing out toilets, their message seemed to be passing over the heads of the working class.

Czech intellectuals had failed to build the connection with the working class that their Polish counterparts had established. In Poland, Adam Michnik, Jacek Kuron and Leszek Kolakowski laid the philosophical and organizational groundwork that made the Solidarity movement possible. Along with the church, they nourished their relationship with the workers in the steel plants and shipyards and kept the spark alive through the long years of repression.

When Lech Walesa, the shipyard electrician, spoke to Polish workers, he spoke to his own. Czechoslovakia did not have a Walesa. Dubček did not come from the shop floor; he had spent his life as a party bureaucrat, an aparatchik who at a crucial moment decided to follow his conscience rather than the dogma that a youth spent in the Soviet Union had hammered into him. But then the Prague Spring did not rise from rebelliousness on the factory floor; it had its roots in the ferment of novelists, playwrights, poets and filmmakers, and the disillusionment of the more thoughtful members of the communist ruling class itself. It was precisely because of this that the Prague Spring was so much easier to eradicate than was Solidarity. All that the Prague regime of Gustav Husák had to do — apart from having Russian tanks around to guard it — was to lop off the head of the opposition, i.e., purge the leaders and keep them off balance by constant harassment. For Poland's General Wojciech Jaruzelski, getting rid

of Solidarity's leaders was not enough; he had to try to root
out the opposition from the dry docks, the machine shops and
the coal pits, and he failed.

The only Czech dissident organization that did manage to
stir mass appeal was very different from Solidarity. It was
Karel Srp's Jazz Section, a club that attracted not only jazz
fans but a broad spectrum of the young. But the Jazz Section
was not looking, as Solidarity was, for a cure to communism's ills; it was merely an attempt to get relief from the
rigors of communist Gleichschaltung. Still, the Jazz Section
was an effective organization that gave tens of thousands of
Czechs a taste of what cultural life in the country could be.
And Srp brilliantly manipulated the Kafkaesque Communist
bureaucracy with a slyness worthy of Švejk's creator, Jaroslav
Hašek.

Though Stalin and his original band of henchmen continually suppressed jazz as an expression of capitalist depravity,
by 1970 it had been displaced in the lexicon of communist de-
monology by rock. Compared to rock, jazz seemed, well, safe;
after all, kids no longer danced to it. And so the authorities
registered Srp's little club as a section of the official Musicians' Union, which they themselves had organized out of
the disbanded artists' unions of the Prague Spring the better
to control the egghead types.

Being an officially approved organization gave the Jazz Section some important privileges. In a society where the state
maintained a monopoly on publishing and reserved the right
to censor everything, cultural organizations were allowed to
publish periodicals for their members without submitting
them to the censors.

Srp used that licence to great advantage with a newsletter
called *Jazz* and a line of paperbacks called *Jazzpetit*. Though
he was limited to printing 3,000 copies, they were passed
from hand to hand and read by tens of thousands of people.
The Section also organized jazz concerts that became popular. Inevitably, it soon crossed the line drawn in the shifting
sands of ideological taboos from jazz to various forms of
rock. Musical groups like the Plastic People of the Universe
and the Prague Selection sprang up and flourished for awhile.

But ultimately they were banned. To the regime, the frenzied masses of young people at rock concerts, however innocent and apolitical, looked threatening. It could not tolerate anything it did not control and could not understand.

The members of the Plastic People band were jailed. But not on political charges — that would have been too embarrassing. Instead, they were found guilty of a criminal offence for having used the word "shit" at a concert, not once but eight times in one song. Similarly, the regime managed to jail Srp by taking a lesson from the life and times of Al Capone, the American gangster. When the U.S. government couldn't nail Capone on charges of murder, extortion and bootlegging, it got him on income tax evasion charges. The Czech regime went the U.S. Justice Department one better: it trumped up a false tax bill high enough to be sure Srp could not conceivably pay it and then convicted him of tax evasion.

The Jazz Section survived these idiocies. Sometimes it was more dead than alive. But Srp and his friends never lost their cunning, their courage nor their sense of humor. When the government, in an effort to kill the Section, ordered its parent body to cease all activities, they just carried on, arguing that a body that had ceased all activities as ordered from higher up could not act on anything. Therefore if it were to disband the Jazz Section, it would be disobeying orders and breaking the law, wouldn't it, comrade?

Much as the Jazz Section discomfited the regime, it was difficult to see how its activities posed any threat to the government. Though it breached the regime's obsessively maintained monopoly on information, it also served as an apolitical safety valve for the frustrations of the young. The Section's publications, besides being apolitical, were also too esoteric for mass consumption: an anthology called *Minimal + Earth + Concept Art*; a book exploring Dadaism; a study titled "The Body, the Thing and Reality in Contemporary Art"; a painstakingly assembled record of "The Music of the Terezín Ghetto," a memorial to the rich cultural life among Jews in Theresienstadt, a concentration camp that the Nazis maintained in Bohemia — until they shipped its inmates off to the Auschwitz ovens in 1944 — as a "model ghetto" to be shown to credulous visitors from the Red Cross. This was hardly the stuff to send the masses running to the barricades. In Canada, such publications would never have made it without a grant or subsidy. But here, in this land starved of any intercourse of ideas, they were snapped up as manna from heaven.

One weekend my crew and I managed to evade our baby-sitter, the watchdog we had been assigned by the government, to attend a cultural festival organized by the Jazz Section at an abandoned farmstead in Moravia. It was an illegal affair because it did not have a permit from the authorities, a permission that would all but certainly have been refused if it had been requested. But there was nothing covert about their *fête champêtre*, no guards posted to warn of approaching cops.

No reticence, either. The music of a rock band is blasting across the fields from what used to be a stable. Iconoclastic art hangs on barn doors for any snooper's telephoto lens to see.

The sons of Smetana, the daughters of Dvořák have picked up on the contemporary sound of the West. But in their own way. As their parents jived to the sound of swing and modified it to the needs of their limitations, so have these Czechs of the eighties adapted rock. They call it experimental rock. The electric guitars are here, so is the urgency of the raucous beat. But the music seems less carnal than Western rock. Instead, the sound is mostly a discordant wail of despondency; the words, a plaint of discontent.

On the walls, among the jumble of wires twisted into mobiles and the collages of cluttered artifacts, declarations of alienation: a blank white canvas entitled *Proof of Identity*; a pair of heavy workman's gloves, spread in a gesture of helplessness and supplication, pinned to a board with bolts driven through their palms as in the Crucifixion.

But this is not a rebellious group. The people here have not come to challenge the government or provoke the police. They came to enjoy themselves, to talk, to play and listen to music. They brought their kids and their dogs. There is not a whiff of the marijuana smoke that blankets so many rock concerts in the West. All is proper, almost prim here. It is more a family picnic, an outing of kindred souls sharing their distinctness, their differences not only with their rulers but also their disdain for the listless passivity of most of their fellow citizens. They wear their dissidence as a badge of self-respect, an amulet to ward off the stultifying effects of conforming to the system.

For all the tranquillity in Czechoslovakia in the summer of 1988, there were pressures on the regime to reform. There were Gorbachev's *perestroika* and *glasnost*, of course, whose fall-out was spreading. But the Czech communists weren't too concerned about that; they thought they could deflect *glasnost* and contain the political implications of *perestroika*. They did worry, however, as they began to realize that they could not go on much longer milking the economy as ruthlessly as they had for decades to deliver the goods that kept the populace mollified. The economy was running down and if something drastic were not done soon, Czechoslovakia would find itself by the end of the century in the mess that Poland was going through. They desperately needed a plan to modernize the economy.

So far, the party had managed to make do with cosmetic changes. Its discredited leader, Gustáv Husák, was shunted aside into the ceremonial presidency. But his replacement, Miloš Jakeš, was no reformer. He had presided over the harsh purges that followed the Soviet invasion. Jakeš was looked on as a stopgap. If the leadership was to survive the pressure of greater expectations generated by Gorbachev, it would clearly soon need a new, uncompromised face at the top.

That is how Miroslav Štěpán found himself shooting up from obscurity to first secretary of the Prague Communist Party and, shortly thereafter, into the politburo. Štěpán was no ideologue; he was an organization man, an administrator, the possessor of a master's degree in business administration, chunky, bulletheaded with a full-blown wattle of a chin, tough, brash, the kind of man, I thought, who under different circumstances might have been mayor of Chicago (*à la* Richard Daley the elder) or president of the Teamsters' Union (shades of Jimmy Hoffa), much like Boris Yeltsin in Moscow, not awed by reputations, not afraid to step on toes. But — unlike Yeltsin — never on the party's toes; the party was all, that much was evident. Štěpán was hardly a natural reformer. He spoke of reform with all the enthusiasm of a glutton who has just been told he must lose weight to live speaks of dieting.

From the reluctant dieter, I went to see the man who was writing the prescription for the diet. Valtr Komárek was the head of Forecasting Institute of the Academy of Sciences, an economist charged by the government with drawing up a plan to bring the country up to present west European economic levels by the year 2010. In other words, if Czechoslovakia ran hard for the next twenty years and if everything went well, it would find itself in the twenty-first century only twenty years behind western Europe. An essential part of the Komárek diet: closing down inefficient plants, finding jobs for their displaced employees, making room for a private sector and forcing state enterprises to compete on the open market. He said his plan was ready but admitted the government had not yet made a decision how much of it to adopt.

Komárek seemed the very opposite of Štěpán, a dreamer rather than a doer. With his pointed beard and a great unruly thatch of hair, he looked like Leon Trotsky might have if Stalin had allowed him to grow old. Komárek, too, was a communist, even though he often seemed in trouble with the party or on the verge of it. But now the party needed people like him who talked of flexibility rather than the dictates of ideology, of incentives rather than production quotas, of the need for a free flow of information, better education, more personal freedom, a better environment. Komárek rejected the American model of capitalism as "social Darwinism." His goal seemed to be Swedish welfare-state capitalism superimposed on a core of sacred-cow nationalized industries. He saw it as the only way socialism could be salvaged from the failures of forty years of Communist party rule.

It was brave talk. But the more he talked, the more enthusiastic he became about his vision, the more I became convinced that the party would not take Valtr Komárek's medicine. It was not his party; it belonged to the likes of Miroslav Štěpán. Reform, real reform would mean giving up power. And power was all the party had left.

I was depressed leaving Prague. I didn't think I would ever want to come back. I might miss a few friends, the fairy-tale loveliness of the city, the melodic sound of the language to which my ears had become attuned once again. But not the rest. This was no longer a place I could call home.

The Czech national anthem sings of home being where "water murmurs across the meadows, forests whisper over rocky mountains." There is more, much more to a homeland than meadows and mountains. Home is, above all, people to whom you feel close. And I no longer had that feeling in Czechoslovakia. The Czechs made me feel like a Rip Van Winkle who woke up and found the future he had been transported into to be too much like the nightmares of his past. It was almost as if the Czechs had all been with my father, my brother and me half a century ago when we spent the night in the washroom of Lobositz Station. Having left on the train the next morning, I had now come back to find them still in the toilet, warm, even comfortable and, for the most part, apparently content to be confined to living in a shithouse.

Not that I was about to blame the victims for their victimization. I hadn't forgotten how meekly I had entered the station toilet with my father. Nor did I think that I was somehow better than they. After all, it was not my doing that I got out on the train. On the contrary, I realized that if I had not been on that train and somehow still survived, if I had not crossed that frozen river a decade later — which was easier for me than for people with families — I would have been just as apathetic as most of them. I knew I never could have found the moral strength of Václav Havel, the fortitude of Václav Malý, the persistence and cunning of Karel Srp. That was what really bothered me. Watching the Czechs, the daily compromises most of them had to make, the apathetic and pathetic meekness that it had brought, what it had done to their lives, what they had allowed the communists to do to them, what many communists — the decent ones among them — had done to themselves, reminded me that there but for the force of circumstances went I.

I had just been lucky. Very lucky.

And yet, dammit, I told myself, it was not just luck. I did do something. I had the gumption to shake off the shackles. I had dared to cross the Rubicon and carve out a new life for myself on the other side.

I was at the airport by then, going through passport control. The border policeman took my passport. I waited. And waited. The policeman was in one of those Soviet style border booths where you can see only the top of the officers' heads while they can watch you. There is even a mirror over your head angled so that they can see your hands. (Are they trembling?) The man was obviously bent over my passport. He put his head up, looked at me and then put his head down again. A few more minutes went by. Then I saw him picking up the phone. Another officer came and entered the booth. They were talking but I could not hear what they were saying. By this time the people in the line behind me realized this was going to take some time, so they moved to other booths.

The two men now left the booth, leaving me standing there alone in front of a locked gate. More time went by, and I started wondering what they were up to. I wasn't worried. There was nothing they could do to me. I was a Canadian now. If they dared mess with me, they'd be up against Joe Clark waggling his wattles at them.

Then a little doubt crept in. The Czechs could, if they really wanted to (and they were unpredictable), just say I was still a Czechoslovak citizen subject to their laws. I had never done anything about renouncing my Czechoslovak citizenship; as far as I was concerned, the country had renounced me. Whenever someone at External Affairs suggested that I had better regularize my status with the Czechs, my reaction was: Screw them, I am Canadian and that's that.

But now I could feel the beginning of something familiar rising in me. It wasn't fear. Not quite apprehension either.

Not yet. Maybe it was more just a little caution like a rabbit pricking up its ears and crinkling its nose in a precautionary sniff. Whatever it was, it was just enough to make me remember how that feeling could grow and gnaw, and what it used to feel like before I fled the country.

Just then the border cop came back. He handed me my passport without a word and pressed the gate buzzer to let me through. I had been standing there no more than twenty minutes, just long enough to remind me that in the end the only difference between me and the 15 million people I was leaving behind in Czechoslovakia was that I had this little booklet in a blue cover with a message inside for all from Joe Clark and the Queen to allow me "to pass freely without let or hindrance."

Once through the gate, of course, I became once again a regular don't-mess-with-me Canuck.

CHAPTER V

We have here [in Canada] no traditions
and ancient venerable institutions. . . .
here, every man is the son of his own works.

Thomas D'Arcy McGee

I had run far. Away from Europe to Canada. Away from the
Atlantic across the continent to the rim of the Pacific. And
beyond, out to sea.

I signed on in the autumn of 1950 as a crewman on the SS
Prince George, a passenger ship that plied the Inland Passage
along the British Columbia coast to Alaska. We would sail
out of Vancouver in the evening as the lights began to ring
the harbor, out under the Lion's Gate Bridge high above our
mast. I'd stand at the stern as the lights of the city fell away
and we headed north to a world of quiet inlets where the
mountains dropped straight into impenetrably dark water.
I had never seen so much space, so much stillness, so much
beauty all but untouched by Man.

Beyond Vancouver, most of the small communities along
the B.C. coast and the Alaska panhandle clung to a narrow
belt of foreshore stingily yielded by the mountains. All were

116

isolated, most approachable only by sea. There were no roads across the mountains to places such as Ocean Falls, a pulp and paper town perched uneasily at the end of an inlet below an almost perpendicular rock. Buildings and roads squatted precariously on wooden platforms glued to the mountainside.

This was still frontier country that made much of the rest of the New World look old. I saw Kitimat when it was enveloped in the stillness of centuries, a stillness that was soon shattered forever by the bulldozers and the drilling machines that came to burrow through the mountains and turn around the flow of rivers to power an aluminum smelter and give birth to an instant town. There was the Saturday night rowdiness of Prince Rupert, a railhead and port with the look and feel of a pioneering town; the salmon migrating upstream right through the middle of Ketchikan; Sitka with the bulbous spires of its Russian Orthodox cathedral, a church whose worshippers had left after the czar had sold Alaska to the U.S. for $7 million almost a hundred years earlier; Juneau, where I encountered my first western saloon with swing doors and none of your Canadian bluenose restrictions; and Skagway, a town with the look of an abandoned movie lot, a place of the lawless Wild West of myth and movies where the ghosts of the cheechakos and the sourdoughs of the 1896 Klondike Gold Rush lurked behind the boarded-up door of the Golden North Hotel. The trains that once carried the gold out of the Klondike to Skagway and the sea still climbed, clinging perilously to narrow mountain ledges and along matchstick bridges thrown across deep gorges, through the White Pass into the Yukon. In Skagway, the local movie house marquee announced that it was "proud to present Shirley Temple in *The Littlest Rebel*."

I was indeed in the New World where the span from news to history and legend was often less than a lifetime. The Alaska purchase took place, after all, in my grandparents' time and my father was alive when the Klondike Gold Rush started. Yet here these all too recent events had become seminal history, the stuff of legend from which the future flowed. Robert Service, the poet and journalist whose ballads celebrated the Klondike Gold Rush, was its Herodotus.

I felt sympathy and empathy for the priest at St. Michael's cathedral in Sitka who, with no parishioners left, had turned tourist guide and loving guardian of the icons and tapestries from a Russia that no longer existed. To him, Leningrad was still St. Petersburg. He was in the New World but not of it, sustained by the shelter he had found among his beloved treasures, prisoner to a lost past.

I had no icons, no relics to worship. I had come to the New World to be free of the past. I had come to a country that was searching, as I was, for an identity, a country that blessedly did not even have a flag of its own.

Flags, to me, were mostly signals of danger, threatening banners that chauvinistic charlatans used to whip up storms of conflict and contention. Even at best, flags were symbols of exclusion that said to people like me: You don't belong. It was comforting to me that the closest Canada had to a flag was a modified British ensign. Its Union Jack provided assurance of the freedom and decency I had found in Britain and yet, looking so much like the flag ships flew on the high seas and faraway ports, it also had the air of having left behind the stuck-up, stick-in-the-mud constrictions of life in Old Blighty. The Union Jack provided protection and the Canadian coat of arms promise. The ensign made being halfway around the globe from the world I was raised in more familiar and reassuring.

At night, as I lay in my bunk in the fo'c's'le rocked by the sea, I knew I had outrun the news at last. News had become nothing more threatening than a storm that flooded basements, a drought that begat forest fires, a brewery strike that threatened the beer supply. People were arrested for holding up banks or doing away with their spouses, not for imagined political crimes or the crime of merely being. From now on, news of great calamities would come from afar, from beyond the mountains and across the seas to be digested safely along with breakfast.

The transition from D.P., Displaced Person, the official term for refugees from Europe that in popular usage became a derogatory label, to acceptance as a member of Canadian society was remarkably easy. It was an astonishing experience, even a shock, when I went to register with the Unemployment Insurance Commission and was asked only my name, age, address and where I was working. There were none of the questions I was used to from Europe about nationality and religion; there was no required slew of documents, no identity card or passport; no one even asked me for proof that I was a legally landed immigrant. Even in Britain, as an alien, I had to register with the police every time I changed addresses. The feeling of freedom in Canada was overwhelming.

What I did not know then, of course, was that I was part of an important change that was sweeping through Canadian society. As the trickle of D.P.s became a flood, they were not only absorbed; they changed the look and feel of many parts of the country.

When I came to Vancouver, Robson Street, one of the main streets in the West End, was lined mostly with Chinese mom-and-pop grocery stores and restaurants that served soup heated straight from the can and soggy hot beef sandwiches. The gourmet's delight of Robson Street was wilted chop suey. Within a few years, the street was popularly known by the German name "Robsonstrasse" to reflect its reputation as a place where central European immigrants came to eat smoked pork chops with dumplings and sauerkraut and to buy their dark rye bread and bratwurst. Pretty soon le tout Vancouver flocked to the Johann Strauss Café to dance to Viennese oompapah music and eat goulash and sauerbraten. O Canada, what did we do to thee?

I had signed on as a mess boy on the *Prince George*. I made beds, cleaned the heads, served meals in the officers' mess. I had a bed, three meals a day, more if I wanted. The abundance of food, the conspicuous abundance of everything in Canada, including freedom, was unsettling. I used to wander down supermarket aisles awe-struck by the quantity and diversity of food, by the fact that, no matter how much people bought, the shelves were always full and the store never seemed to run out of anything. The first time I saw the galley helpers on the *Prince George* throw huge quantities of leftover food over the side of the ship, food that elsewhere would have been saved, I was so appalled by the waste that my stomach churned as I watched the circling, diving seagulls gobble it up.

I did not realize it then, but my time at sea helped me to recover from the debilitating effects of my experiences. For four years I had thought mostly only of surviving, wondering whether I'd ever be able to walk again, concentrating on getting out of hospital, getting out of Czechoslovakia without being caught and jailed, hiding my hip ailment from immigration officers to get out of Europe, and finding a fingerhold in the new society into which I had been dropped. Under such conditions, everything — energy, willpower, ambition — is sucked up by the all-consuming instinct to survive. The year I spent at sea allowed me to recuperate, to realize that my existence was no longer threatened, to start thinking ahead beyond tomorrow.

I decided I needed an education, and in the fall of 1951 I ventured ashore and enrolled at the University of British Columbia. I was going to become — don't ask me why! — an economist.

It was the start of a new life for me, a normal, peaceful, sometimes frustrating, overwhelmingly happy, productive, up-and-down (but more ups than downs), blessedly ordinary personal life, and it's been that way ever since. I've gone through the usual experiences of a middle-class Canadian existence: two marriages, the first ending in divorce, the second the lasting source of my happiness and stability; two kids grown into thoughtful, decent and resourceful women; a house with a mortgage and such once undreamt-of sybaritic self-indulgences as a fridge that, when tickled by a glass, dispenses ice through the door. I went from itinerant and impecunious journeyman to established media figure, from beer and rye with ginger through plonk and martinis to a weakness for single malt Scotch, Médoc wines and VSOP cognac. All comfortably and comfortingly humdrum, thank you.

I came back to news, but this time for the fun, the interest, the excitement and not for the need of it. One day, shortly after I arrived at UBC, I wandered into the offices of the campus newspaper, the *Ubyssey*, out of curiosity. And I stayed. I had found a new home.

I discovered there was more to journalism than just news. There was opinion, inquiry and imagination. And you didn't have to be serious all the time. Or, for that matter, if you had the wit and the talent, any of the time. The *Ubyssey* was irrepressibly irreverent and disrespectful of authority. It covered the frolics of its constituency: the frosh festivals, pool dunkings, homecoming parades, Mardi Gras, engineering student antics and other rites of post-puberty initiation. But it also attacked the university administration, the student council, sororities and fraternities, the Canadian Officers Training Corps, the provincial government, the athletics department, the Russians and the Americans, communism and liberalism, in fact any -ism at all. And it had no inhibition about making a fool of itself. The targets of its pique were predictable and so were the reasoning and the writing. But the freedom and the feistiness were infectious. News didn't have to hurt to be news. I was hooked. Within a year, I was the editor of the paper.

What we didn't know at the *Ubyssey* then is that for many of us the time we spent at the UBC Publications Board, or Pub, would turn out to be more useful than any of the courses we were blithely skipping. Or that the *Ubyssey*, which a prominent preacher once denounced as "the vilest rag you can imagine," had become the breeding ground for what would one day be known collectively as the Ubyssey Mafia. Some Pubsters gravitated to politics, as John Turner and Pat Carney did. Many turned to the law. There was even a poet, Earle Birney. But what the *Ubyssey* did best was to turn a long line of layabouts into good journalists, a line that started with Norman DePoe, Pierre Berton, Ron Haggart, Val Sears, and Eric Nicol. From the *Ubyssey* that I edited came Pat Carney, Allan Fotheringham, Helen Hutchinson and Sandy Ross.

Economics had lost its allure. Besides being editor of the *Ubyssey*, I was also part-time campus correspondent for the *Vancouver Sun*. The following year, besides carrying a full course load as a student during the day, I also worked nights as a police reporter. I didn't even wait to graduate to turn to journalism full-time. First, I worked at the *Sun*, where I was quickly fired for not showing any talent for the business, and then at the Vancouver *Province*.

Newspapering in Vancouver belonged to the whoop-and-holler school of journalism. The three newspapers — the *Sun*, the *Province* and the pauperly and terminally ill *News Herald* — combined the timidity of boosterism and babbitry with the brashness of the press-card-in-the-hatband style of journalism. The newsrooms were a refuge to clones of the tough-talking characters out of *Front Page*, editors whose most important tool of the trade was a hip-pocket flask of rye and reporters known more for their imagination than enthusiasm for truth or objectivity. Some of them were more colorful than any of the people they wrote about. I knew I had made the grade when the rewrite desk chief invited me to the washroom and offered me a slug of whisky from his flask.

Journalism in Vancouver was not a calling for the money-hungry, or, for that matter, the serious-minded. Murders, bank robberies, Red scares, gory accidents, goofy stunts, sob stories, Sasquatch hunts and tales of survival in the wild: those were the glories of the Vancouver newspapers. I did my share of these stories and loved it. Most of the time, I worked night shifts, mostly on the police beat, covering murders and bank robberies, fires and ship sinkings, riots at Oakalla prison and criminal trials. Once I unearthed a potential murder witness whom the police had missed, a story that didn't exactly help me in maintaining good relations at the cop shop. Another time, the *Sun* threatened to bring theft charges against me because I had "borrowed" — very tempo-rarily, you understand, just long enough for the *Province* to make a copy — their exclusive photo of a bank robber being arrested. The Vancouver police chief, Bill Archer, brushed off the *Sun*'s complaint with the remark that it made no sense charging me since he had always known that all newspapermen were thieves.

I also tried my hand at writing editorials, which showed where my real interests lay. When the 1954 partition of Vietnam set off a flight of refugees from the communist North, I wrote in the *Province* that "the nations which aided and encouraged their migration southwards have a responsibility towards these people. . . . If the communists should gain control of southern Vietnam, we must not forget these people. The communists certainly will not." This was twenty years before the fall of Saigon.

When eastern European countries started buying wheat from Canada, I wrote: "No excuse can be found in 1955 for the fact that Hungary, the country of the fertile Great Danubian Plain, one of Europe's best wheat areas, must import wheat — no excuse but communist incompetence."

Sometimes I did "silly season" features. When bankers boasted they would cash any kind of cheque, no matter what it was written on, I took in a cheque written on the back of a shirt and insisted they cash it. They did. When Canada was smitten by uranium fever, I spoofed about it by going out into the streets of Vancouver with a Geiger counter and finding that the flowers in front of the courthouse gave off the most clicks in town. "Thar's uranium in them thar geraniums," said the story.

As much fun as it was, I felt I needed something more than newspapering in Vancouver could give me. In 1958, I moved to Toronto and for two years I worked for the *Toronto Daily Star*, mostly as a City Hall reporter. Toronto City Hall was — and, I suspect, still is — a great place to oberve the practice of politics at its most pragmatic. The rulers of Metropolitan Toronto were disciples of Machiavelli, Darwin and P.T. Barnum.

For years, there had been a fierce rivalry between the *Star* and the *Toronto Telegram*, the kind of rivalry that is closer to war than just competition. But the *Tely* was now bleeding — mortally, it would turn out — and the *Star* was walking away from the fight the way a matador who knows he has the bull spooked contemptuously turns his back on the beast and saunters away. The *coup de grâce* can wait.

The *Star* turned from being scrappy to being earnest. It did some wonderful things. Pierre Berton and Ron Haggart wrote columns that were a delight. In the meantime, I was covering endless hearings on plans for the new City Hall and Bloor subway, filling whole pages of the *Star* with more details of the haggling and niggling than anyone would ever want to read. But the overkill served to tie the *Star* to the community; no one could accuse it of neglecting Toronto.

For me, my five years of working for the *Province* and the *Star* had been valuable experience. I had learned how to compose low-fat, high-cal sentences; how to make the banal look interesting and the interesting sound fascinating; how to extract the kernel of what mattered from the minutiae of reams of material, be it evidence at a trial or a royal commission report; how to persist in getting information out of people who did not want to part with it; how never to take no for an answer — at least not until your head started hurting from being banged against a wall; how to bring order out of chaos (no two eyewitness accounts of anything ever seem to jibe with each other); how to spot the wiles of publicity hounds and not let yourself be used; how to make sure you got the little things as well as the big ones right (I had to overcome a weakness for getting addresses wrong by transposing house numbers).

In short, I had learned the finger exercises of journalism. Now I was ready for something more challenging. Personally as well as professionally. I had recovered from the hurts of Europe. I had become a Canadian in a wider sense than just having a piece of paper saying so. Canada had changed my outlook, my set of references for looking at the world and my place in it. I was more self-confident and optimistic, less prone to looking over my shoulder. I was ready to tackle the world once again.

It was a warm January night in Paris, so warm that after

dinner my friend Bill Boyd and I decided to have a drink outside at a café on the Boulevard St. Germain. Suddenly, across the square, behind the ancient church of St. Germain des Prés, an explosion. I looked up and saw flames and smoke billowing from an apartment building.

I jumped up, excited, my reportorial glands flowing. But all around me there seemed to be only a mild curiosity. It was 1962, and Paris was used to bombs.

The OAS, the Secret Army Organization, a terrorist group dedicated to keeping Algeria part of France, was bombing the homes of its opponents and killing policemen. The OAS was made up of Frenchmen — colonists in Algeria, soldiers waging a war against Arab and Berber guerrillas fighting for independence, generals, politicians and senior civil servants — who felt Charles de Gaulle had betrayed their cause.

The breach started when de Gaulle told the French colonists of Algeria at a huge rally in Algiers, *"Je vous ai compris,"* I have understood you. That simple statement was to arouse as much controversy among the French as the general's *"Vive le Québec libre"* would nine years later in Canada. The colons, the so-called *pieds noirs*, or black feet, not being used to the subtleties of de Gaulle's Delphic pronouncements, took his statement as a pledge of support for their campaign and cheered him. The cheers turned into screams of outrage when they discovered that what the general understood about their cause convinced him that France should give up Algeria. And so they declared war on him and his government, a war they carried from North Africa to the streets of Paris.

There were checkpoints everywhere. Policemen wore bullet-proof vests and stood guard behind armored barriers that looked like portable versions of the metal pissoir kiosks that dotted the streets of the city. When the police stopped your car at night and checked your papers, there was always one officer pointing an automatic weapon straight at you.

There were bloody demonstrations for a Free Algeria and equally bloody demonstrations for a French Algeria. *Al-gé-rie Fran-çaise*, the crowds would chant, and hundreds of beeping car horns would pick up the rhythm.

The demonstrations had their own Parisian rhythm. First,

a broad river of humanity flowing down the boulevards, dignified and peaceful. Then a flurry of impatient radicals taunting
the police, sometimes with a barrage of torn- up paving stones.
Finally, the police would break up the demonstration with tear
gas and truncheons if it got really serious, or by using their
dandyish capes as flails if it was not. The capes were effective
— their bottom edges were lined with weights to make sure
the cape did not cling but fell stylishly from the shoulder and
swished elegantly with a turn of the arm or body. But when
the edge of the cape hit you, as it did me while I was covering
a demonstration in the Latin Quarter, you knew the capes
were not designed just to keep out the cold and the rain. They
combined elegance and force in one neat package, persuasion
Parisian style.

That January night at St. Germain des Prés, however, the
violence of Paris was all new to me. I had just arrived in
Paris that day to start a new job as a copy editor at the
Herald Tribune, the famous Paris *Trib*. And right there in
front of me, even before I had started work, was a story.
It did not take long to find out that this was not just an
ordinary bombing, that the apartment that had been the target of the terrorists belonged to none other than Jean-Paul
Sartre, the existentialist philosopher, the reigning king of the
French intellectual world. But Sartre was not at home when
the bomb exploded; he had prudently moved elsewhere in the
expectation of such an attack. The only serious casualty was a
child in a neighboring apartment.

I phoned the *Trib* newsroom. The editor at the other end of
the line listened, but when I told him that Sartre was unhurt,
that he had not even been there, he lost interest. And so did
the patrons at the Café des Deux Magots and the Café de
Flore, just around the corner from the bomb blast, the cafés
where Sartre and Simone de Beauvoir used to spend their
days and much of their nights. The king of the Left Bank was
safe, and the people at the Deux Magots and the Flore went
back to their Pernods and café-calvas. The bombing around
the corner, the maiming of a child, was just another routine
atrocity, and life on the Boulevard St. Germain went back to
normal.

For me, the bomb blast at St. Germain des Prés was my welcome back to Europe. It seemed a reminder of something that I had forgotten in Canada — the existentialist idea that to be free is to suffer and that life, in Sartre's view, is futility, nothing more than an "ineffective passion." In Europe, it all seemed plausible. In Canada, if I had thought about it at all, it would have been nothing much more than pretentious prattle.

I had gone back to Europe not as a European returning home; I went as a Canadian observing a journalistic rite of passage. Going to Europe to travel around the continent and, if possible, to work there for a year or so was what many Canadian newspapermen did between leaving university and settling down to a family, career, mortgage and taxes. A European tour seemed almost a prerequisite, much like having to pass the obligatory first-year maths course, only much more pleasant.

Europe was the Last Big Fling before you settled down. You worked just long enough at home in Canada to save up for it. With luck and a good deal of belt tightening, you could save enough to buy a small European car. You paid for it in Canada — you got a new car tax-free that way for less than $1,000 — and picked it up in Europe at the beginning of the summer.

Then off you went, riding along the back roads of Europe, eating bread and cheese, drinking lots of local wine and sleeping it off because, as a good Canadian, you weren't used to drinking wine morning, noon and night. Perhaps you camped, or you slept in student hostels or cheap hotels, $3 a night if you felt extravagant. You spent your days going through cathedrals, castles and art museums, and nights in cheap but interesting bars, good and cheap restaurants, and bad and cheap nightclubs.

All tours were different but they all had four "musts": London, Paris, Rome and a beach, preferably not in Spain, because the cops there, Franco's dreaded and dreadful Guardia

Civil, had not yet quite got used to having to tolerate that scourge of fascist civilization — women in bikinis.

The hard part — the one that differentiated us from more ordinary tourists — came in September when it came to either finding a job or going home. Journalistic jobs on the continent were scarce, particularly for unilingual anglophones, so most of us ended up looking for a job on Fleet Street, London's journalism row. Britain was still kind to Canadians in those days. The cost of living was low by Canadian standards and there were none of the present restrictions that make it difficult for Canadians to get permission to work in Britain.

In the late fifties and early sixties, Fleet Street was full of young Canadian journalists, particularly veterans of the *Ubyssey*. Canadian parties in London sometimes looked like a reprise of Ubyssey Pub parties in Vancouver. Some Canadians worked for the Fleet Street newspapers, but most got jobs at the Reuters news agency.

I found a job with United Press International as an editor on the agency's European desk. It was neither a well-paid job nor an exciting one. My job was to shoehorn the huge volume of reports from UPI's bureaus worldwide into one comprehensive service that provided the material that would be of most interest and use to UPI's European clients. This came down to taking the output of paper spewed out continuously by half a dozen teletype machines and boiling it down to what one machine could put out. That meant a lot of fast rewriting and even more arbitrary slashing of long, complex stories into a few simple paragraphs.

But the most important tool of the job was the wastebasket. If the first paragraph didn't grab your attention, out went the story into the basket. If you didn't act quickly and ruthlessly you would find yourself being strangled by gigantic snarls of teletype paper demanding attention and editorial decision. If you threw out the wrong story, of course, you soon heard about it. The wires would be buzzing with angry messages asking why the AP or Reuters had the story while UPI didn't.

It was a system that trained people to think quickly and act decisively. But once you mastered it, it became dull and insufferably boring. For a while, the charm of London, for me mainly the theatre, the richness of its bookstores and the variety of its newspapers, made up for the boredom of the work and the poor pay. But by the fall of 1961, after a year in London, I was ready to go home, back to Canada.

The offer of a job in Paris with the European Edition of the *New York Herald Tribune* changed my mind. And my life.

The City of Light put light into my life. I met my wife, Mike, in Paris. She is an American, a Wisconsin Swede, who had joined the U.S. Foreign Service and had been posted to the Paris embassy after assignments in Colombo and Moscow. Both our children were born in Paris. And so, in a way, was my career. The job at the *Trib* fitted my talents and my experience.

The *Trib* or, as it is known in French, *L'Herald*, is a Paris institution, a century-old newspaper of solid reputation and zany tradition, the newspaper that sent Stanley to the depths of Africa to look for Livingstone and Art Buchwald to London to see his Savile Row tailor in his new, made-in-Hong-Kong suit. Stanley found the famous explorer in the jungle and made "Mr. Livingstone, I presume" part of the English language. When Buchwald's snobbish tailor clapped his eyes on the horror of Hong Kong tailoring, he expressed his anguish with: "Mr. Buchwald, Mr. Buchwald, you've been in an accident."

The *Trib* was at a crossroads when I joined it. The *New York Times* had launched its own European edition a year earlier to challenge it. Since the *Times* was rich and the parent *Trib* in New York was hemorrhaging, the outlook for *L'Herald* was perilous. The owner of the *Trib*, Jock Whitney, a multimillionaire New York financier, dabbled in horses, New York politics, diplomacy — he had been President Eisenhower's ambassador to the U.K. — as well as newspapers. He appointed a new editor to rejuvenate the Paris *Trib* and meet the challenge of the *Times*. I was hired as part of that rejuvenation.

The *Trib* was both an American newspaper and a European one. It provided Americans in Europe and elsewhere with news of home. It also gave foreigners a glimpse into American affairs and thinking. It was read by European politicians and businessmen. It was read in the Kremlin. It was read in Cairo and Damascus, as well as Tel Aviv. And it had to speak clearly to all these constituencies.

I was a natural for the job. I knew something of both Europe and the U.S., and yet I was of neither. I had the experience to spot the hurdles of linguistic, political and social incomprehension, large and small, that might stump some of the paper's readers. I was likely to be more understanding of the varied interests of its constituencies than some of the American journalists who came wandering to Europe for the first time.

Within a year, I was the *Trib*'s news editor. A year later, I was the assistant managing editor.

Our resources were much weaker than those of the *Times*, and we survived on the strength of the paper's tradition in Europe and by our wits. By the time I left the *Trib* in the fall of 1966 to return to Canada, we had beaten the European edition of the *Times*. In New York, the *Trib* died, and the *Times* went from strength to strength. In Paris, the *Times* gave up, the *Trib* survived and became the *International Herald Tribune*, a paper that now girdles the globe.

In that underdog fight against the *Times*, I had found my calling: foreign news, interpreting it, clarifying it, demystifying it, making it interesting and relevant.

When I went to register the birth of our first-born, Léah, at the town hall of Neuilly-sur-Seine, the suburb of Paris where she was born, the town clerk asked me whether I wanted to register the baby as a French citizen. He seemed upset when, without hesitation, I answered, "No." He looked at the form I had filled out and said, "Well, since it's a girl, it doesn't matter; it would have been different if the child had been a boy." A baby boy was important to the French as draft fodder for the army; girls, it seemed, were dispensable. Even so, the clerk reacted to my abrupt refusal of what he undoubtedly considered a privilege granted to undeserving foreigners by the excessive generosity of the French Republic by turning on the corrosive peevishness at which French functionaries excel.

The clerk had no idea how much his suggestion that my child become a French citizen had thrown me. I loved living in France. Mike. The baby. The job. The town. I was besotted by life in Paris. Have you ever seen Gene Kelly dancing with Leslie Caron in the movie *An American in Paris*? What Caron and Kelly performed on a movie lot with a Paris backdrop, Mike and I lived in Paris. We danced along the Seine embankment below the flying buttresses of Notre Dame Cathedral to the music of moonlight. We danced to the crunch of gravel in the gardens of the Château de Chenonceaux in the Loire Valley. We celebrated Bastille Day by dancing on the cobblestones of the Quai Voltaire to the crackle of fireworks exploding over the Louvre. We were living a dream. Paris, the real Paris, was our backdrop with every stone, street and café put there, of course, just for us. I could have gone on dancing in Paris forever.

But settling in Paris was a different matter, and that was the prospect the Neuilly town clerk had raised. Having a French child implied a certain commitment that I knew I could not make. It wasn't that I had anything against France. On the contrary, I had come to love France even if not necessarily the French. What bothered me, what held me back was the idea of binding my family, my offspring to Europe once more. The European garden was lovely again. But I could never forget how easily and quickly it could become choked with dangerously noxious weeds.

Life in Europe was pleasant as long as I was camping out there much in the same way as I had stayed in the Rakouš household in Prague after the war. I could enjoy it because I knew it was not forever, because I was always aware that I would return to Canada, that Canada was home to me. And once we had a second daughter, Ann, I brought my family home in 1966. To nest.

It lasted four years. A job with the CBC in Toronto handling foreign news. A house and backyard. Happiness at home; restlessness on the job. Back to the *Star* as foreign editor. Stuffing kids into snowsuits. Back to the CBC as executive producer of *The National*. Kindergarten and the PTA. Up the ladder at the CBC to boss of TV News. The contentment of summer on the shores of Lake Muskoka. At work, meetings, meetings, meetings and hardly a sniff of news. No dancing for the deskbound.

In 1970, I jumped off the ladder I had been climbing back into the thicket of news. I went off to the Far East bureau of the CBC. And reporting foreign news is what I have been happily doing ever since.

Dancing, still dancing.

CHAPTER VI

When you start on the journey to Ithaca,
Pray that the road will be a long one,
Full of adventures, full of knowledge.

Konstantínos Pétrou Kaváfis

If you got a large enough map of El Salvador, a good wall-size map, you would have found Guarjila marked on it even though Guarjila no longer existed. Even when it was there, it wasn't much, a few ramshackle houses, hovels really, straddling a road that looked like a road only on the map and was, once you got on it, more like a course for cross-country motorbike rallies. But Guarjila did have a church and it had a school of sorts and it had people, several hundreds of them, and so it belonged on the map because a map of El Salvador without communities such as Guarjila would be mostly just large empty splotches.

Guarjila was a place largely disconnected from the twentieth century, a place without television or telephones, electricity or running water, tractors or doctors. When it finally did run into the modern world, the major manifestation of twentieth-century technology it encountered turned out to be

133

machines of death — planes and helicopters, machine guns and rockets.

Guarjila is north of San Salvador in the province of Chalatenango at the foot of the hills that crest along the Honduran border. Chalatenango is where the war between the army and the leftist rebels started in 1980 and it has been one of the main battlegrounds ever since. Shortly after Ronald Reagan became president of the U.S. in 1981, his crusade against communism came to the hills of Chalatenango in the form of marauding troops, helicopter gun ships and planes. Though no one ever said officially that the campaign was aimed at depopulating large parts of the province, that is what it did.

Mao Tse-tung used to preach that guerrillas could survive and prevail only if they lived among the people like fish swimming in the sea. Moving among the peasantry gave them a source of food and manpower and, most important, camouflage to shelter them from indiscriminate attacks by their enemies.

What the Salvadoran army tried to do was to siphon off the sea. The Americans had tried it before them in Vietnam with the "strategic hamlet" program. They moved several million people out of their villages into armed stockades, ostensibly to shield them from intimidation by Viet Cong guerrillas. The abandoned guerrilla-controlled areas were then declared free-fire zones, allowing U.S. and South Vietnamese forces to shoot at will at anything that moved in them.

The Salvadorans did not even bother with anything as ambitious and costly as resettlement in fortified hamlets for the people of Guarjila and many of their neighbors. They just bombed their villages to bits. "They killed you if you stayed," a peasant from Guarjila recounted years later, "and they killed you if you fled, because, as far as they were concerned, if you were caught running around the mountains you had to be a rebel." Hunted and terrorized, the villagers fled to Honduras and much of the Chalatenango countryside became a killing zone.

In Honduras, the people of Guarjila and thousands from other Salvadoran villages lived unhappily in deprivation in refugee camps. They couldn't make a living in the camps and they were not permitted to move out of them. They were guarded and harassed by the Honduran army and resented by the local population. People disappeared mysteriously, people starved, suffered, vegetated and pined for their homes.

Then, in 1987, they heard about the Central American peace plan, which, among other things, called for the repatriation and reintegration of refugees. They had also heard that El Salvador had become a democracy, that the country now had a freely elected president, José Napoléon Duarte, a Christian Democrat who had been, as they had, a victim of military persecution, and that this had led to the Salvadoran army no longer killing people by the thousands as it used to do in the early eighties.

Thousands of refugees decided it was time to go home and headed for the border. At first, the border guards would not let them in. But there was such a press of returnees at the border crossing — and so many journalists to witness the event — that the political embarrassment of not letting them in would have been more than the government could afford. So the Salvadoran authorities relented and let the villagers return.

When the people of Guarjila got back to what had been their village, all they found was a clearing on the road between San Antonio Los Ranchos and San José Las Flores with only a few stubby ruins of the walls of the church still standing. They planted their fields first and then set about rebuilding the community with whatever was at hand — sheets of tin, palm thatch, bits of wood, stone and plastic. While they waited for the crops to ripen, they were kept from starving mostly by supplies from foreign charitable organizations.

The new Guarjila was not much to look at — from the distance you might have mistaken it for a garbage dump — but it was alive.

At first, the villagers were encouraged by evidence that the Salvadoran military had indeed changed. It had been forced to change its ways under American pressure, under threat that the U.S. Congress would cut off aid if the Salvadoran armed forces and police continued committing what the North

Americans called human rights violations, that is to say if they continued to behave as they had always behaved. So the army, which was all but totally dependent on American money, had become more circumspect.

The people of Guarjila had not been home long, however, before the army came to remind them that though it may have changed its ways somewhat, it still looked on them with suspicion and regarded the village as a potential shelter or base for the guerrillas. Helicopters circled the village again every once in a while firing their machine guns. Only this time, they at least did not fire their bullets directly into Guarjila but instead sprayed the fields around it with machine–gun fire as a warning. For the villagers, it was a reminder of old horrors and it scared them. If they sympathized with the rebels — and many did — it was mainly because they hated the soldiers for what they had done to them years before. But the last thing they wanted was to become embroiled in the war again. They just wanted to be left alone.

But the army, along with its attempts to intimidate the villagers, also tried to woo them. One Sunday shortly after the people of Guarjila had returned home, an army convoy pulled into the village with an army band and trucks of food and clothing. As the band played, soldiers distributed the goods they had brought and an officer made a speech about friendship between the people and its army. The band even played dance music, and the soldiers asked the local girls to dance. But the girls wouldn't, and most of the soldiers had to dance with each other. The troops had more success with the village children, who flocked around soldiers handing out candy. The scenes of smiling soldiers surrounded by happy children looked impressive when Salvadoran television showed a report the next day prepared by the army camera crew that had accompanied the troops visiting Guarjila. The population of Guarjila, Salvadoran TV reported, appreciated the help of the army in resurrecting the village from the damage done to it by the communist rebel war.

When we got to Guarjila two days later, the village elders were livid. They felt that they had been used and that the army had taken advantage of the vulnerability of their hunger and of their children. Some of them, they said, had refused to take the food the soldiers offered even though they knew it was a useless gesture. They were afraid that the TV pictures showing the army's seeming generosity and commitment to helping civilians would now be used against them, and that any complaints they might now have against the soldiers, however legitimate, would be dismissed as ungrateful whining. They said that even while the officer in charge was making his friendly speech for the TV camera, other soldiers made no bones about it in private that this sociable visit was all for show and that the army would go after the *campesinos* (peasants) of Guarjila whenever it got the chance. Their only protection and guarantee against attack, the village elders said, was the attention of foreigners, the frequent comings and goings by volunteer workers from charitable organizations and the publicity generated by the occasional visiting journalist.

"Tell people in your country," said an old man who, judging from his reaction to us, had never heard of Canada, "tell them that we rely on them watching out for us. As long as the army knows the world is watching, it won't start butchering us again."

The old man could not have known how little attention Salvadoran colonels pay to righteous thundering from Ottawa.

Guarjila to international summits with a lot of territory in between. That is what I do. From talking to the old man in Guarjila as we squatted under the shade of a tree to interviewing Ronald Reagan in the East Room of the White House under the glare of TV lights and the anxious scrutiny of a gaggle of hovering presidential aides.

I can't remember a thing President Reagan told me the couple of times I interviewed him because, whatever it was, I had heard him say it before, in one form or another, at news conferences and in speeches. No matter what he was asked, he would regurgitate the familiar and the facile, or — he was very good at it — evade the question. On Canada, Reagan could always be relied upon to fall back on talking about the world's longest undefended border. Reagan was an exciting politician. But what he said, while always smooth, was eminently forgettable.

But I will not forget what the old man in Guarjila said, because he talked to me before a TV camera knowing that speaking up about the Salvadoran army's penchant for violence could cost his life. He talked to me not because he had any assurance that I or my story could help save his village, but because he had become convinced that to stay silent would be to condemn his children and grandchildren to the certainty of recurring violence.

That, in part, is why this book deals with my experiences reporting on such subjects as the survival struggles of Guarjila rather than with the power politics of Washington. As fascinating as it has been to cover North America and western Europe with their sophisticated societies, their sleekly prosperous economies and their contentious but generally benign and beneficial politics, the events that stay most in my memory are the tragedies and the triumphs over adversity that I have witnessed. And though there are tragedies and adversity in peaceable and prosperous societies, they are less frequent, less widespread, less endemic than those that I saw in places such as Czechoslovakia and El Salvador, Vietnam and Iran, Lebanon and China.

As troubling as it is to see people lose their livelihood in a land of plenty, it is much worse watching a whole country falling into the grip of penury. It may be painful when the annual rate of inflation gets to the double digits, but it is catastrophic when it hits three digits per month. It is outrageous for anyone to be unjustly jailed; it is monstrous for whole countries to be turned into jails. It is shocking to see one person murdered; it is devastating to watch a society dying.

Yet we have got used to it. It used to be that these tragedies didn't bother us because they were far away. All we knew of them, we learned from cold print. "1,000 die in India," the headline would say in print so small you barely saw it. Even when the headline was bigger and the story longer, the limitations of journalism in style and often of writing talent insulated us from the sting of reality. The pictures were static, in black and white, and their impact was further blunted by the fuzziness of newspaper reproduction.

Now we have the opposite problem. Television has brought so many searing images into our living rooms that we have become inured to misery because it has become too familiar. For all the sharp precision of the images, they are so ubiquitous that they turn to fuzz in our minds. Shock as schlock.

This is only partly the fault of television. It is mostly the result of our mindset, the way we look at the misery of distant masses of foreigners. Being there, rather than watching it on television, would not necessarily help. George Orwell caught the way most whites tended to see people from the Third World:

"When you see how people live, and still more how easily they die, it is always difficult to believe that you are walking among human beings. . . . The people have brown faces — besides, there are so many of them! Are they really the same flesh as yourself? Do they even have names? Or are they merely a kind of undifferentiated brown stuff, about as individual as bees or coral insects? They rise out of the earth, they sweat and starve for a few years, and then they sink back into the nameless mounds of the graveyard and nobody notices that they are gone."

Differentiating that "brown stuff," giving the brown faces names and the sweating, starving bodies voices, that is what the TV camera is good at. By zooming in, it can force the eye to look at what it might prefer to have left out of focus. The challenge to the reporter is to give the eye a compelling reason to stay focused on the screen, to give the situation meaning, context and relevance.

Television news is probably at its best covering big, important occasions, historic moments, being there when it happens, preferably live. *Aïda* rather than *La Bohème*. But I prefer the close-up lens to the wide shot, working on smaller stories that tell a larger point. Getting close to the problems of places such as Guarjila, trying to explain them, tracing them back to their causes and putting them into the context of their time and place is what I like doing best. Television is well suited to this cameo format. The problems of little people in small places can often illustrate larger problems — problems of war, of government misrule, of the pain of social change and economic dislocation — much more clearly than do the pronouncements of politicians and bureaucrats. Or statistics.

When the Salvadoran government or the U.S. embassy in San Salvador issued statistics to show that the human rights record of the Salvadoran army — i.e., the number of civilians the soldiers have killed in situations other than the heat of a battle — has improved considerably, it was wise to talk to the peasants of the villages such as Guarjila to find out how valid the figures were. They may not have known the whole truth, but they were almost certainly closer to the truth than the dispensers of statistics in San Salvador. Any reporter who ever attended the Five O'Clock Follies in Saigon during the Vietnam war at which American officers served up their infamous enemy body counts knows that much. In Saigon, they inflated the body counts to show how well the U.S. and South Vietnamese armies were doing. In San Salvador, they liked to keep the count of civilian dead low.

If the killing had indeed abated, the *campesinos* in the countryside would have sensed it long before the statisticians in the capital. Only they could tell you what it meant to their lives not to have to worry when they woke up about whose body would be found dumped in a ditch with bullets in it.

Trying to illustrate larger societal problems with anecdotes, or "people" stories, is an old journalistic technique. It is widely used by newspapers and magazines but it suits the smallness of the TV screen even better. Many see these vignettes as a journalistic vice because they tend to generalize from the particular. Vignettes can distort a situation, but they need not. They can never encompass the whole truth; nothing can. But when done properly and honestly, they can capture as much of the truth as most statistics, with infinitely more vividness.

Guarjila's problems may not have been representative of El Salvador as a whole. Even by Salvadoran standards, Guarjila was out of the mainstream, an isolated, impoverished and embattled place. The people of Guarjila were, to use a dismissive and yet devastatingly accurate Spanish term, *los marginales*, marginal people. Despite this, their experiences were valid as a metaphor for what ails Salvador. While Guarjila suffered more than most communities, its suffering would not have been unfamiliar to any impoverished community in Salvador.

Reporters are taught to stick to facts and leave the sermonizing to editorial writers and the thundering to columnists. But facts often carry messages more effectively than sermons. The plain facts of much of what has been happening in our world, when displayed on television, carry a tremendous emotional wallop and the essence of truth, from watching the man in Beijing who single-handedly confronted a column of tanks at the time of the Tiananmen Massacre going back nearly a quarter of a century to pictures of U.S. marines setting fire to a Vietnamese village with Zippo lighters.

These messages do not by themselves alter the course of history. But they have a cumulative effect that hurries history along. The images of protesting blacks being set upon by police dogs, of fire hoses being turned on demonstrators helped bring about civil rights reform in the U.S. The brutal images of the wars in Vietnam, Nicaragua and El Salvador helped teach Americans the truth about their involvement in those countries. Television pictures of Western prosperity and freedom that penetrated the Iron Curtain brought home to the people of eastern Europe the bankruptcy of their regimes. And as they started rebelling, the news and images of one nation rising up spread and encouraged its neighbors from Warsaw and Budapest to Berlin and Prague, from Sofia to Bucharest, and into the Soviet Union itself.

Few people become journalists to carry messages or preach. Most of us are in the business because we are curious. We want to be witnesses, sometimes perhaps even voyeurs. Above all, we are in journalism because we hate to be bored.

Journalism is exciting. More than forty years after I first walked into the Prague bureau of the AP, I am still excited by the prospect of the next assignment, the next story, still surprised sometimes that they even pay me to do what I do. I have done just about every job there is in journalism. I've worked on newspapers, for news agencies, on radio and television. I worked night shifts for years on end. I have been a reporter, rewrite man, wire-service slotman, newspaper editor, TV producer and editor. I've written editorials, magazine pieces and newspaper columns. For awhile I was even the part owner of a newspaper — a suburban weekly in Vancouver — and sold advertising space for it and sometimes even set type. Just about the only editorial job I have not done is to make the pictures, whether it be operating a TV camera or drawing cartoons. And after all these years, I can still say that for me my work has been an undying love affair.

There is the excitement of chasing a story and nailing it down, getting it first and getting it right, chipping away at mangled copy until it shines with clarity, making up a front page that tells it all as it should be told, honing the pictures and pruning the words until you get that special magic that television can bring to journalism. There is the delight of words, of fiddling with phrases, polishing paragraphs, refining ideas, of matching words with pictures, of searching for just the right word and the elation of finding it, the pleasure of trying to capture a mood or a milieu, a sound or a rhythm on paper and then lifting it off that paper to make it sing. It isn't great literature, it may not be profound, but good journalistic prose is clear, robust, entertaining and informative.

Ultimately, though, the joy of journalism has less to do with the finished product and how it is perceived by readers, watchers and listeners, or even editors, than it has with the pleasure of learning, of being constantly bombarded with information about every subject under the sun, of being able to wander through fields of ideas and forests of events, of always being confronted with something new and fresh, of being where things happen.

The curiosity of journalists, usually more roving than probing, may be the intellectual equivalent of joy-riding. But what a joy and what a ride. It gets in your blood. Somewhere out there is always another adventure, another exciting story to be found, an elephant to be ridden.

Norodom Chatangsey was a Khmer prince, an uncle of Prince Norodom Sihanouk, the pixyish one-time ruler of Cambodia. Chatangsey was a rich man. He reportedly made his fortune running a gambling casino. The prince was also a politician with a mission, a belief that large dollops of money could keep the Cambodian peasantry from going Communist. But when I met him in the spring of 1972, he was first and foremost a colonel in the army of Marshal Lon Nol, who had overthrown Sihanouk and was fighting the Communist Khmer Rouge with American help.

Colonel Chatangsey, the commander of the Cambodian army's 13th infantry brigade, was in the spring of 1972 one of the rare success stories of the Lon Nol regime. He and his troops had managed to wrest control of a large chunk of territory around Kompong Spey, south of the capital of Phnom Penh, by developing his own way of fighting the war. His principal weapon: pigs.

When his forces captured a village, he would call a village meeting and present each family with a pig, paid for, he said, out of his own pocket. His theory was that the pigs represented an investment that the peasants would not risk losing by siding with the Khmer Rouge, who were likely to confiscate it to feed their troops. Sometimes, it was said, he even paid for new wells and pumps. And he founded schools in villages where there had been none.

He also ran a propaganda war with posters in which the Khmer Rouge were portrayed as murderous foreigners from Vietnam. His most effective propagandists were his soldiers. Where most units of the Cambodian army had difficulty finding recruits, Chatangsey had none. He could pick and choose because he supplemented the official army pay of $14 a month with a supplement that he said also came out of his own pocket. And when he couldn't get enough weapons from Phnom Penh, he would buy weapons for his men on the black market in Vietnam.

The colonel was rich but he wasn't rich enough to change the course of the war. And the Lon Nol regime, which received billions of dollars from the Americans, had its own method of conducting the war, much of which consisted of lining the pockets of its leaders, possibly including the colonel's.

The Americans, too, had their own priorities and their own highly mechanized ways of fighting the war that were anathema to the colonel and many other officers in Cambodia and also in neighboring Vietnam. The colonel believed that the helicopter gun ship strikes that killed innocent civilians and sweeps by motorized patrols that damaged crops only antagonized the uncommitted peasantry. So he devised his own mobile force — mounted on elephants. And that is how I came to grief.

I arranged with the colonel to accompany one of his elephant patrols. An elephant may look clumsily massive but compared to a half-track armored personnel carrier, it is a delicate creature indeed. Where the half-tracks chewed up rice paddies, the elephants left relatively tiny footprints.

Each animal in the patrol of a dozen elephants carried two soldiers seated on a wooden platform. Watching how the soldiers squatted on these platforms cradling their rifles, it all looked pretty easy. But when I mounted one of the beasts — none too elegantly — I ran into a problem. While the elephants seemed to move with gyroscopic smoothness, the ride was actually more like sailing a choppy sea with nothing to brace yourself against. Paddies are divided from each other by small dikes. Sometimes, the elephant I was riding would step right across them. But every once in a while he would mount the dike and descend on the other side, sending me slithering across the platform to hold on by the edges.

Finally, it happened. The beast surprised me and I found myself falling off the animal, sliding down his forehead, vainly trying to hold on to something — its eyebrows, I think — past the trunk, down into the dry paddy. As I lay there, surprised, the breath knocked out of me, there was much yelling of commands and the whole herd came to a stop.

Except for my dignity, I was unhurt. I got up, dusted myself off and with the help of two solicitous NCOs clambered up onto the platform again. As the column started off across the paddies into the forest, I could see a score of Cambodian soldiers snickering about the clumsiness of round-eyes. On we went with me sitting cross-legged, arms crossed casually, muscles aching, cheeks aflame, riding by dint of rigid concentration with a semblance of dignity if not ease. Noblesse oblige.

From riding elephants to riding desks, there is something in journalism for every taste. Just as gabby lawyers are likely to end up in trial work and bookish ones may bury themselves in contract law, or bold doctors become surgeons while shy ones may prefer to keep the company of cadavers in the morgue, so do journalists usually drift where talent and inclination take them.

The garrulous ones are likely to end up as political reporters, buttering up their sources, cohabiting with their contacts for so long that ultimately you can't tell many of them apart from the pols they cover. The orderly ones, the ones who like some order in their personal lives, will retire to newsroom desks. The assertive ones may become investigative reporters or bosses; the studious ones, once they've had the addiction to constant adrenalin stimulation knocked out of them, get to be editorial writers. The restless ones — those who don't become itinerant journeymen wandering from newsroom to newsroom — are the ones likely to end up as foreign correspondents.

There are two kinds of foreign correspondents. There are the resident correspondents, those who for several years, sometimes even a lifetime, live in one foreign land and report all but exclusively on the affairs of that country or region. And then there are the really restless, the floaters who rush from crisis to crisis, drift from country to country, from war to war. They are called firemen.

I am a fireman. I have been one for twenty years. "Have laptop, will travel," is the firemen's motto. Firemen — be they men or women — must be adept at adapting and surviving. They need good legs and cast-iron stomachs more than they need good brains. Being ingenious and devious helps, though. They don't have to be polyglots — it would be impossible to learn the languages of all the countries they drop in on — but they must be able to get past the barriers of language to have an understanding of people who not only speak differently but who almost always also think differently. They are expected to get out an account of what happened fast. But they are not usually expected to think too much about the meaning of what they saw. Firemen are the cannon fodder of journalism.

Fireman work is to journalism what the 100-metre hurdles are to track sports. Only tougher. For one thing, the hurdles are not fixed; they just keep throwing new obstacles at your feet as you go along. And then, when you've done your distance, you are likely to find that they've moved the finish line right to the other side of the track and you've got no choice but to keep on running.

A crisis breaks out somewhere — revolution, earthquake, war, flood, you name it. The first problem is getting there. All planes are likely to be fully booked, or all flights cancelled or the local airport closed. So do you charter a plane, putting a big hole in the budget? If you do, will you be allowed to land? And when you do get there, will they let you in? Do you have a valid visa? If not, can you sweet-talk your way in? Good luck!

Tuesday, November 6, 1979. Washington. I am trying to put

together a story for the CBC on the takeover of the U.S. embassy in Teheran two days ago by radical students. American officials are worried but try not to look it. They point out that when the embassy was similarly overrun several months ago, the Iranian government quickly ended the affair.

Wednesday, November 7. I am in Boston covering Senator Ted Kennedy's announcement that he is running for the presidency. It's the beginning of a year-long election campaign.

Thursday, November 8. In Ottawa to cover a visit by President Jimmy Carter. Carter cancels at the last minute to concentrate on the Teheran hostage affair, now promoted to a full-blown crisis.

Friday, November 9. Back in Washington. I cover a demonstration by Iranian students in front of the White House. I leave straight from the White House for the airport to fly to London en route to Teheran.

Saturday, November 10. London. No Iranian visas but we have assurances from Sadegh Ghotbzadeh, the head of Iranian TV, that he will have visas waiting for Don Dixon, my producer, and me when we land in Teheran.

Sunday, November 11. Teheran. No visas for us at the airport. Immigration officials say we have to return to London. On the phone, Ghotbzadeh's office says hang on, someone is on the way to the airport to arrange visas. Canadian ambassador, Ken Taylor, says hang on, the embassy is working on it. Still no visas. The plane for London is about to leave. The immigration officers are insistent. They hustle us onto the plane and we take off.

Monday, November 12. Back in London. We get visas at the Iranian embassy. Back to Heathrow airport.

Tuesday, November 13. Teheran again. Good to get off a plane for awhile. Seven days, a different city, a different country every day. It's been a long week.

When you finally do manage to make it into the country of your editors' fancy, you may find there's no transportation available at the airport and the phones are not working. You can't walk to town carrying half a ton of TV equipment. Eventually, your producer manages to find a guy with a truck who, out of the kindness of his heart and a small consideration worth not more than his previous two months' pay, will consent to take you into town.

By the way, do you have a hotel reservation? You do? Good. Well, actually not really good enough, because, dollars to dineros, the desk clerk will tell you they never got your reservation. See, pal, I told you so! You have a telexed confirmation with a reservation number? Forget it! What do you think this is? Chateau Lake Louise in off-season? Try crossing the reception clerk's palm. And, while you're at it, you'd better make it greenbacks!

So you made it. Congratulations. Never mind that the electricity in the hotel is the wrong voltage (your crew will have brought transformers), that there are frequent power cuts in the city (find the hotel's emergency generator and run a line to it; it may take a little baksheesh but do it!), that the local TV signal transmission company has no record of a satellite feed order from Canada (by transmission time, after much screaming over the phone, they'll have found it), that their TV equipment is not compatible with yours (your crew will find a way of jury-rigging it), or that the phone system won't let your laptop talk to the mother computer back home (never mind, you were around before computers and managed).

Oh, one more small detail: You are supposed to have a story on the air tonight. You know, a little something on whatever it was that was supposed to have happened here today. And pictures, too.

(By the way, do you know anything about the country? Not much, you say? I guess that means next to nothing. Too bad. But that won't do as an excuse, you know. You'd better learn fast! And get it right! There are thousands of people from this place living in Canada, and if you get it wrong, you'll hear about it. Worse still, so will your bosses.)

Outside, you can see the sun will be down in an hour or so, and you're starting from scratch. Panic, panic. While you and the camera crew have gone off to look for information and pictures, the producer is busy collecting pictures that are already available: pool transmissions received in Canada earlier, dubs of material from local television, begging extra footage from friendly and allied crews (there are video recorders mating all over the place), or borrowing tapes in exchange for favors past and future. With luck, you may now have enough material for the barest semblance of a coherent story. The producer and the tape editor will already have screened the tapes and shot-listed them. You roll through the tapes, fast, fast, fast, and bash out a script. You go out and shoot the stand-upper, the summing up done by the reporter standing before the camera. The sun has already gone to bed, and they have a powerful light glaring right into your eyes.

I get to the end of what I have to say. I sign off, "Joe Schlesinger, CBC News," then stop. My mind has gone blank. I yell: "Anyone know where the hell we are?"

Somehow the report gets finished. The producer and the tape editor take the edited cassette to the feed point. They are late. Half of our fifteen-minute satellite window has already gone. There are other people lined up, cassettes in hand, waiting like pigs at a trough for their turn. Wait! Canada isn't seeing our signal. Damn! The money clock is ticking as we wait. Now they do see us. We roll the countdown to the report. Now the pictures are flicking past. Stop tape, they yell over the phone from the other end. They don't like the sound quality. We rewind to the start and adjust the sound output levels. Time is running out. We try again. Finally, it works. We are off the satellite with twenty seconds to spare.

We collapse. No, collapse is the wrong word. Deflate is more like it. We may feel like collapsing into bed. But we can't. We're still flying high. We need to come down slowly. Somebody remembers we haven't eaten since we got off the plane. We eat, we drink, we talk about plans for tomorrow. No, not tomorrow; it already is the next day. We'll need local press credentials; otherwise we'll never get through the military roadblocks or into government news conferences. The producer has an interpreter lined up for the morning. The interpreter's English apparently isn't all that good but she knows her way around. I shrug; it's a fair enough trade-off.

We will need an interview with someone in charge. And an expert who can explain it all. And for God's sake, let's make sure we get someone who speaks English!

I go to bed, taking a batch of background files on the country with me. I don't get past the first paragraph before I fall asleep.

In the morning, we start all over. Only more efficiently this time. Less panic. The pieces of the jigsaw puzzle start coming together. A human interest piece, reports on the background of the crisis, the political fall-out, the economic consequences. Within a few days, our operation will be humming along, and I may even have an idea of what I'm talking about. By then, of course, the story will be over. And we'll be packing up again.

For the past twenty years I have lived a split professional life. One part has been spent riding elephants and rickshaws, exploring life in Brazilian slums, dropping into besieged outposts in Vietnam, learning about the importance of nightsoil in Chinese farming, bumping along the back roads of Lebanon looking for PLO fighters or the hills of Nicaragua for contras. It has been a Walter Mitty kind of existence that has brought out the Boy Scout in me even as my hair grew grey and my paunch ever bigger.

In that life, the style is casual: jeans and sports shirts, chinos and safari jackets bulging with overstuffed pockets. In my other life, I wear a suit and tie and carry a briefcase and I go to news conferences, background briefings, protest demonstrations, conventions, election rallies and committee hearings. Or just watch them on video feeds or read background papers and transcripts of what was said. In this life, I cover the people who make the decisions that make or unmake the upheavals I report on in my other, tieless life. This more sedentary existence also has its rewards and sometimes even the thrill of watching history being made.

I was in Geneva when Ronald Reagan first met Mikhail Gorbachev and watched in Washington and Moscow as the

Great Cold Warrior warmed up to the leader of the "evil empire." I interviewed the Ayatollah Khomeini when to most of the world he was only an obscure cleric calling for the overthrow of the Shah of Iran. Later, surrounded by a million frenzied Iranians, I rode in his cortège when the Ayatollah returned to Teheran from exile to take power. I followed Richard Nixon across the Middle East and the Soviet Union in his final weeks in power when he acted as though by just keeping on moving he could stave off his downfall. I stood in the Indian parliament in New Delhi as Indira Gandhi was garlanded in triumph after her country's victory over Pakistan in the war that gave birth to Bangladesh. I have followed Pope John Paul II through five countries and dozens of pontifical masses. I had Reagan fall asleep on me as I sat next to him on a campaign bus. I have watched Pierre Trudeau strutting his stuff; Gerald Ford tumbling down steps; Leonid Brezhnev mumbling; Charles de Gaulle, Valéry Giscard d'Estaing and François Mitterand, chins up and lips pursed, being as arrogantly imperious as Louis XIV; Jimmy Carter smiling vacuously as his presidency was sinking; Anwar Sadat and Menachem Begin being acclaimed at the height of their power; Helmut Schmidt sternly lecturing and Helmut Kohl amiably nodding; Mao Tse-tung waving weakly and Chou En-lai manoeuvring deftly; Brian Mulroney playing the Cheshire cat; Deng Xiaoping being pixyish, Mikhail Gorbachev devastatingly charming and Margaret Thatcher just devastating.

After all this name-dropping, I should add that I don't know any of these people. Mostly I only see them at news conferences or so-called photo ops. Or at a distance at some ceremony. Sometimes I may get to shake their hand and exchange a few mumbled words at a reception. Even when you interview them, it is more a ritual dance than a conversation. You are not likely to get behind the political mask. As a Viennese satirist once noted, "Politics is what one does to hide what one is."

Besides, firemen rarely stay around long enough to get to know anyone really well. Their critics would add that they also move so fast they never get to know any thing well.

Certainly my knowledge of many countries is no match for that of the resident correspondents who have spent several years there. But sometimes I have the advantage. Having travelled widely and long, I am likely to be better equipped to compare one country or one situation with another.

When I first went to El Salvador in early 1982, I knew little about the country or the war. The guerrillas, the government and the resident correspondents were all talking about the fighting having reached a decisive stage; the rebels even announced they were launching the final offensive that would take them to victory. Having seen similar fighting in Indochina, I saw quickly that the war was still in its infancy. Furthermore, given the prevailing level of political and material support for it in Washington, it was inevitable that the fighting would escalate and last for quite some time.

Neither side had hit its stride yet. The headquarters of the army high command was so lightly defended — a few lounging guards and a couple of strands of barbed wire on top of the wall — that my first reaction when I saw it was how lucky the Salvadoran commanders were that they did not have the Viet Cong to contend with; an experienced Viet Cong sapper squad could have taken the place apart in ten minutes.

The Salvadoran army didn't even have sandbags in the early stages of the war. Soldiers on guard duty protected themselves by building breastworks of stone. If hit, the rocks would send stone chips as well as bullet fragments ricocheting in every direction instead of absorbing the shots as a sandbag would. If anything heavier hit the stonework, it was likely to produce a storm of flying rocks.

By the late eighties, of course, the Salvadoran army did have sandbags and a lot more. Army HQ by then was surrounded by all the military gadgetry that American money could buy: peeping TV cameras, armored guardposts, and an entrance equipped with electronically controlled barriers that rose out of the ground at the touch of a button. And the war was still not over.

As a lifestyle, the wandering correspondent's job can be

both wonderful and terrible at the same time. Wonderful because one gets to see many exciting and interesting places.
Terrible because the travelling and long work days take their
physical toll and, worse, place a heavy load on the correspondent's family life.

When I worked in the Far East in the early seventies, I was
the sole CBC news correspondent covering a territory that ex-
tended from Japan south and west across the rim of Asia —
China, Indochina, the Indian subcontinent and the smaller
countries in between and beyond — to the Khyber Pass on
the Afghan-Pakistani border. When I was posted in Paris in
the late seventies, my territory stretched from the Khyber
Pass across the Middle East through southern and western
Europe to the English Channel. For all but the last couple of
years of the eighties, I was the sole CBC TV News correspondent assigned to cover everything in the Western hemisphere from the Canadian border to the South Pole.

Both Hong Kong and Paris are wonderful places to live.
But for me, they were only rest stops; I spent most of my
time elsewhere. There is little news in Hong Kong except
for the imminence of what may be its demise, and even that
was hardly news enough yet when I lived there to keep me
in town. As for Paris, the Parisians may think the city is
the centre of the universe — and as far as some of its more
pleasurable aspects are concerned, I would even agree with
them — but as a world news centre, it is second-rate and still
fading.

When I was assigned to Washington at the start of the
eighties, my work pattern changed. Washington generated
so much news that it was often difficult to get out of town to
cover news elsewhere. The days without a worthwhile Washington story were few and far between. The city's impact
was felt just about everywhere in the world, and almost anything important that happened around the world was likely
to have reverberations in Washington. As fascinating as it
is, though, Washington is in many ways an artificial city, a
place preoccupied with power, politics and gossip. From time
to time, it becomes necessary to travel back to the real world.

To Guarjila and beyond.

As the years go by, the summits and conventions, the crises and elections, the scandals and investigations, the negotiations and confrontations fade from memory. The summits with all their hoopla blend into each other as one giant glittering photo op with a revolving cast of characters.

The politics, the policies and the process that are so engrossing while they are being played out become fuzzy memories. After all, what counts about politics and policies is not the process but their effects on the lives of people. It's not the date of the battle, the names of the generals or even the spellbinding tales of derring-do that are the most important; it's why the war took place in the first place and what its outcome led to.

In political battles as in war, it is the battle and its immediate outcome that preoccupies its participants. Once the battle is over, once a policy has been set or a law promulgated, the policy makers go on to something else. The policy lives on, sometimes successfully, sometimes not. More often than not it will have unintended consequences. (When the framers of the U.S. Constitution proclaimed the right of Americans to bear arms in defence of their liberties, they surely could not have imagined that Americans would come to use this right to shoot each other in ever greater numbers.) Sometimes the original intent of a law is subverted by the bureaucrats who administer it. (Did McCarran and Walter have amiable and innocuous iconoclasts like Farley Mowat in mind when they drew up their bill to keep dangerous foreigners out of the U.S.?)

Once a policy is in effect, though, it is not likely to gain the attention of the decision makers again unless it goes seriously wrong and starts hurting politically. In well-run societies, the politicians and bureaucrats will tinker with it and adjust it before any irreparable harm is done. If not, it will fester until it bursts.

I usually come in where the process has run amok. We have enough problems keeping up with the details of our domestic political processes without being all that interested in the minutiae of the everyday politics of foreigners. (It can be dangerous to reporters' careers if they become too involved in the affairs of the countries they cover; they may be seen at home as having gone native.) By the time reporters are dispatched to the scene, the situation is likely to have reached malignancy. Foreign correspondents, particularly the firemen among them, are not so much pulse-takers as pathologists. By the time we arrive, the symptoms are all too evident: demonstrations, riots, war, fallen governments, or hyper-inflation. But to get to the cause of the disease you need to get away from the hullabaloo of events to some quiet corner where the hurt is.

In Iran, when the Shah's regime was falling in 1978, I tore myself away for a day from the daily demonstrations, the shootings and the propaganda war in Teheran to Mahmoudabad, thirty-five kilometres away. Mahmoudabad, I had heard, was a place that had benefited from the Shah's rule. Its landless peasants had got land under the Shah's White Revolution land reform program. Yet despite this, Mahmoudabad too had turned against the Shah.

I learned why, sitting on a carpet with some of the farmers around a *korssi*, a low round table that has a coal brazier underneath it. In rural Iran, people eat and sleep in the winter around quilt-covered *korssis* with their feet tucked under the table to keep them warm. As the men talked, the women of the household, their faces veiled, served us tea silently. I sat there with my feet toasting under the table, being careful not to get them too close to the coals, and listened. I would have liked to know what the women thought but I knew better than to ask. If you as much as looked in their direction, they would scuttle away.

At first, the farmers said, they were happy to have their own wheat fields and apple orchards, however small they were. But then the Shah ran into a problem in the cities. The city dwellers were unhappy about the price of bread. So the Shah started importing cheaper foreign wheat. The farmers found they could no longer compete, that they had to get jobs in factories to be able to feed their families.

They said they were worse off than they had been before the White Revolution. At least then they could make a living in the fields working for a landowner. Now they had to travel hours to work in awful factories and often didn't get to see their families for days. Many of the young men had simply given up and moved to Teheran. The Shah, to whom they had once been grateful for giving them land, had chased many of them off their land. And they hated him for it.

Now they were hoping that Ayatollah Khomeini and the rule of the Koran would make it possible for them to quit their factory jobs, for their sons to come back from the city and for them all to return to their fields and orchards.

In Teheran, there was talk of revolution and holy war and ranting about infidel foreigners, satanic Americans and the indecency of the Empress Farah Diba's décolletage. In Mahmoudabad and the many places like it that make up most of the country, they seemed concerned about more mundane matters. In Mahmoudabad, it was the price of wheat and being able to keep worms out of their apples. That's where it usually starts — with a worm in an apple.

There is another factor at work in journalism — forgetting. The cycle from story to story, from crisis to crisis has accelerated, and news has become ever more perishable. Today's story obliterates yesterday's.

"The bloody massacre in Bangladesh quickly covered the memory of the Russian invasion of Czechoslovakia," the Czech writer Milan Kundera wrote in *The Book of Laughter and Forgetting*. "The assassination of Allende drowned out the groans of Bangladesh; the war in the Sinai desert made people forget Allende; the Cambodian massacre made people forget the Sinai; and so on and so forth, until ultimately everyone lets everything be forgotten."

Remembering and reminding — that, too, is what journalism is about.

CHAPTER VII

They made a wasteland and called it peace.

Tacitus

If you woke me up in the middle of the night and said "Vietnam," I'd probably respond with "Huey." The Huey helicopter, the workhorse of the Vietnam war, was surely one of its most pervasive images. Even people who never were in Vietnam, who saw the war only on TV news and in films, have had the images etched into their brains. Swarms of Hueys clattering into jungle clearings to disgorge GIs. Huey gunners spraying paddies with machine-gun fire. Or setting the countryside ablaze with napalm. Cobras, the gun-ship version of the Huey, firing rockets into a hamlet of hutches. And then there is the searing image of that last chopper of the war plucking people off the roof of the U.S. embassy in Saigon.

For those who were there, the Huey loomed even larger. For the Vietnamese fighting the Americans, it was the ubiquitous bird of death and destruction and they lived for years with their ears attuned for the first faint sounds of its ominous clatter. For the Americans and their fellow travellers — and those of us who covered the war travelled with the

157

Americans and depended on them however much we may
have disapproved of their war — the Huey was much more
than just a means of transport or even a weapon of war; it
was often a life-saving *deus ex machina*. I still remember
standing in a clearing in the middle of nowhere, Lord knows
where, trying to get out because it was about to get dark and
dangerous, and signalling a passing Huey with my thumb to
hitch a ride and then watching in amazement as it actually
came down and picked up my cameraman and me.

But my most vivid memory of a helicopter ride, the one
that occasionally still flashes through my dreams, is of being
lifted out of An Loc. I am on my belly, having just flopped
myself aboard as the Huey came down for a brief lull in the
shelling and then rose again abruptly like a bird frightened by
gunshots. I look around the compartment. My cameraman,
Brian Hosking, is there beside me. But I can't see Gerard
Hébert. I look down and there he is still standing on the
landing pad as three mortar shells explode nearby. I watch
as he gets smaller and smaller and then both he and An Loc
disappear.

For the moment, I am too relieved to be out of the besieged
town and jubilant about having come out of it with an exclusive story to worry much about Gerard not having made it. I
tell myself, no harm done, he'll get out on the next chopper.
To celebrate my escape, I pour the last of the drinking water
I had been hoarding in my field flask over my head. I lick my
lips and the dripping water mixed with sweat and dust tastes
better than any champagne toast ever did.

When Brian and I got back to Saigon, I was busy with our
scoop. An Loc, where Communist troops had 5,000 South
Vietnamese soldiers bottled up, was hot news. Our pictures
of the besieged town were shown just about everywhere
around the world.

I was elated. But I was also beginning to be concerned about
Gerard. He had not made it back to Saigon. There was no
news from him or of him. Not from the South Vietnamese,
not from the Americans. There had been no more choppers
out of An Loc the day Brian and I got out. And none the next.
Too much shelling. Only a radio report from the garrison that

North Vietnamese tanks had broken into the town. They had overrun half of An Loc before air strikes and the anti-tank weapons of the South Vietnamese managed to destroy several of the tanks and forced the others to retreat.

Now I was really worried about Gerard. I felt responsible for him — not only because he was my friend, nor even just because I felt that I had got him into this mess since it was I who had come up with the wild idea of trying to get into An Loc. I realized that I felt protective about him because I thought he needed me, which on the surface was ridiculous because Gerard was what the French call a *débrouillard*, someone who is extremely resourceful and able to look after himself. I knew he had done things I had never done, been in situations I had never experienced. But long before we went to An Loc, I regarded him as vulnerable and in need of protection.

Yet at the same time, I also depended on him. We had, in a way, complementary talents. The closest I can come to explaining our symbiosis is to say that if we had been lost in a forest, Gerard would have known which berries and roots to eat to survive and I would have had the compass in my pocket to help us find our way out of there.

I admired Gerard, but I also patronized him. I was condescending when it came to his professional skills. Gerard was a news photographer who did not seem to know all that much about photography and certainly didn't have much of a clue about journalism. Much of the time in covering the war he did not know what he was looking for. But he knew the basics of photography, and his employers at UPI liked him because as a freelance he came cheap, a bunch of film and $15 for every photo they used, barely enough for a few bowls of *pho*, an anise-flavored beef and noodle soup, and a modest room over a store on Tu Do Street.

Moreover, Gerard didn't mind taking assignments no one else wanted, the ones that took time and showed very little promise of reward. They were covered because the Saigon bureau felt it had to protect itself in case headquarters in New York asked why they had no pictures of that two-bit firefight that AP had had on all the front pages of the United States that day, to say nothing of ancillary play in the boondocks of Europe, Canada, and South America. It's not as if UPI didn't have its hotshot photographers. But they wouldn't waste their best talent, people who were paid salaries, even if they were only UPI salaries, on stories with only dog-bites-man potential. Worse yet, if they did send one of their staffers on such an assignment, it might lead him to conclude that if UPI couldn't find better ways of using him, he might as well go and work for someone who paid real money.

So amateur paparazzi like Hébert had their uses. There were plenty of them in Vietnam: greenhorns burning to make their reputation; ex-GIs who stayed or returned once their tour of duty was up because they could not face what awaited them at home; men who had a woman, women, cheap sex and/or drugs they would not or could not leave; people who liked the life in Vietnam despite the war; and those who liked Vietnam precisely because it did have a war.

For most journalists in Vietnam, as in other wars, danger was the price of covering the war. "If one writes about war," Graham Greene wrote in *The Quiet American* about an earlier stage of the Vietnam conflict, "self-respect demands that occasionally one shares the risks." But there were quite a few in the Saigon press corps for whom journalism was only the price, or at least only the means, and danger the reward they were looking for. Few of them were reporters; most had chosen the camera as their weapon. The camera was an all but unlimited licence to go where the action was.

The role model of the war lovers was Sean Flynn, who played out in real life the swashbuckling roles his father, Errol Flynn, used to perform in the safety of Hollywood studios. Sean became a legend. He did not just take pictures of the war; he also fought in it. At one time he is supposed to have led a successful charge against a fortified North Vietnamese position. He would go on his "hunts" in tailor-made combat fatigues with hand grenades clipped to his belt. At other times, he would go off to war in shorts, plastic flip-flop sandals and love beads. What he was after, he once told his editors, was "*la seule grande aventure: celle de la guerre et de la mort.*" Flynn finally managed to catch up with the final adventure of death in the spring of 1970 in the Parrot's Beak, a piece of jutting Cambodian territory aimed at Saigon like a dagger from which the Viet Cong used to launch attacks across the border. He was last seen — by Bill Cunningham, my predecessor as CBC Far East correspondent — at a Cambodian roadblock. Flynn was berating his travelling companion, Dana Stone, a cameraman, for wanting to turn back because going ahead seemed too dangerous. "Of course it's dangerous," Flynn said, "but that's what makes it a good story." They both gunned their motorcycles and roared off towards Viet Cong territory, never to be seen again.

For all the good pictures the flamboyant sensation seekers did manage to get out of places where no one else went, they were not an assignment editor's delight. Given their motives and predilections, they were not prone to take orders and were, in their editors' eyes, often not reliable. Gerard was and that was why the photo editors at UPI liked him. He may not have had a great eye or editorial judgment, but he was available, reliable, and his bright smile and ingratiating, self-deprecating ways often got him into places where others could not.

The Vietnamese military, particularly those of the Airborne Division, also liked Gerard because he did not behave like the other *mũi lõ*, long noses, the Vietnamese term for whites. He was prepared to live as the Vietnamese did and stay out in the field as long as they did, eat their food and even drink the same brackish water they drank, a strict taboo with most of the rest of us. Gerard was not like the other foreign *bao chi* (Vietnamese for press), including me, who would come in expecting action right away, pronto, and were likely to leave before nightfall, because they either got it and had to get to Saigon to file it, or because they didn't and wouldn't want to waste any more of their time waiting for something to happen that might not happen.

Soldiers in dangerous places are usually friendly to reporters and camera people who drop in on them. After all, few other people would visit a position under fire of their own free will. So when journalists do come and share the danger when it seems to the soldiers that they don't have to, that no one would court-martial or shoot them if they refused to stick their necks out, they are welcome. But underneath the friendliness there frequently lurked resentment. The troops knew that by the next day or sometime soon, we would be back in Saigon, drinking whisky and eating good food instead of field-ration slop, sleeping in a dry comfortable bed, probably with some woman, possibly their woman or their sister.

Gerard, though, managed to escape the brunt of this envy because of his simple and solitary ways. Most other journalists were conspicuously privileged. They always had cigarettes and sometimes carried their own food, water or beer. The TV correspondents came with a crew to boss around. The print reporters were accompanied by interpreters. Quite frequently, there was also an escort officer to guide them. And always — well, almost always — the journalists had some means of getting out again. Even if they shared what they had with the soldiers, it set them apart.

Gerard, by contrast, usually travelled alone, carrying nothing much more than his camera and film. He cadged lifts, he cadged food, he cadged cigarettes. That made him dependent on the soldiers and their willingness to share what little they had. It made him different; it made him known; it made him accepted; it made him, in his vulnerability, almost one of them.

I think the Vietnamese also sensed that Gerard was a rarity: a foreigner who was in Vietnam simply because he wanted to be there. All the foreigners they had ever known came to Vietnam because they wanted something. They either wanted to conquer it, or to save it from paganism, communism, dictatorship or from the Vietnamese themselves. Everyone wanted to profit in some way. The latest crop of foreigners had come to seek glory or advance their careers so they could become generals or sergeants, or win the Pulitzer Prize. All the GI Joes wanted was to get out but all too often they took it out on the Vietnamese for being stuck in the country. Gerard, however, expected nothing from the Vietnamese and accepted them as they were.

Gerard was also popular with South Vietnamese officers because he was Canadian, rather than an American as most foreign press types were, and because he spoke French. That was important to some of the older officers — the generals and the colonels — who had been trained in the French colonial army. They no longer got much of a chance to speak French. They missed speaking it because while French may not afford the nuances of rank and respect that Vietnamese does, it does it much better than English.

What also pleased a lot of South Vietnamese officers about speaking French to foreign journalists was being able to speak to "long noses" in a language other than English. English, for many of them, was the bane of their lives. They had to learn English to talk to their American advisers. If they did not, they were put into the humiliating position of having to rely on the interpreting skills of subalterns to conduct one of the most crucial relationships of their command. What riled South Vietnamese officers particularly, even those who spoke English proficiently, was having to defer to their American advisers and to their insistence that things be done the American way. There were Vietnamese officers who had enough political pull in Saigon to defy their advisers. Complaints by American advisers about being stymied and frustrated by Vietnamese political machinations and corruption were legion and legendary.

The most profitable corruption was the prerogative of officers who had a fiefdom — garrison commanders and, above all, the province chiefs, military men who had almost unlimited power over the civilian government of their area. Combat unit officers, whose outfits were moved from hot spot to hot spot and were never in any area long enough to develop the political clout to extract tribute from the population, were more dependent on the advisers than the better connected local garrison commanders.

The American advisers were always, as a matter of protocol, one rank junior to the Vietnamese officers they advised. South Vietnam was split into four military regions, each headed by a three-star general who had a two-star American adviser. And so it went down the line to the division, brigade, battalion and often even company level.

The advisers had crucial powers. They could bring in critical American air, artillery or logistical support, or have a large say in withholding it. Many South Vietnamese officers resented this hold the Americans had on them. None more so than the older officers, who did not have the understanding and camaraderie with their advisers that the junior officers had. The more ambitious captains and majors were more likely to have been trained by the Americans and to be able to speak colloquial English.

Resentment of the Americans spilled over to the American media. American brashness and the habit of American correspondents and camera crews to try to extend to Vietnam their concept of access and the freedom of the press as guaranteed under the First Amendment of the U.S. Constitution did not sit well with the Vietnamese. Add to that the not inconsiderable threat, implied or explicit, that lack of co-operation would result in unfavorable publicity that might rile Washington and set in motion the retributory machinery of U.S. headquarters in Saigon.

It's no wonder then that many South Vietnamese officers and officials looked on what the Americans called "third country nationals," i.e., people who were neither American nor Vietnamese, more kindly. They could reject us with impunity; they could talk to us without fear of the consequences. And that gave us — the Canadians, British, French, Swedes, and others — a special entrée. And to no one more so than to Gerard because he was conspicuously a loner without any powerful sponsors in Saigon. Gerard always came in with a cheery "Bonjour, mon colonel" or, even better, addressed the colonel by his Vietnamese rank, *daita*, called him *vous* and allowed himself to be addressed as *tu*. That was an expression of inferiority of rank but also one of friendship and patronage. More than anything, I suspect, ARVN officers liked Gerard because he gave them the respect few other Europeans, certainly not many Americans or Frenchmen, had ever showed them. The result was that Gerard usually ended up getting help that other foreign reporters and photographers did not.

It was hard to tell how old Gerard was. He had a lean, hard, smooth-skinned body but his face had the slightly sunken cheeks that sometimes come when age does not run to swelling flab. He was small — five foot eight at most — and had dark luminous eyes, smooth black hair and the rolling walk of a sailor. He had come to Vietnam from Montreal where he had worked for the French network of the CBC. His wife had died, he said, while his two sons were still children. He raised them, and when they finally went off on their own, he said, he quit Radio-Canada and took off. Vietnam seemed to him as good a place as any to shed the responsibilities he had carried.

By adopting the airborne division — or having the paras adopt him — Gerard had chosen well. The paratroopers were one of the elite units of ARVN, the acronym the Americans used when they spoke politely about the Army of the Republic of Vietnam. As such they — and other elite units such as the rangers and the marines — were constantly being moved around to trouble spots, a battalion perhaps along the Cambodian border and another on a sweep in the Central Highlands.

Considering that the ARVN was propped up by American power for so long and that it collapsed ignominiously once that support was withdrawn, "elite units of the South Vietnamese army" sounds like an oxymoron. Despite what happened and the contempt the Americans had for the ARVN, there were South Vietnamese soldiers and units that fought well, bravely and to the end. Given the nature of the Saigon regime, its corruption, its lack of political direction, it was a wonder that they did. Considering that as individuals they didn't just fight for a one-year hitch or two at the most as the Americans did; that many of them had been fighting for as long as a decade; that, when wounded, they didn't have the medical care, the prostheses, the pensions that the Americans had; that they didn't have the huge U.S. logistical "tail" — for every American in combat there were nine others in the rear, many of whom had an easy and sometimes even pleasant and profitable war; that the Vietnamese had fought the war not for six years as the Americans had by the time I arrived in Saigon in 1971 but for more than fifteen, it is no wonder that the South Vietnamese were tired of the war. The Americans certainly were. Many of them were doped up and some were murdering each other. So many disgruntled enlisted men took to killing unpopular officers that a new word was invented to describe it — fragging, from the fragmentation grenades that were the easiest way of doing the job.

By the time I got to Vietnam, the American presence had been drastically reduced and the war was being "Vietnamized" to appease opposition to it in the U.S. There were now fewer than 100,000 American troops in Vietnam, down from a peak of 550,000. And more were leaving every day. Only air crews were still heavily engaged in the fighting. The few remaining American ground combat units were mostly confined to defending U.S. air and naval bases.

The story now was how well the South Vietnamese would do as they took up more of the burden of fighting the war. When the war used to be all but completely an American war, journalists could rely on the Americans for the air transport and other services they so generously dispensed. In fact, without U.S. military help — grudgingly given as it often was — the war almost certainly could not have been as thoroughly covered as it was.

The giant American complex of military transport flights, of choppers that would get you there and get you out, of officers' clubs where, as an accredited journalist — as a courtesy, all journalists were given the simulated rank of major in the U.S. Army — you could get a cheap steak dinner and a free bed, was being wound down now that the war was being "Vietnamized." Good contacts in the ARVN had become essential. Gerard had the contacts and I had a couple of things he needed: a vehicle to get him to where he could tap the contacts and the editorial savvy to know a story when we ran into one. So we teamed up several times in the fall of 1971 for ARVN sweeps near the Cambodian border.

Once we went on an operation across the border into Cambodia. When we landed with the first wave of choppers, Brian Hosking and I stayed around to film the next wave landing, then followed the troops into the trees for a while. When nothing untoward happened, we got on a chopper that had brought in the third and last wave and got out. We had nice pictures, no action except for three bullet holes in one of the choppers and a ho-hum story about the ARVN gingerly returning to an area where they had been clobbered a few months earlier, resulting in one of their three-star generals losing two of his stars.

Gerard, in the meantime, had walked into the jungle with the 200-man force, hoping they'd run into something that would make it a story. We couldn't stay because a film camera and sound gear are a lot heavier than a 35-mm still camera to haul around on a lengthy trek and there is no place in the jungle to recharge the batteries that TV cameras use. Besides, our bosses would have taken a dim view had we stayed in Cambodia for several days and come back, as Gerard did, with nothing more to show for it than a bullet nick in the leg. But the Cambodian hike helped Gerard in strengthening his links with the paras.

There were many Gerard Héberts in the Saigon press corps by then. The ambitious and well-connected reporters and photographers who had flocked to Vietnam during the war's heyday in the late sixties, when it was big news, had mostly gone. There was little interest, no glory and no money in the war. There was nothing but a lull, a lot of talk and speculation. Everyone was saying the communists were just waiting for the Americans to go away before they made their next big strike. And, of course, if and when they did, the world — and certainly the U.S. — would not care very much any longer because the Americans were no longer directly involved in the ground fighting. Vietnamese killing Vietnamese certainly would not have any great impact as a news story or as a burning global political problem.

I was in Cambodia when, much to Washington's and Saigon's surprise, the communists struck at South Vietnam on March 30, 1972, with a force of 120,000 North Vietnamese regulars supported by tens of thousands of Viet Cong guerrillas. They came in from the east in Cambodia and Laos and from North Vietnam through the demilitarized zone, the famous DMZ. They had Soviet heavy artillery, rockets and tanks. This was no longer the guerrilla war of old; this was a conventional offensive on a big scale. Washington remained serene. General William Westmoreland, the army chief of staff and former commander of U.S. forces in Vietnam, predicted the offensive would falter in a few days because "the staying power of the enemy is not great."

When I got back to Saigon, the city was stunned. The communists had captured Loc Ninh, a town a little more than 100 kilometres north of the capital, then advanced a few more kilometres down Highway 13 and surrounded An Loc, a rubber plantation town.

Hébert was distraught. His friend and room-mate, Michel Dumond, also a photographer, was missing at Loc Ninh. There had been a radio message from the American advisers there before their bunker was overrun. They reported that the ARVN garrison had fled and that "Frenchie is here with us." Then the radio went dead.

(Dumond, it turned out, was taken prisoner and marched to a North Vietnamese base along the Ho Chi Minh Trail in Cambodia. He was held much of the time in a bamboo cage that was so small he could only crouch in it. When he was let out, he was at first unable to straighten out and crawled around on all fours like a dog, to the great amusement of his guards. Luckily, Michel had a powerful uncle, General Jacques Massu, the French paratrooper who was a hero of both the losing French wars in Vietnam and Algeria. With Massu's influence, Dumond was released on July 14 as a Bastille Day gesture of goodwill towards France.)

I was all over South Vietnam those first few days of the communist invasion: up along the Dong Ha River in the north where the South Vietnamese were trying vainly to hold the south bank to keep the city of Quang Tri from falling, in the beleaguered town of Kontum and besieged fire bases in the central highlands and on Highway 13, the road to An Loc.

Everyone was on the road to An Loc. Or, to describe the situation in the pidgin of Vietnamese-American communication, beaucoup ARVN (pronounced as a word rather than initials), beaucoup VC, beaucoup NVA, beaucoup bao chi, beaucoup merde incoming and outgoing. Translated that means lots of South Vietnamese troops, Viet Cong guerrillas, troops of the North Vietnamese army, correspondents and cameramen. La merde was ordnance of many calibres from various weapons-delivery systems. There were ARVN 105-mm howitzers, Viet Cong sniper fire, NVA 60-mm mortar shells, bombs from American B52s, rockets from SouthVietnamese F-5 fighter-bombers and fire from the guns of Cobra gun ships. At night, Spookies, planes equipped with rapid-fire Gatling guns, would spray the countryside just to make sure the communists kept their heads down.

In addition, there were Vietnamese vendors on the road selling noodle soup, beer and pop. The peddlers showed up quickly wherever a battle that stayed still for awhile was going on. They were a good-luck omen. As long as they were around, as long as you did not go far beyond the last cold-pop cart, you were relatively safe. You could take it as a given that their analysis of the military situation was sound. When they started pulling out, that's when you had to start worrying.

One day, another kind of peddler showed up, an American two-star general with a sales pitch. He stood on top of a pile of dirt by the side of the road like a baseball pitcher on the mound. Not a bad position for what he was doing. It forced the TV cameramen around him to point their cameras up at him, making him look more commanding. The line he was pitching for the evening news programs in the U.S. that day was that the communist offensive had been blunted and that South Vietnamese forces were about to break the siege of An Loc.

Life on the road to An Loc was interesting enough. But once you had seen it, once you had reported on it, it was the same day after dreary day. For reporters, it was taking chances of getting hit with nothing much to show for it. The place to be, quite obviously, was not on the road to An Loc but inside the town. Especially if you believed, or even half-believed, the American general's message.

The only way into An Loc was by helicopter. I had seen a few Hueys and Chinooks clattering their way towards the town, presumably going in with supplies and reinforcements and returning with the wounded. The trouble was finding someone

willing to give us a ride. It was clear that neither the South
Vietnamese command nor the Americans wanted reporters
inside An Loc. That meant finding someone who didn't know
or didn't care too much about what Saigon wanted. When I
broached the idea to Gerard, he was eager to go because the
Fifth Division, which had been in Loc Ninh, had retreated
to An Loc and he thought he could find out more from them
about the fate of his friend Dumond. So once again Gerard,
Brian and I went hunting for a sympathetic South Vietnamese officer. We found him a few miles back on the road at an
army base at Lai Khe. The colonel, a paratrooper, was amused.
Yes, he said, he was just about to send a chopper with six of his
men into An Loc. If we were crazy enough to go, he'd give us a
lift. But he warned us that all he had were one-way tickets.

Off we went, nine of us crowded into the back of a Huey
along with some equipment and munitions boxes. Hueys in
Vietnam almost always flew with the doors of the back compartment open to allow the two gunners with seats on either
side to fire. The rest of us and the gear just sat on the floor
with some of us, including me, dangling our feet out the door
into space.

Normally, there is no more exciting and pleasing way to
travel than being perched at the open door of a chopper.
The whole world is at your feet. At the speed and height
helicopters usually cruise, you can examine the earth below
the tips of your toes in ways you never could walking, riding in a car, and certainly not looking at it from a speeding
plane. You see the ground better than the pilots in the front
cabin do because you haven't an instrument console as a bar-
rier in front of you, there are no instruments to watch, there
is no restraint of a seat belt. You feel free because everything
below you seems within reach. After all, all you would have
to do to join the people down there is to slide out as if getting
out of a chair. You hover, watching at your leisure the world
unfolding.

The earth becomes a map come alive. You can see over
walls and around corners that the dots of people beneath
you cannot. You can see the lay of the land, its contours and
colors, the shapes of roofs, the turns of roads, the traffic on

them, the twists of rivers. In Indochina, when the chopper dipped low, the dots below became bullock carts, women — or at least the tops of their conical straw hats — doing their laundry by the river bank, children splashing in the water, water buffalo wallowing in the mud. There were also in this Asian landscape reminders of foreign intrusion: the miles of straight-as-straight-can-be rows of trees in the rubber planta- tions left behind by the French and the huge ugly scars of craters made by bombs dropped from B52s.

But not all was visible and pleasing to the hovering eye. There was the jungle, an impenetrable dark green carpet. In the jungle, in the clumps of trees and other heavy veg- etation, and sometimes under innocent-looking roofs, there lurked danger: the Viet Cong, the North Vietnamese and their anti-aircraft guns and, lately, the Soviet SAM missiles whose heat-seeking mechanism loved the exhaust gases of chopper engines.

Where ground fire could be expected, there was no lei- surely hovering. In heavy fire zones, chopper pilots had two choices. One was to fly low, at treetop level. Coming in low and fast cut the chances of the communists getting in a well- aimed shot. The other method of avoiding danger was to fly high above the ceiling of the most effective light anti-aircraft weapons and then come cork-screwing down at what felt like the speed of a plummeting stone. That is how we came down at An Loc. We all just hung on for dear life as supply boxes slid back and forth along the floor, hitting and pushing bodies that didn't have much to hang on to.

As we dropped, the communists opened up on the landing zone with mortars. They missed, but as we landed they came close enough to let us know that getting out was not going to be easy. If we needed proof, there was the American sergeant we literally bumped into as we jumped off the chopper. He was trying to get on. But helicopters landing under fire don't stay on the ground for more than a few seconds. I could al- most swear that our chopper never touched the ground. The sergeant, big, fat and clumsy, just wasn't fast enough. He got left behind. He was almost in tears with anger and frustra- tion. The sergeant, a radio specialist from the U.S. base at

Bien Hoa, had made the classical mistake of military life: he had volunteered for a job. Nobody told him the location of the radio he was supposed to fix. To his great surprise and shock, he suddenly found himself in a besieged town under fire. It took him only a few minutes to fix the radio, he said, and he had now spent two days trying to get back out.

It didn't take us long to realize that the main defenders of An Loc were not the troops inside the town. What kept the North Vietnamese at bay at An Loc — and everywhere else in South Vietnam — was American air power. American Phantom jets came in low, bombing and rocketing communist positions in the rubber plantations surrounding the town. So did the occasional South Vietnamese propeller-driven Skyraider and Spookies whose Gatling guns sounded like giant toy rattles as they hosed down the rubber trees with bullets to discourage surprise infantry attacks. Even more deadly was the work of the big B52s. They flew so high you couldn't see or hear them. You knew they were there when you saw the earth explode beyond the town.

The Americans, I found out later, flew 100 tactical strikes in the An Loc area that day. In addition, there were eleven B52 missions, which meant they dropped more than a million pounds of high explosives. All that explosive power did not, I would imagine, kill many North Vietnamese. One of the first things one learns about war is how easy it is to kill a human being and yet how difficult. You can kill a man with a fraction of an ounce of metal, yet with luck and ingenuity he can survive having tons of explosives dropped on top of him. He can dig in and hide, he can move and fake. Most of the bombs dropped around An Loc the day I was there probably did nothing more than displace lots of dirt.

Yet the American strikes kept the North Vietnamese off balance. Instead of being able to bring up their heavy 175-mm artillery and pounding An Loc into submission, they had to make do with lighter and more mobile mortars and rocket launchers. A few hundred rounds a day or so. Enough to keep heads down. And kill. But nowhere near enough to take the town. If they wanted to do that, they'd have to do it the hard way, by storming it.

We got our pictures: the diving planes and bomb bursts; an incoming chopper greeted by mortar fire; a mortar shell hitting a compound; spouts of earth shooting up as a stick of B52 bombs hit beyond the town; dead bodies being covered by ponchos; bodies being carried away. You could feel the tension. After all, people were dying all over the place. But in pictorial terms, as TV news, it was undramatic, unemotional, like clearing up after a traffic accident.

Television is not always as good at conveying the drama of war as it is supposed to be. What looks dangerous on TV is not necessarily so. A scene showing a reporter with shells exploding in the background looks dramatic even though the explosions are safely a few hundred yards away. If the reporter were under small-calibre fire — presuming he or she were insane enough to stand there — the TV shot would look mundane, unless, of course, one of the bullets hit home. Besides, TV news rarely shows the real gore of war: close-ups of bodies with parts blown off, the agonies of the wounded and dying, to say nothing of the smell of the dead.

Our An Loc story was no gung-ho war-movie stuff with blood splattering all over. But it was what was happening, it was the news and it was exclusive.

I needed an interview explaining the situation, preferably with the garrison commander. But at headquarters, instead of getting an interview with the Vietnamese commanding general, we got an earful from his American adviser, a colonel. He came steaming out of the command bunker wanting to know what the hell we were doing there and how the hell we got there. What's more, the colonel said, he'd make sure we got the hell out of there. And he detailed a Vietnamese lieutenant to make sure we caught a chopper out the next morning.

The colonel's expulsion edict suited me. I had the story; now I needed to get it out. Staying longer would have been useless. Our batteries were all but dead and there was no way of recharging them.

The paras offered to take us in for the night in their bunker. We turned them down. The bunker was already overcrowded. Besides, we figured we would be better off somewhere away from what seemed like a prominent, even if solidly protected, target. We slept in a flimsy hut that couldn't have stopped a thrown brick. But it was also out of the way and inconspicuous. As I was falling asleep that night, I could hear the shells coming in and the Gatlings rattling.

The next morning, we found out that a shell had hit the paratroopers' bunker during the night, killing three of the paras with whom we had flown into An Loc and wounding the other three. We never got to see the survivors. Our guardian, the young lieutenant, was in too much of a hurry to get us out of town and rushed us off to a helicopter landing zone. They kept changing the landing pads to make it more difficult for the communist gunners to zero in on them. There aren't all that many places in a besieged town where helicopters can land and what kept An Loc open to choppers was that the American air strikes also kept the North Vietnamese mortar crews hopping around.

The few choppers that came in were equipped with cargo slings they would drop as they hovered without landing. Brian and I waited in a trench by the landing zone, ducking our heads when the choppers came and drew fire. Gerard, though, sat on the edge of the trench, his feet dangling into it, a cigarette pasted to his lips, the picture of Gallic insouciance, not taking any notice of the incoming fire. I kidded him about having watched too many Humphrey Bogart and John Wayne movies.

I still don't know how he failed to catch a ride out with us when a chopper finally did set down for a few seconds. I remember running as fast as I could across the landing zone. But Gerard should have been there ahead of me. Not only was he in better physical shape, but my hip was giving me trouble again, slowing me down considerably. At first I told myself it may have been the leg wound Gerard got in Cambodia that held him back. Or perhaps he stayed because he thought he would get better pictures, even perhaps scoop us, his buddies. But I knew I was only kidding myself. Gerard stayed behind simply because there was action. After all, he had not come to Vietnam for the journalism, certainly not for the money, or even, as Sean Flynn had, in search of fame and glamour. I had come to believe he was there simply because it was deadly.

Five days after we had last seen Gerard, I got a phone call that he was in the U.S. military hospital in Saigon. I went to see him. He had two wounds, one in each shoulder, neither of them too serious.

He got the first wound, he said, when the communist tanks came. He got a few shots of tanks lumbering into the town square before he got a bullet in the shoulder. For four hours, as the battle raged around him, he hid in a burning building and watched several tanks being destroyed by South Vietnamese infantrymen. When the battle was over, he made it to the field hospital only to be wounded again by shrapnel from a round that hit the building. He lay there for three more days before a medevac helicopter picked him up.

The chopper, loaded with sixteen wounded men, had barely lifted off when it was hit. This time his luck turned. The craft didn't crash; it sank slowly to the ground. Unfortunately, it landed beyond An Loc's defence perimeter. Gerard, sure that the communists would be there quickly to round them up, scampered off, heading for cover among the rubber trees. Just then another helicopter came by, picked him up and flew him to safety.

Gerard had a terrific story, an exclusive eyewitness account of the day the tanks came to An Loc and were beaten back. He had looked inside one of the damaged North Vietnamese tanks, he recounted, and found the dead driver chained to his seat. A sensational story if it could be shown to be true. But there was a serious problem with the story. Gerard had no pictures. He had lost both his cameras when he was wounded. For a photographer, that is as bad as it gets.

UPI made the most of the story of communist soldiers chained to their posts. And Gerard got a few hundred dollars out of it. If he had had pictures, though, he could have made himself a lot more money, enough to pay off some of his debts and buy himself better photo equipment. As it was, he was still all but broke and, worst of all, without a camera.

When he got out of hospital, I lent him my still camera to tide him over and lectured him on being more careful where he stuck his head. But I knew by then that it was probably no use, that for reasons that I would never know Gerard Hébert did not care whether he lived or died.

I was on leave in Thailand when he was killed.

It happened as it was bound to happen. He was up north, covering the battle for Quang Tri. As usual, he was with airborne troops. They were having lunch when the communist big guns opened up. The North Vietnamese gunners stepped their fire towards their position and as the shells started landing closer and closer, everyone dived for shelter. Gerard did not. He just kept on eating. When the shell hit, a piece of shrapnel blew his head off.

That's when we found out that Gerard Hébert wasn't who we thought he was. All attempts to contact his sons in Montreal led nowhere. The addresses he gave for them were phony. Messages to his sons broadcast by a Montreal radio station brought no response. He had worked for the CBC in Montreal for some time but that was all that was known about him.

Then it came out that Gerard had left some effects for safekeeping with the Corsican owner of one of the many bars on Saigon's Tu Do Street. Among them were papers that made it evident that Gerard Hébert was not his real name, that he was not Canadian, that he had got his Canadian passport under false pretences, that he was a Frenchman who had left France after getting into trouble with the law.

All of a sudden, no one wanted anything to do with his body. The airborne division people, who had originally offered to bury him in their cemetery, a gesture that would have delighted Gerard, withdrew the offer. The Canadians said that since he was not Canadian, they could have nothing to do with him either. The French said they would have to check it all out. So the body lay in the morgue unclaimed.

Finally, they buried him in the old Catholic cemetery of Saigon, a place where French and Vietnamese lie side by side. He must be one of the last Frenchmen to be buried in this cemetery built for Frenchmen.

The place fit the man and vice versa. In an odd way, Gerard completed the cycle of the rise and decline of European colonialism in Vietnam. The first Frenchmen to be buried there

— soldiers of Napoleon III — had come to Vietnam for more or less the same reason Gerard had: because of troubles at home. Not theirs, but their emperor's. Napoleon turned to overseas adventures to try to draw attention away from his domestic problems. He had managed to anger French capitalists, conservatives and churchmen. Even his own wife, the Empress Eugénie, had turned on him because his intrigues had let down the pope. To Napoleon, whose manoeuvrings in Europe seemed to misfire whatever he did, Indochina must have seemed like a good, safe place to recoup. And he had an excuse. The Vietnamese emperor Tu Duc had beheaded a French missionary. The French retaliated by storming Saigon and spreading from there throughout Indochina.

The French used Vietnam after the Second World War for a second time as a means of resolving some of their domestic problems. France was at a low point in its history. The French had been humiliated by their defeat at the hands of Germany in 1940 and by the slights they had to put up with from the Allies during and after the war. By retaking Vietnam, which they had lost first to the Japanese, then to Vietnamese nationalists, they hoped to regain some of their prestige. The French army, in particular, was eager to cleanse itself in Vietnam of the stains of its defeat in Europe. Dien Bien Phu put an end to that.

What Louis-Napoleon Bonaparte did in the 1860s in pursuit of France's *mission civilisatrice*, Lyndon Baines Johnson was to do in the 1960s to further the crusade against communism. Vietnam was not Napoleon's enemy; the Prussians, Russians and Austrians were. Neither was Vietnam really LBJ's enemy; the Soviet Union and China were. But since the Americans couldn't very easily take on the Chinese and the Russians, they made do with sticking pins into the Vietnamese. Vietnam was only a substitute, a metaphor.

But Vietnam was not used just by the French and the Americans. Just about everybody did it. The Chinese had abused Vietnam for centuries. The Russians would use Vietnam to get at the Chinese. The U.S. Army used it to test its mobile warfare theories just as Hitler and Mussolini had tested their weapons in Spain. And Vietnam was the only place where

the U.S. Air Force could test the effectiveness of its B52s. If
Gerard Hébert used Vietnam to find the end of his problems,
he at least had not hurt any Vietnamese, except perhaps the
feelings of a few ARVN paratroopers.

Now Gerard lay in a grave surrounded by the history of the
century between Napoleon's *poilus* and LBJ's GIs. The graveyard by that time had the look of an archaeological dig for
the relics of an extinct society. First, the French conquerors
who were buried, it is said, tilted towards France in one last
salute to *la patrie*. Next, the graves of the church's warriors:
the priests and nuns who died transplanting their faith to the
tropics. Quite a few died as martyrs, some by the sword but
more to the soul-searing miseries of dysentery, cholera and
malaria. The biggest battalions in the graveyard, though, are
the French civil servants who for ninety years ran Vietnam
and brought to Saigon such achievements of French civilization as sidewalks, mosquito netting, the baguette, croissants,
red wine and syphilis.

The grandest tombs didn't belong to those who conquered
Vietnam; they were built in honor of those who lost it:
South Vietnam's politicians and generals, descendants of the
converts the missionaries had recruited. These were people
whose acquired religion had set them apart from most of their
countrymen. South Vietnam was largely run by Catholics, former colonials trying to perpetuate the system the colonizers
had left behind.

I never did go to see Gerard's grave. I knew it had his
real name on the headstone; that made it the grave of
a man I didn't know. I preferred not to know his real
name, to go on remembering him as Gerard Hébert, a
Canadian photographer with a smile and seemingly not
a care in the world, a good friend with whom I shared
and who shared with me, and a man with a fatal taste for
danger.

For fifteen years I resisted the urge of curiosity that is the
one common denominator of all journalists. I knew how to
find out what Gerard's real name was. I just never asked.
Finally, thinking I might return to Saigon, I did ask.

I know now that if I should ever get back to the town they

now call Ho Chi Minh City, I shall have to look for the grave
of Gerard Arroux.

I don't know whether, after all that's happened in Saigon
since he died, the gravestone is still there. But I do know of
one memorial to Gerard Hébert. It is in the U.S., a tree in
the Arlington National Cemetery across the Potomac River
from Washington, just behind the Tomb of the Unknown Soldier, a tree planted "in memory of journalists who died while
covering wars or conflicts for the American people." Gerard's
name is on the list of those it memorializes. But the Americans got his name wrong; they anglicized it to "Herbert." As
with so much else in Vietnam, they made Gerard their own.
It's a wonder they didn't call him Jerry as many Americans in
Vietnam did.

Not that Gerard would have minded. Jerry Herbert would
have seemed to him as good a name as any other. And if
he couldn't be a Vietnamese hero, a Canadian hero or a
French one, he would have been quite happy to be remembered as an American hero. I can just see him laughing at the
thought.

There are still two Vietnams, even though the South Vietnam and the North Vietnam of the war are long gone. The
way I count it, the first Vietnam is a country in Southeast
Asia inhabited by a people called the Vietnamese. The other
is the Vietnam of Americans, of those who went there, most
to fight, and those who never even saw the country but were
also profoundly changed by it, not only as individuals but as
a nation.

There are, of course, other countries that have had such
an effect on foreign interlopers. The influence of India on
the British imagination, for instance. But India is so much
larger than Vietnam, and the Indians and the English were
locked in a bittersweet embrace for so long that they got to
know each other, took from each other and even gave to each
other. When they finally parted, they kept much of what they
had gained from one another, first and foremost perhaps, the

vivid resonances of a shared history.

In India and Pakistan, the reminders of British rule are still everywhere. And not just in monumental stone. You can see the British were here in the way many Pakistani officers carry swagger sticks with English insouciance. You can detect the British traces in the courts in India, in the Parliament in New Delhi, or watching tea-plantation managers take tiffin at their clubs. Not so in Vietnam. Apart from a taste for American cigarettes and jeans, all the Vietnamese have left to remind them of the once overwhelming American presence are the stigmata of their suffering: ruins, graveyards, war trophies preserved like bronzed baby shoes and the human detritus of the war, cripples and abandoned Amerasians, the much disdained offspring of GIs and Vietnamese women.

For the Vietnamese, the American adventure in their country was only a short but intense interlude in a long series of foreign invasions to be fought, repulsed and then set aside, if not forgotten. From long Chinese occupations, they got their culture; from their days as a colony of France, a liking for baguettes; from the short American stay, a weakness for chewing gum.

Americans returning to Vietnam these days are often amazed at the lack of bitterness towards them. This forgiveness seems due more to indifference than to a generosity of spirit, more to a need for American help than a yearning for reconciliation. The fact that the departure of the Americans did not bring peace, that Vietnam almost immediately found new enemies to fight among its own people and foreign allies, also helped dilute the animosity towards Americans.

The Vietnamese were, after all, at war before the Americans came and they have been at war almost constantly since they left, in Cambodia and on their border with China. Even when the fighting died down, they were still preoccupied with the dangerous power vacuum at their front door in Cambodia and with the Chinese propensity to kick in their back door from time to time. Compared to the millenial threat of the Chinese, the American intervention was to the Vietnamese much as Ho Chi Minh saw the French presence in his country in the forties: "Better to sniff a bit of French shit than eat Chinese shit for the rest of our lives."

The war against the Americans has a less important place in Vietnamese history than Americans like to think. The Vietnamese had, after all, fought many wars of national liberation over the centuries. Even in this century, the American war was for them only a replay. They had done it all once before against the French. They shed the chains of colonialism and gained their independence by defeating the French at Dien Bien Phu.

What was at stake in their war against the Americans was a different problem of Vietnamese history, the division of the country. Sometimes the Vietnamese had to share their country with Chinese invaders. At other times, they caused the split themselves, as they did in the sixteenth century when the Nguyen family took over the south, leaving the house of Trinh to run the north. The French, the better to rule by dividing, broke it up into three parts, the colonies of Cochinchina in the south, Annam in the centre and Tonkin in the north.

So the partition between North Vietnam and South Vietnam agreed upon after Dien Bien Phu by the West, the Soviet Union and China at the Geneva conference of 1954 was not something new. Neither was it unnatural. It merely resuscitated an old rivalry. The north, centred on the Red River and Hanoi, was the cradle of Vietnamese civilization. The south of the Mekong River delta and Saigon was new territory wrested from the Cambodians in the seventeenth and eighteenth centuries. The conflict between Hanoi and Saigon, between the Red River rice bowl and the paddies of the Mekong delta continues to this day despite reunification under the communists.

The drive to unify the country might have remained a purely domestic struggle if it had not been for the ideological Cold War elsewhere. It became an international issue once it became clear that Ho Chi Minh, the nationalistic communist ruler of the North, was a far more effective organizer and more popular leader than Ngo Dinh Diem, the nationalistic president of South Vietnam, a remote and austere Confucian

Catholic. The authoritarian Diem regime was not so much
falling apart under communist assault; it never really started
functioning as an effective government. The Americans felt
they had to prop up Diem to save Vietnam from communism. When it became apparent that his regime could not go
it alone, they sent U.S. troops.

Though the fighting was between communists and anti-
communists, it was not really a class war and certainly not
a struggle between capitalists and industrial workers; there
were precious few of either in Vietnam. Nor was it a case of
landless peasants rebelling against the land-hogging classes
as in El Salvador. Not once in Vietnam did I encounter a
situation in which the war was played out simply as a struggle between the haves and the have-nots.

For one thing, most of the leading anti-communists in Vietnam detested capitalism almost as much as the communists
did. To people like Diem, the competitive individualism of
liberal democracy was an evil that disrupted harmony in
society. As Confucians, they believed that society must be
a co-operative egalitarian enterprise in which their role, as
mandarins, was to act as patriarchal guardians of the common good.

On the other side, Ho, too, was unorthodox, more driven
by nationalism than conventional Marxism. What had attracted him first to communism was not *The Communist
Manifesto* but Lenin's *Thesis on the National and Colonial
Question*. He was won over by the Russian's argument that
in colonial societies the nationalist struggle for independence
took precedence over anti-capitalist, anti-bourgeois revolution. "It was patriotism and not communism that originally
inspired me," Ho wrote years later.

In the struggle between these two different conceptions of
Vietnam's future, the arrival of the Americans tipped the
scales towards Hanoi. It is easier to recruit people to fight
foreign enemies than it is to persuade them to fight their
own countrymen. The presence of Americans enabled Hanoi
to turn a domestic fight for power into a war of national liberation. People who would normally have had nothing to do
with communists now flocked to them. GIs came to play the

same role in Vietnam as the redcoats did in the American revolution, as foreign occupiers from whom the revolutionaries bravely plucked freedom. The British redcoats and the American green berets both became the props of legends, the backdrop of myths spun to inspire future generations. In stories of valor, they were nothing more than stuffed figures into which boys plunged bayonets to become men and heroes. They became machines of evil that manufactured national martyrs. Domestic opponents, whether they be Loyalists in eighteenth-century North America or anti-communists in twentieth-century Vietnam, never could have fulfilled the role of serving the mythos of nationalism as well as foreign occupiers did.

To put George Washington on the pedestal of history, though, did not require that Lord Cornwallis and his redcoats be forever hated. Similarly, Ho's status as the savior of his country did not require hatred of General William Westmoreland and his GIs once the immediate postwar period was over. So Hanoi has shoved them into the shadows as cardboard figures to be used when needed for target practice by the myth-makers. One day, perhaps, that lack of heat in the hatred of Americans will enable a successor to Lyndon Johnson and Richard Nixon to be welcomed in Vietnam as warmly as the descendants of George III are lionized nowadays by Americans.

For the Vietnamese communists, of course, winning the war against the Americans was not the end of their problems. It was rather the beginning of painful new ones, many of them self-inflicted. Once the foreign invaders had left, the Vietnamese went back to what they had been doing when the soldiers of Napoleon III so rudely interrupted them more than 100 years earlier: trying to take over what was left of Cambodia.

Six years after the war, Vietnamese Prime Minister Pham Van Dong confided ruefully to Stan Karnow, an American journalist: "Waging a war is simple, but running a country is very difficult."

For the Vietnamese, it still is. That's probably the main reason why they put the sufferings of war against the Americans behind them so quickly. The pain of today is so great that it has pushed aside remembrances of the pain of yesterday.

For the Americans, on the other hand, the pain lingered on because they had been hurt as a nation where they had never suffered hurt before. In their pride. In their confidence in themselves.

Fred Downes sat rubbing his artificial left arm as if it itched. He was recalling how happy he had been when he came out of hospital with the arm he had been given to replace the flesh-and-bone one that he had lost in Vietnam. He was determined to catch up with his life. He would get a university education and forget the terrible things that had happened to him in Vietnam. But his countrymen would not let him forget, he said. Right from the start. It began the day he arrived on the university campus. A man came up to him and wanted to know about the arm. "He pointed at my hook and said, 'Did you lose that in Nam, man?' I said, 'Yeah, up in Chu Lai, near Tam Ky.' He looked right at me and said, 'Serves you right.' I was stunned.

"The one dream we always had in Vietnam was going back to the real world. This was the world. And it was not what we thought it was. We were shattered."

Fred Downes and tens of thousands of other GIs returning home from the Vietnam war found themselves in another war: America at war with itself. This, too, was a war they felt they could not win. They had gone to Vietnam because it was expected of them, because they did not have the education to avoid the draft, or the pull to get a cushy posting, or the gumption and desire to flee to Canada. They had come home to find that instead of being heroes as their fathers had been when they returned from the Second World War and their grandfathers were after the First, they were looked upon as spaced-out bums and baby killers.

Most Vietnam veterans were convinced they knew why they were being treated as outcasts. In many ways, it had nothing to do with them. Most Americans were angry because for the first time in its history their country had lost a war. So they took it out on the soldiers who had fought the war as if they were the ones who had lost it. The soldiers, especially the officers, felt, as had so many soldiers in so many losing wars before theirs, that it was the fault of civilians — craven politicians and, in this case, also anti-war radicals. But in this war, unlike in Germany after the First World War, the civilians had the upper hand in the blame-laying. After all, the American generals had said time and time again that if they were only given more men, if they were only allowed to bomb North Vietnam more fiercely, they could win the war. Again and again, they were given most of what they demanded until they had more than half a million men, and they still couldn't win. All the excuses they would offer afterwards was that if they had only been given even more, they would have won.

To many of the civilians who had opposed the war, who had dodged the draft, the substantiation of the worthlessness of those who had fought it was the final justification of their own stand. As for those who had supported the war, it made them feel better to think that the U.S. had lost not because it was the wrong war and certainly not because of some fault in the country itself but because the men who fought it were not the A team. Vietnam had no Sergeant Yorks and Audie Murphys, those bemedalled sharp-shooting, devil-may-care heroes of the two wars in Europe. If there was a prototype of the Vietnam soldier, it was to many Americans Lieutenant William Calley, the leader of the platoon that had massacred 567 unarmed civilians in the village of My Lai. A bunch of Lootenant Calleys, that's what many Americans called their Vietnam soldiers.

Rejected, many Viet vets turned inwards. Some crumbled, dropped out of society, debased themselves in various ways or even committed suicide. But most led normal lives, coping by putting their Vietnam past into the closet alongside their uniforms.

They would come out of the closet eventually. Just hesitant peeks at first. Things were happening in Indochina and elsewhere that were slowly changing American attitudes. In Cambodia, the Khmer Rouge were massacring their own people by the hundreds of thousands, even millions. Everyone who knew anything, was anything, owned anything was on the communists' death list. Teachers, doctors and ordinary folks, too. Just owning a pair of reading glasses was reason enough to be killed as an intellectual. Then there were the terrible stories from Vietnam itself about desperate people fleeing in rickety boats. The boat people defied sharks, pirates and death rather than live under the rule of the government that supposedly fought the war only so that all Vietnamese could live in peace and unity. Not only did the "peace-loving" communists oppress their own people, they even rekindled the Indochina war by attacking their erstwhile allies in Cambodia. It made many Americans come to the conclusion that even though they may have fought the wrong war, they had at least not been fighting the wrong enemy, as the "peaceniks" and Jane Fonda had been telling them.

Then came the Iranian revolution and further humiliation. The whole U.S. embassy was held hostage for days, weeks, months, then a year and more. The U.S. was gripped by the fury and frustration of helplessness. Out of the indignity of the whole country being held hostage by what Americans saw as a gang of grubby fanatics led by a malevolent, glowering mullah came Ronald Reagan with his mission of "making America stand tall again." The slogan "No More Vietnams" was suddenly and stunningly turned around. Where before it had meant not getting trapped in more foreign involvements, its new Reaganesque meaning was no more retreats, no more turning the other cheek, no more humiliations.

If there was a single event that brought the Vietnam vets out of the closet, it was the return of the American hostages from Teheran. They watched with astonishment as the country welcomed the freed diplomats as heroes. They, the Vietnam vets, had fought, been wounded, a lot of their buddies had been killed, and all they got when they came back was a Bronx cheer. Yet here were these civilians who had also got the country into a humiliating situation, who had done nothing but sit around for a year waiting for someone to get them out, and now they were getting more confetti showered on them than Charles Lindbergh did when he came home after flying the *Spirit of St. Louis* to Paris. To the vets, it looked as if the same Americans who covered up their embarrassment over Vietnam by blaming them for the fiasco were glossing over this latest national embarrassment by pretending that the end of the humiliation of the U.S. at the hands of Ayatollah Khomeini was a triumph. The Viet vets decided that they had enough of eating crow, that their hour had come.

For their comeback, the old soldiers copied the methods of the anti-war demonstrators of the sixties, the people who during the war had called them names. The new demonstrators, their faces, their beards, the casual and even sloppy dress often looked the same as those of their mentors of the anti-war movement. They didn't burn flags, but they marched like them, they raised their fists and yelled slogans, they staged sit-downs. They wanted better care for their disabled and compensation for victims of Agent Orange, the defoliant chemical that had been sprayed over Vietnamese jungles to deprive communist troops of cover. What they wanted most was their dignity back. And a memorial to their dead.

It was not easy. Sometimes they themselves did not know what they wanted. When the winning design for the war memorial was made public, most of them were outraged. In their hurt, in their sensitivity to slight, they saw the black polished, below-ground-level retainer wall that was to be built on Washington's Mall as an insult.

"A hundred years from now," one of them complained at a congressional hearing, "every visitor to the Mall will see it for what it is, a black hole in the ground, and they'll have no trouble understanding what America thought of Vietnam veterans. We are going to be a black splotch in the history of this country."

The veterans' organizations wanted something more grandiose, a statue, perhaps, to proclaim the glory of those who had died in this most unglorious and unglamorous of wars. But definitely not the black hole that was being dug for their dead.

They were wrong.

The Vietnam memorial has become in a few short years a monument to rival the vastly more grandiose Lincoln monument beside it. Its austere simplicity speaks with a subtle eloquence. Yes, it is only a plain stone wall, but it is a moving place. It is also, literally, a touching place. People touch it and it touches their hearts. They kiss the names that are engraved on it, the names of all the Americans — 58,175 of them — who died in Vietnam. They caress the black stone. They make rubbings of the names, names of their brothers, their sons, their fathers, their comrades-in-arms, and, here and there, of their sisters and daughters, too. This is not a monument to the abstraction of an Unknown Soldier; it is a memorial to every dead soldier, for many the only gravestone they will ever have. For each of them there is a place here, a place for a mother to kiss, for friends to lay flowers and flags at the foot of the wall below the name.

With its ground-hugging modesty and lack of militaristic bombast, the Vietnam memorial also speaks of other things than remembrance of the dead. It speaks of the price of vainglory, of the folly of the American *idée fixe* that the U.S., as the Last Great Hope of humankind, had the God-given mission to spread democracy and free enterprise to every nook of this world and plant it there by whatever means it took.

Not even Ronald Reagan spurring on Americans with his pep talks could resurrect the careless gung-ho jingoism of the country's innocent youth, that stirring mixture of altruism and aggressiveness whose last poet laureate was John F. Kennedy. Occasionally, Reagan would try to resurrect that spirit. His attempt in Nicaragua to have his contra proxies overthrow the Sandinista government failed. He was more successful with the invasion of Grenada but that was merely a comic opera re-run of Teddy Roosevelt's charge up San Juan Hill.

The Grenada operation served mostly to distract attention from the historically more meaningful business of the quick withdrawal of American power from Lebanon. Faced with the first taste of determined opposition — the bombing of the U.S. Marine barracks in Beirut — the Americans retreated only days after Reagan had declared he would never cut and run.

For all his bombast, Reagan had instinctively learned the limitations of U.S. power. He substituted the high-risk poker that Kennedy played in the Cuban missile crisis and that Johnson and Nixon practised in Vietnam with low-ball adventurism. As punishment for Colonel Muhammar Ghadaffi's dabbling in terrorism, Reagan bombed Libya, which was ill-equipped to strike back. But he didn't bomb Iran, whose support of terrorism was much more extensive than Libya's. If Iran had been attacked, Ayatollah Khomeini had the means of retaliating effectively and there was little doubt he would have.

The biggest deterrent to high-risk military adventures, though, was probably a U.S. military made more cautious by its Vietnam experience. Curiously, the main lesson the U.S. Army came away with was not so much improving the means of combatting guerrilla insurrections and wars of national liberation as the need to avoid being caught up in them. Its new dictum is never to allow itself to be sent to a war that does not have popular support at home.

Time after time since Vietnam, the armed forces have demurred when the politicians and the diplomats started talking about sending them into small crises that had the makings of an unintended major confrontation. It was the State Department and not the Pentagon that pushed for the dispatch of the marines to Lebanon. Similarly, the U.S. Navy was less than enthusiastic about its mission of protecting tankers in the Persian Gulf from Iranian predators; it saw the potential of a dangerous escalation. The Pentagon was also cool for a long time to the State Department's enthusiasm for confronting General Manuel Noriega, then the dictator of Panama. In fact, it was not until General Colin Powell, a long-time presidential adviser who had absorbed much of the diplomatic and political culture of civilian Washington, became chairman of the Joint Chiefs of Staff and until one of the armed forces' own, a marine lieutenant, was killed by Noriega's men, that the armed forces took up the mission of invading Panama. And for all the chest-thumping since then, routing a vastly out-manned bunch of thugs who have never done anything but beat up on civilians is hardly a feat of glory for a professional army.

Presidents are still free to send the army on little forays against puny foes, such as Grenada and Panama. At the other end of the scale, they can, with the consent of Congress, use the armed forces in a fully declared war against a major power. But only with great difficulty and against flagrant provocation can they use the army for anything in between. And certainly not for another surreptitious Vietnam.

For Americans, little by little, the wounds of Vietnam have healed. They have adapted to the lessons it taught them and come to accept, as have all powerful nations before them, some of the limitations of their power. They can now talk about Vietnam without confronting each other bitterly. They can not only write sensitively about Vietnam but also have their books published and read. Vietnam is now even an acceptable subject for commercial television without having to use, as the producers of "M*A*S*H" did, the subterfuge of shifting the war to Korea.

But if Americans have been facing up to what Vietnam did to them, they have not yet fully confronted what they did to Vietnam. When they talk of the tragedy of Vietnam, they usually mean what the war did to them, of their trauma, not that of the Vietnamese. When they talk of the damage done to humans by Agent Orange, they talk of the injury done to Americans. Only rarely have I heard talk of the much greater injury done to Vietnam, where not only the people who were sprayed but the very land was poisoned. Vietnam reportedly has one of the world's highest cancer rates, especially among women living in areas sprayed with Agent Orange.

Even the question of a peace settlement with Vietnam is bogged down over an American obsession, the issue of MIAs, of those missing in action. A peace treaty is unlikely until the question of what happened to all of the missing Americans is resolved. It is understandable that the families of the missing would want their remains back. But the idea that has driven U.S. policy on this issue, that somehow the Vietnamese are holding the bones of dead Americans hostage, is almost as ridiculous as the Rambo fantasy, not confined to the movies, that some of the missing Americans are still being held prisoner in the jungle. There is something almost obscene about putting the onus on the Vietnamese to find the remains of a few Americans in a charnel house brimming with the bones of Vietnamese killed by Americans.

The Vietnamese are also short-changed in most American novels and films about the war. In many of them, the Vietnamese characters are almost as woodenly two-dimensional as are the Americans in Vietnamese propaganda. The films star American pain; Vietnamese pain is for the extras. American suffering comes in close-ups with the Vietnamese writhing in agony in the background. Books, too, concentrate on American anguish. In American literature, there are no Vietnamese protagonists as developed as the Indians of English literature, figures such as E.M. Forster's Dr. Aziz in *Passage to India*, or Hari Kumar from Paul Scott's *The Raj Quartet*.

One day perhaps there will be an American book about real Vietnamese with hearts and brains and stories to tell, a story of the real Vietnam, the one in Southeast Asia where Americans once so briefly sojourned, not the one of their self-absorbed national nightmare. It could help them lay Vietnam to rest into the quietude of history.

CHAPTER VIII

The beast called the dragon can be tamed and trained
to the point where you may ride on its back.
But on the underside of its throat it has scales
a foot across that curl back from the body,
and anyone who brushes against them is sure to die.

Han Feitzu

A noise outside wakes me. There is barely a hint of light, and I lie in bed listening, trying to figure out what the noise is and, more importantly, where I am.

I have awoken before and since on a thousand-and-one mornings aware in those moments when consciousness struggles to penetrate the sleep-sodden brain that I am not at home and wondering where it is that I am and why.

Slowly the clues accumulate. The weak, dying whir of an air conditioner fighting a losing battle against the mustiness of the tropics? Probably Managua or Phnom Penh. An elaborate armoire dimly perceived through a barely lifted eyelid? The Hotel Raphael in Rome. Or perhaps the Ritz in Lisbon.

Stuck to the frying pan of a hard board bed and tangled in mosquito netting? Feels like Can Tho in Vietnam's Mekong

Delta. Police sirens? Lots of them? In the morning? Must be New York. The sound of Big Ben? If it's not the radio tuned to the BBC World Service, it's surely the Sheraton in Buenos Aires, which has the English Tower with its Little Big Ben just outside its windows.

Slathered with sweat and encrusted with bedbug bites? No use even trying to strain the brain; the possibilities are endless. The smell of obsessive cleanliness, of wood polish, brass polish, poly-polish and tutti-frutti cleaner? The Okura in Tokyo or the Mandarin in Hong Kong are prime candidates. A flowery thermos bottle on the night table? China, no doubt about it. A lone siren that wheezes like an asthmatic? Oh, just about anywhere in Europe. The Gestapo seems to have left them behind everywhere it went.

This particular morning, though, the sound is of human voices, indistinguishable squawks that finally sort themselves out into "yi, er, yi, er, yi, er." Ever so slowly the translation oozes forth. It's Chinese for "one, two, one, two, one two."

Of course, this is, this has to be Peking. After years of closing itself off to the world while it writhed under the torments of Mao Tse-tung's Cultural Revolution, China has opened the door a little to let in a few foreign journalists. We arrived in the city after midnight, sneaking in by the light of a few weak streetlights that showed not a sign of life.

But now it is dawn, a noisy dawn. I jump out of bed to take a look at the source of the noise.

Hundreds of people are marching under my window in winding columns heading every which way. At the head of each column, a figure with a red flag. And all the marchers, men and women, marching and counter-marching, are identically dressed in blue pants and jackets. As they march, they kick up clouds of dust, shrouding the scene in a grey haze that battles the weak rays of the rising sun. It's a Brueghel painting come to life with frenetic motion and piercing sound.

"Yi, er," the column leaders shrill. It's part morning rush hour, a ritualistic going-off to work, part communal exercise. But more than anything else, it is the party and Mao Tse-tung imposing the group on individuals before they have time to rub the sleep out of their eyes on their own.

To me, China this morning looks like the other side of the moon. I can hardly wait to get out there to find out what kind of cheese it is made of. It is Easter Monday, 1971.

The previous week, during the festival of Ch'ing Ming, the festival of tomb-sweeping, when the Chinese tend the graves of their ancestors, I stood with Mike on the waterfront in the Portuguese colony of Macao looking wistfully beyond a Chinese gunboat in midstream to China on the other side. It was only a few hundred yards away but it seemed a thousand miles.

The Chinese were allowing in only a few foreign journalists and those they did let in operated under severe limitations, even tribulations. The British news agency, Reuters, had closed its bureau after its correspondent, Anthony Grey, spent two years under humiliating house arrest during the height of the Cultural Revolution. Only three Western news organizations — the Toronto *Globe and Mail*, a German news agency and a French one — still had correspondents based in Peking. And even now, with the Great Proletarian Cultural Revolution having quietened down, the five Western journalists there were still mostly confined to sitting in their bureaus in the capital waiting for someone to talk to them, pleading to be let out of their ghetto cages to travel.

Most Western reporting of China was done from Hong Kong. There were thousands of China watchers in the colony: academics, diplomats, spies, businessmen and journalists. They culled clues of what was happening inside China from broadcasts, newspapers, texts of speeches, transcripts of show trials, the scribblings on wall posters and travellers' tales. They exchanged information and traded rumors, and often the wildest rumors were tame by comparison with the phantasmagoric reality of the Cultural Revolution.

Most of the membership of the Hong Kong Foreign Correspondents' Club had been waiting for years to get into China. Almost all of us had a standing visa application filed with the Chinese, and we devoted much effort to wooing the staffers of the Hong Kong bureau of Hsinhua, the official New China News Agency that served as a stand-in for the Peking government in the British Crown Colony.

I was thrown into the frustrating exercise of visa chasing the moment I arrived in Hong Kong in October 1970. There were meetings of the Marco Polo Club, the forum for encounters between the semi-official representatives of Peking in the colony and their Western supplicants. Aside from handshaking and smiling a lot, the activities of the Marco Polo Club required nothing more than listening patiently to speeches in praise of Mao and trying to keep awake during screenings of puerile propaganda films about China's accomplishments under the Great Helmsman.

Most of our wooing, though, was done individually over restaurant tables with Hsinhua officials. There would be much polite chit-chat about "mutual understanding." Every journalist would try to press his national advantage. The Americans argued that if China wanted to emerge from her isolation, Peking would have to attract the attention of Washington, which didn't even recognize the communists as the government of China. The Europeans — the British, the French and the Swedes mostly — reminded the Chinese that, having recognized the Communist government early, they were the new China's oldest friends.

My main argument was that since Canada had recently disavowed the Nationalist regime in Taiwan as the government of China in defiance of the U.S. and had recognized the communists as the sole legitimate rulers of China, we were Peking's newest friend. Canada was about to open its embassy in Peking and this historic widening of China's relationship with the rest of the world should be recorded and publicized.

I argued my case over dim sum, "a bite to please the heart," the lunch tidbits of Canton. At the CBC's expense. I argued my case over lamb stir-fried with noodles and onions, Peking style. Hsinhua's treat. Over braised prawns *à la façon de Shanghai*, I tried to convince the Chinese that allowing the CBC to report on the changes in their country would afford them an entry into the North American information network without having to tackle the delicate political question of hosting Americans who did not deign to recognize their legitimacy.

The men from Peking gave me a gastronomic tour of their country. Sizzling rice soup from Szechuan. But no Szechuan. Mongolian Hotpot. But no Mongolia. The steamed buns of Peking. But no Peking. My hosts and guides always chose for me the most delicious morsels of the delicacies on the table and passed them to me politely with their chopsticks. But no visa. They would never say no. The Chinese are too polite to say no outright, but they know dozens of ways of closing the door without ever quite letting it click shut.

That is what was depressing me in Macao. The door was not slammed shut. But neither was there a glimmer of daylight to be seen.

But by the time my wife and I got back to Hong Kong on Good Friday from our short holiday in Macao, everything had changed. It was if I had fallen into a daydream. Instead of me chasing the Chinese for a visa, they were suddenly after me, imploring me to please, please go to China. And to hurry. I had messages from Hsinhua and urgent messages from the official China Travel Agency waiting for me. My application for a visa to cover the Peking International Table Tennis Tournament, the messages said, had been approved.

Ping-Pong tournament? I had not even heard about a table-tennis tournament in Peking, never mind applying for a visa to cover it. A visa? No time, the man at the travel agency said on Saturday.

"Here are the tickets for you and your cameraman," he said. "Please show up at the Kowloon railway station tomorrow morning. And don't worry about visas."

And so my cameraman, Bob White, and I went to China. Without visas. Also along on the trip was Mark Gayn of the *Toronto Star* and three Americans: John Roderick of the AP, John Rich and Jack Reynolds of the National Broadcasting Company. In a few days, a growing journalistic contingent would join us.

We were to be the main conduits of a new Chinese diplomatic initiative to reach out to the rest of the world that would lead to the admission of China to the United Nations and eventually to the establishment of relations with the United States. The Chinese effort came to be known as "Ping-Pong Diplomacy," the first hesitant step in the long process of opening up China.

The imperial dragon of China, it is said, had nine sons, each different. One is the dragon of burden; you will see him on the base of monuments. Another is the dragon of fantasy, and he sits on roof gables staring up at the sky. One brother appears on bells, another on rice bowls. One is the spirit of rivers, yet another the guardian of jails. The youngest dragon is the custodian of closed doors.

The ninth dragon, the dragon who upstaged his older brothers during the Great Proletarian Cultural Revolution, was suddenly in retreat.

The train from Hong Kong to the Chinese border started from the waterfront of Hong Kong harbor. It rolled past the gleaming towers and the highrise slums of Kowloon, the main population centre on the colony's mainland; across the paddies and past the hills of the New Territories, the hinterland where the colony grew produce that was too perishable to bring in by ship and of too little value to fly in; along the pipeline from China that brought Hong Kong most of its water and made it so vulnerable to pressure from the Chinese hand on the tap; and then, barely an hour later, as the steward served you the last gin and tonic you would have until you left China, into the border hills guarded by a brigade of Gurkhas, those most loyal mercenaries of the defunct British Empire, to Lowu Station and the Chinese border.

At Lowu, a small, pastoral railway station and a short, narrow railway bridge over the river Shumchun, a brook almost, form the border. No passenger trains crossed the bridge. You walked.

This tiny bottleneck was, in effect, China's main gateway to the world. There were few other easy ways of getting into China. There was a weekly Air France flight from Paris and a

Pakistani flight from Karachi. But there were no flights from Hong Kong, or Tokyo, or London, or Vancouver, certainly none from New York, and the traffic across the border with the Soviet Union was all but strangled by the ideological and border disputes between Moscow and Peking.

So isolated was China at the start of the seventies that this tiny gateway was hardly overburdened. In fact, most of the traffic across the bridge was local. There were people working in the colony visiting relatives in Kwangdong province and local peasants, mostly from the lowly Hakka tribe, who farmed land on both sides of the border.

The Hakka women, their eyes hidden behind the short, black veils that hung all around the broad brims of their straw hats, came and went with sniffy disdain for both Mao's soldiers in their shapeless tunics and Her Majesty's Chinese border policemen in their spiffy British colonial short pants and bare knees. So did the amahs of Hong Kong, the six-days-a-week, twenty-four-hours-a-day, $100-a-month, ubiquitous household servants who made the leisurely lifestyle of the rich Chinese and Europeans in the colony possible. The amahs scrimped, saved and cannily played Hong Kong's crazily volatile stock market until they could afford to go home to their villages in Kwangdong, loaded with bags of goodies unobtainable in China, to bask in their munificence as "aunties" to their extended families.

Here and there among the locals were foreigners. Diplomats heading for Peking, an assignment that would test their masochistic mettle under Chinese water torture. Politicians looking for ways to exploit the Maoist mystique. Businessmen trying to turn a buck out of the dross of revolutionary unrest. A sprinkling of overseas Chinese looking for their roots. The only tourists were Western bourgeois devotees of Maoism, pilgrims yearning to worship at the fount of ideological purity. And now, once again, a handful of journalists, the forerunners of a horde panting to capture in words and pictures this newest reincarnation of the alluring Mysterious Orient.

Across the bridge, a few steps from the stiffly starched creases of the defenders of British Hong Kong, a different world. Slouchy guards in slovenly uniforms. Red flags. Yellow stars. Loudspeakers blaring propaganda in slogans and song. Loudspeakers at the customs shed. Loudspeakers on the train. There is no escape. Not even on the plane from Canton to Peking. I try to catch a cat nap. But the moment I rest my head against the bulkhead, a loudspeaker next to my ear blasts me awake. "Workers of the world, unite," the voice bellows into my eardrum. And then comes music. Always the same music and always loud.

There seem to be in this world only two tunes: "The East Is Red" and "Sailing the Seas Depends on the Helmsman." They come in two rousing versions: a shrill choir accompanied by brass, with lots of crashing cymbals, or brass band only. And there is only one form of dress: a shapeless tunic and baggy pants for everyone, men, women and children. And only three colors: green for soldiers, blue for civilians, and, for the more privileged in this officially privilege-free society, an almost elegant alternative: grey.

There is not a skirt to be seen, not a tie, not a bangle, nothing, not even a show of an awareness of sex nor any touch of personal panache that would say: see, I am I and not some interchangeable, indistinguishable part of a mass of a billion parts.

Pinned to every breast, all those hundreds of millions of them, a badge with a picture of the Helmsman. And for every hand, except for a dispensation for those as yet too tiny to clutch it, the *Little Red Book of the Helmsman's Thoughts, Quotations from Chairman Mao Tse-tung*.

In books, Mao. On walls, Mao. In songs, Mao. In poetry, Mao. In the news, Mao. And nights, in lights, more Mao.

Mao, Mao everywhere and not a thought to think.

"A revolution is not a dinner party," Mao says in his *Thoughts*.

But that spring in Peking it was. At least it was for those of us, the table-tennis players and the journalists who had been invited to the party. It was more than just a dinner party; it was a whirl. Dinners of Peking duck. Tea parties. Lavish ten-course banquets. And at every occasion, throat-searing toasts of fiery maotai liquor to "friendship among peoples." Peking resounded to the call of "kanpei," bottoms up.

In the table-tennis arena, too, it was party time. The Chinese were among the best in the world, far ahead of anything that Canadians, the Americans or the Europeans could bring to the green table. And yet, again and again, Western players who knew they would be doing well against the Chinese if they lost by less than a five-point spread found themselves coming closer, and some even won squeakers. And not just in single games. The Canadian women's team managed a tremendous upset. It beat China.

The Canadians knew, however, that their victory was a gift, that the Chinese had for political reasons taken a dive. At times, when the Canadian players fell behind, they would suddenly find themselves unable to lose a point. No matter how bad the shot, it came up a winner. The beneficiaries of this burst of Chinese altruism were not fooled. They knew that even if they had been tempted to pretend that they had done so well on the strength of a sudden burst of hitherto unsuspected talent, the Chinese would not have let them forget what really happened. The Chinese players were letting up in their pursuit of victory at the Ping-Pong table because they wanted to win in a more important arena. They had had their orders from the Party. Those orders were expressed in the slogan the Chinese had made their theme for the tournament: "Friendship is more important than competition."

Ping-Pong diplomacy was clearly a propaganda campaign. But it was meaningful and important propaganda. Peking was signalling that China was about to change, that the leadership, or at least its more rational faction, was looking for a way out of the self-inflicted, almost suicidal frenzy of the Cultural Revolution that Mao had launched five years earlier, and that the only way out was to start by ending the country's isolation from the rest of the world.

The message was reinforced by Premier Chou En-lai at a reception for the foreign table-tennis players and journalists in the Great Hall of the People. Outside, the posters everywhere still called us "running dogs of imperialism." But inside it was tea and sympathy.

The setting is familiar now. The big over-stuffed chairs with the fussy Victorian doilies. The spitoons beside them. The tea mugs covered with lids on the side tables. The interpreter hovering over the Chinese leader and his guests. The high-pitched translation of the pleasantries. It has become the sine qua non ritual of the growing stream of VIP visits to China.

But it was new and news then. The Number 3 in the Chinese hierarchy greeting Westerners, American paper tigers as well as Canadian running dogs, with smiles and kind words. It was the Americans, though, who were the centre of his — and everyone else's — attention. First, a little chit-chat to put the young Americans at ease. In defiance of all that was sacred to the Cultural Revolution, Chou spoke approvingly of rock and roll, that symbol of bourgeois decadence. Then came the important part, a message to the U.S. government: "You have opened a new chapter in the relations of the American and Chinese people," he said. "I am confident that this beginning of our friendship will certainly meet with majority support of our two peoples."

After twenty years of nothing but name calling between Washington and Peking, Chou was suddenly talking about friendship! True, he had said nothing about friendship between governments. But the message to the Americans was clear: Let's talk!

It turned out later that Chou and Mao had tried before to send a signal to Washington. The previous fall, on October 1, China's National Day, Edgar Snow, an American journalist who had become a friend of the communist leaders in the thirties, was invited to stand next to Mao on the reviewing stand at Tiananmen Gate. Mao apparently intended this unprecedented honor to symbolize the importance and urgency he attached to resolving China's differences with the U.S. But the Nixon administration missed the signal.

"They overestimated our subtlety," Henry Kissinger, who was Richard Nixon's national security adviser at the time, says in his memoirs, "for what they conveyed was so oblique that our crude Occidental minds completely missed the point."

This time Chou made sure the obtuse Occidentals couldn't miss the point. And he was eager to get his message spread as widely as possible so it wouldn't be missed. But China's isolation made getting it out difficult. Telex lines were swamped, and phone service was antiquated and poor. But newspaper and agency reporters, by and large, were able to get their dispatches out, and I succeeded in filing radio reports by phone.

But the Chinese wanted more. They were very much aware of the growing power of television and they badly wanted worldwide TV coverage. Unfortunately, they had neither the knowledge nor the means of getting it. They had not a single television transmission link with other countries. No satellites. No land lines. What is more, I could not even ship my TV reports to Hong Kong. Shipping agents said they could not guarantee transshipment of film from the plane that would carry it to Canton to the train that would take it from there to the Hong Kong border. Even if the film did get through, they added, it would take several days.

That was obviously unacceptable. So I set off to carry my film to Hong Kong. The Chinese, eager to help, agreed to allow me to come back once my reports had been filed. But they were not ready to give a similar guarantee of a re-entry permit to the Americans of NBC.

There is nothing that draws journalists closer to each other, especially when they are far from home, than arbitrary, unfair treatment by authority. Out of sympathy for the NBC crew's plight, I volunteered to carry their film to Hong Kong. After all, the CBC was not in direct competition with NBC, and the NBC producer, Jack Reynolds, was a friend of mine. My friendly gesture, however, nearly led to my undoing.

Unbeknownst to me, the CBC had accepted an offer from CBS to let me use their Hong Kong facilities to process my film, edit my reports and send them by satellite to North America. In return, CBS wanted first use of my material in the U.S. To NBC in New York and Hong Kong, that naturally made me a competitor. So now I not only had to cope with the chaotic inefficiencies of China; I was also about to face the implacable efficiency of the dog-eat-dog competition of American network television.

My first hurdle: the lack of a timely connection between the Peking-Canton flight and the Canton-Hong Kong train. Chinese transportation was in such a mess that the once-a-day scheduled flight from the capital to Canton arrived in China's southern metropolis after the daily train to Hong Kong, the destination of many of the Peking plane's passengers, had left. That forced the Hong Kong passengers to spend a night in Canton waiting for the next train.

The situation brought out in me all the worst of the "foreign devil" elements that the Chinese see in all Europeans. I fretted. I fussed. I fumed. A car, I said, I want a car to take me to the border.

I knew better, of course. I knew that there was not really a road to the border, that it was a series of all but impassable cart tracks that made a car trip at best an uncertain venture. But somehow in this business that I am in we are conditioned to keep on trying, to push and never to fail for lack of trying. It's pounded into us early with assignments from city editors to knock on doors of families that have just had someone killed in some particularly gruesome way and to screw up the courage and the gall to ask for a picture of the victim and never to take the first no for a final answer. If you don't ask, if you don't press, you'll never know, that's the dictum.

One never knew. Perhaps, without my knowing anything about it, the Chinese had recently improved the road to Hong Kong and were keeping it a secret. Perhaps I could get my hands on a four-wheel drive vehicle or a half-track even. They eventually did build a road, of course. But not that day, not in time to do me any good.

The next morning, when I arrived in Lowu by train, there was a welcoming party waiting for me. CBS was there. And so was a man from NBC. I handed over the NBC film bag to him, and the race was on. The CBS man pushed me into a Jaguar. The NBC man jumped into another car. The two cars raced down a narrow country road to a golf course at Fanling, near the border. On the golf course, two chartered helicopters.

One for CBS, the other, NBC. I jumped into the CBS chopper and it took off. But the NBC helicopter managed to get a head start on us.

When we landed on the helipad in the centre of Hong Kong, there was a Rolls-Royce waiting for me. From there, we hummed our way through the usual dense Hong Kong traffic to the film lab. And that is where the problems of capitalist competition caught up with me.

The color news film lab in Hong Kong was controlled by the three American networks on a first-come, first-served basis. Others could use the lab, but the Americans had priority. NBC got into the lab first and processed its China films. When CBS tried to put my film in as theirs, NBC argued that it was not CBS film and therefore would have to wait until film they and ABC had to process had gone through the machine. CBS protested but ABC, miffed because they had been shut out of China, sided with NBC. ABC and NBC then tied up the processing machine to keep my film out of the hands of CBS. And so I was forced to cool my heels for several precious hours while the problem was being sorted out between Hong Kong and network headquarters in New York and Toronto.

But we made it. By dawn, when it was time to feed the satellite for the evening's TV news in North America, I had four reports ready: on Chou En-lai and his tea party in the Great Hall of the People; on the Ping-Pong tournament and the political self-sacrifice of China's champion players; on the Cultural Revolution and how it affected factory workers and university students; and one from the Great Wall, which had been closed to foreigners until we were taken there.

"The Wall may now be the preserve of VIPs," I said in my report, "but the fact that it has been opened to table-tennis players and, above all, the fact that the Chinese invited the Americans to come along may mean that one day soon the Great Wall of China may become a crowded tourist attraction."

That evening, the CBC ran the first two of my reports; it planned to save the others and dole them out over the next two days. The "CBS Evening News with Walter Cronkite," though, that same evening did something that was unprecedented in

North American network television. To get across the importance of the message from Peking, CBS ran all four of my
reports, one after another, all on the same program.

Nixon and Kissinger got the message.

"The whole enterprise was vintage Chou Enlai," Kissinger
wrote in his memoirs. "Like all Chinese moves, it had so
many layers of meaning that the brilliantly painted surface
was the least significant part. At its most obvious the invitation to the young Americans symbolized China's commitment to improved relations with the United States; on a
deeper level it reassured — more than any diplomatic communication through any channel — that the emissary who
would now be surely invited would step on friendly soil.

"In many ways the weeks following the Ping-Pong
diplomacy were the most maddening of the entire tortu-
ous process. Only the President and I understood the full
implications of Chou Enlai's move. . . ."

They took Chou up on it and within three months, Kissinger
was on his way on a secret mission to Peking. The American
rapprochement with China would become the foundation of
his reputation as a diplomatic magician.

We were coming back from the Great Wall, impressed. You
can't help but be impressed if you walk on top of the Wall
of China, seven metres thick at its base, topped by a road
six metres wide, wide enough to accommodate five horses
abreast, stirrup to stirrup, a wall nine metres high that, before most of it collapsed from centuries of neglect, used to
snake thousands of miles over hill and dale. It was there before the Christian era was born. It was greater than all the
pyramids of Egypt. It was the only thing that Man had built,
it used to be said, that could be seen from the moon.

So when you have just seen that wall and you are riding in
the rickety bus back to Peking with the current representative

of the people who built it, a man whose ancestors were there when the Mongols breached it and the Ming rebuilt it, you tend to listen to him even if he is a somewhat wimpish and owlish young man — Li is the name — who is only parroting the collected sayings of Mao, the latest ruler of the Middle Kingdom.

Li is telling the occupants of the bus, the Canadian table-tennis team, about the New China, the new morality of the Maoist Man, and Mao's injunction to "serve the people." The talk, inevitably, turns to love, to sex and marriage. Li talks about China's problem of overpopulation, of the efforts to get people, mostly rural people who have always seen having many children as insurance against a poverty-stricken old age, to postpone marriage, preferably until they are thirty, and then limiting themselves to having one child.

"Do you mean to tell me," Derek Walls, the captain of the team, wants to know, "that the Chinese are supposed to abstain from sex through their twenties and that they are actually doing it?"

"Not all of them, of course," Li answers, "but most people are responsive to the teachings of the party and the needs of their society, and they wait for their proper moment."

Walls reacts with sudden, unexpected vehemence. "I was beginning to believe what you were saying about the New Chinese Man," he tells Li. "I was beginning to fall for it. But though I may not know much about politics, one thing I do know something about is sex. And when you tell me that most Chinese are putting off having sex until they are nearly as old as I am, all I can tell you is that you are full of shit."

For a moment, the spell of China is rudely broken. The idea of Mao undertaking to stem the sex drive of the young evokes visions of King Canute trying to stop the tide from rushing in. It brings on titters of disbelief.

But the disbelief is not strong enough to break the allure of China for very long because, for North Americans and Europeans, China is a landscape of the mind that escapes the realities that hold true for their own lives.

It is a dream landscape that has been all but bred into us, a place of willows and bamboo, of bridges that look as if made

from lace, of improbably shaped mountains piercing majes-
tic clouds, delicate scrolls showing a tranquil land peopled by
bearded Confucian sages, a vision of a paradise glimpsed in
the sheen of blue and white porcelain.

Then came the fall of the dream, the end of the serene society celebrated by Marco Polo. If the willow-patterned China
of our imagination was shattered, we knew that it was in large
part because Westerners had come along and raped and plun-
dered the country, forced opium on the Chinese and reduced
them to a nation of starving coolies and peasants, emigrant
purveyors of chop suey, and left them with nothing stronger
than "no tickee, no shirtee" to threaten our well-being. Worse
yet, there were periods, most particularly in the fifties, during and after the Korean War, when many in the West were
scared into half-believing that poor, devastated China consti-
tuted a Yellow Peril that was about to engulf them.

The West felt guilty. Consequently, when the Chinese re-
belled and set out to build a new society along the communist model, many Westerners, even fervent anti-communists,
were understanding. Communism in Europe may not have
been acceptable to them; it was seen by more and more people as a doctrine of tyranny imposed where democracy could
have and should have been allowed to flourish. But somehow
the communism that Mao built seemed tolerable because it
was, after all, a rebellion of cruelly exploited peasants, not
against democracy or any hope of it, but against the hopeless-
ly corrupt rule of warlords. Except for the "Who lost China?"
crowd of the American right, China's peasant revolution was
accepted in the West because it carried no threat to the established Western industrial and political order.

Mao, with that benign look on his moon face, was, after all,
no Stalinist monster. He had not made his way to the top the
way Stalin had done by plotting, scheming and murdering; he
had earned it the hard way. He had fought his way to power in
open battle and was the leader of the Long March, an heroic
odyssey worthy of standing alongside the other great legends
of Chinese history.

If Mao did launch the Cultural Revolution that ate its children as had the Russian one before it — and, of course, the

French Revolution, too — it was argued that Mao's revolution was different. In China, people were not arrested secretly in the middle of the night and then shot in the nape of the neck in some hidden cellar before dawn, as in Moscow. The Red Guards, the ruffians, so the argument went, may have been guilty of brutal excesses. They harassed people, they paraded them in public and harangued and humiliated them by dressing them in dunce's caps, but they did it in daylight. For all the atrocities they committed, they were seen as young revolutionaries mistakenly drunk with the enthusiasm of their cause, not professional secret police killers.

If anything, the Cultural Revolution was aimed at purifying the ideals that Leonid Brezhnev had defiled in the Soviet Union by turning the dictatorship of the proletariat into an institutionalized tyranny in which party bureaucrats became the permanently entrenched ruling class. Mao had perceived what the Yugoslav communist Milovan Djilas had seen and articulated before him, that once the revolution had been achieved and consolidated, it was soon hijacked by a New Class of communist commissars. Hence Mao's Cultural Revolution was a revolution to purify the revolution, to keep it going because revolutions, just like Nathan Detroit's floating crap games, had to keep moving along to stay in business.

Mao's heir, President Liu Shaochi, was purged. So was the party's secretary-general, Teng Hsiaoping. Behind them, legions of party and government officials, managers, scientists, teachers, the whole elite of the country was shoved aside. Universities were closed, schools disrupted and turned into workshops. Rank was abolished in the armed forces. Anyone doing anything that was not strictly manual labor had to take a turn at working on a farm or factory floor to have any hope of ever doing again what it was that he or she was qualified to do. Society was turned on its head. It was chaos.

When Mao saw the anarchy he had created, he pulled back. The army was called to tame the Red Guards. Mao's young storm troopers were disowned and sent out to the countryside to work in communes and rot.

With Mao's blessings, Chou En-lai reduced the speed and intensity of the Cultural Revolution.

The onset of Ping-Pong diplomacy became the signal that the greatest chaos of the Cultural Revolution had run its course. China was seen as trying to enter a new stage of tranquillity and development. Mao had retained the Mandate of Heaven, and China became to the Western bourgeois imagination what the Soviet Union had been to many in the West in the twenties and thirties before the realities of the Stalinist tyranny had disillusioned and embittered them. A new Western delusion about China was being born in which the elegance of Confucian cobalt blue was replaced with a robust Maoist red.

A new tranquil and serene China was being presented to us. The returning Old China hands accepted it readily because the last time they had seen China — in most cases before 1950 — it had been in turmoil. Starvation and corruption were everywhere. Women turned to prostitution to feed their children. Children were being killed at birth because their parents had no hope of feeding them. Now, though many people were still in rags, no one seemed to be starving. And everywhere there were beguiling apple-cheeked, healthy children and government guides to explain how much conditions had improved since Liberation in 1949.

The New China hands like me were also impressed and, of course, even more impressionable. My last assignment before China had been to Calcutta and Dacca, cities that are showplaces of human misery and the degradations of abject poverty, places that batter Western complacency and scar all but the most impervious conscience. By comparison, China seemed caring and almost prosperous.

I was not blinded, of course. I knew that all was not as it seemed to be. I was suspicious of our guides and translators. As someone who spoke four European languages, who could always find someone in any European country who spoke one of them, I was frustrated by my inability to speak Chinese. Yet I knew quite well that even if I had spoken Chinese, it wouldn't have done me much good. I knew from my experiences of the communist society to which I had belonged that no Chinese in his right mind would tell me what he really thought. Not in private and certainly not in the presence of a scary television camera and the omnipresent official guides. But there was enough to see and much of what we saw was different not only from Marxist models elsewhere but also from what I knew of Chinese elsewhere, in Hong Kong and throughout the rest of Southeast Asia.

I reported what I saw and what I was told, which, in itself was both interesting and telling. Even the disingenous Chinese propaganda. Inevitably, the holes in the legend showed and, at times, I would stumble into the real China, sometimes by accident.

On June 21, 1971, the Canadian ambassador in Peking was called to the Chinese foreign ministry, where the director of the ministry's information department expressed concern on behalf of the government of the People's Republic of China about an unfortunate incident that had occurred to a citizen of Canada, one Joseph Schlesinger, a week earlier on the Shuan Wang Agricultural Commune, in Shansi province, in the county of Wei Nan, near the city of Sian. Chinese officials accompanying the above-mentioned Canadian citizen, the foreign ministry spokesman said, had regretfully failed in their task of protecting him.

Ambassador Ralph Collins assured the Chinese diplomat that no harm had come to Mr. Schlesinger and that neither the Canadian government nor Mr. Schlesinger attached any blame whatsoever to the Chinese officials involved. Throughout, His Excellency, in the best manner and tradition of the Canadian diplomatic service, kept a straight face.

And so ended the affair known to the Canadian community in China at the time as The Shit Pit Incident.

To put it plainly, I fell into it.

The story of my misadventure came to be retold to newly arrived Canadian correspondents as a cautionary tale. To Old China hands, it was a perfect example of a newcomer who literally didn't know China from a hole in the ground.

We had been on a trip to north-central China to visit the caves of Yenan, where the Chinese communists, led by Mao, had consolidated their positions after being hounded by the Nationalist forces across thousands of miles in 1934–35 in what became known as the Long March. We had been shown the cave in which Mao slept, his bed, the house in which he worked, his desk, his brush and inkwell, his calligraphy and endless exhibits of photographs of the Great Man.

It was fascinating but it wasn't news. Since we were one of the first Western television crews in China since the Cultural Revolution had started, just about anything we aimed our camera at was acceptable as a novelty even if it was not news by any traditional definition. But there were limits. Still, after more than two months of crisscrossing China, we had not yet managed to get a story on how a Chinese commune farm worked, so we humored the Chinese officials in Yenan by filming Mao memorabilia ad nauseam. As a reward, they finally consented to take us to an agricultural commune. Chosen by them, of course. On the way to it, we passed farms that seemed interesting, where peasants were threshing grain by hand with flails. But our guides wouldn't stop. They were ashamed of the backwardness of Chinese agriculture and were determined to show us the most modern farm they could find.

The Shuan Wang commune was the pride of Shansi. None of your old-fashioned hand threshing; Shuan Wang had a threshing machine, a steam-engine model that could not have been much older than half a century or so.

The irrigation system was even older. The ditches were fed by a water wheel driven by water buffalos. As my cameraman, Brian Hosking, was filming the irrigation system, I was taking still pictures of the wooden water wheel. I crouched to get a better shot, stepped back . . . and fell into the pit. It was filled with two metres of nightsoil — otherwise known as organic fertilizer — that was distributed through the same irrigation ditches as the water.

I went down. Right down. Over my head. I resurfaced by myself (certainly none of my friends was about to make any move to touch, never mind rescue me). I came up sputtering, oozing manure. I still consider it one of the minor triumphs of my life that, after a few moments of trying to catch my breath, I was able to laugh at the ridiculousness of my situation. So did my cameraman and other Canadian reporters. But our Chinese hosts were distraught.

As I rolled around in the irrigation ditch trying to wash off the worst of it, our interpreter kept repeating: "We have failed in our work. We have failed to take into account the teachings of Chairman Mao."

"A shower," I yelled. "Take me to a shower."

That shows how little I knew about Chinese farms. In all the 356 households of the Shuan Wang commune there was not a single shower. When I needed a shower more than I had ever needed one in my life, or was ever likely to, I had to do with the Chinese bringing me a relay of half a dozen small enamel washbowls of lukewarm water and a stack of hand-sized towels. By the time I was reasonably clean, my hosts had a Chinese peasant's best Sunday outfit ready for me: blue cotton pants, white shirt, underpants held up by a drawstring, all at least a size too small for me, and plastic sandals.

They had also procured a doctor who gave me a tetanus shot, stuffed me full of pills and marvelled that the city boy from the capitalist West was not prostrate from nausea. As a father who used to have a hard time changing his children's diapers, so did I.

The Chinese guides, meanwhile, were still wringing their hands over what had happened to me. They took my soiled clothes, shoes, camera, wallet and notebook away to be cleaned. After I had returned to my hotel and had a real shower, they brought my things back. They had not, they said, been able to fix my camera because the area's camera repairman happened to be out of town. But everything else was there, including my laundered money, my bleached notes and my belt and shoes as stiff as boards. I threw the shoes and the belt into the wastebasket.

(When I was leaving the next morning, a hotel employee came running after me holding up the shoes and belt, insisting that I take them with me. It took fifteen minutes and a good deal of eloquence to convince him, the hotel management and

our interpreter that the shoes and the belt were of no more use
to me and had not been left behind as an insulting gratuity.)

A couple of hours after the shower, there was a knock
on my door. An official delegation had come to talk to me.
There was a man from the foreign ministry, another from
the provincial revolutionary committee, an official from the
commune brigade committee and an interpreter. They had
come to apologize, they said, because they had failed me.
My accident had shown shortcomings in the work of the interpreters, guides and members of the commune. They maintained they should have known that foreigners like me would
know nothing about Chinese fertilizing methods and should
have posted warning signs at the pit. I told them that it was
all my fault, that signs in Chinese, or, for that matter, since I
was moving backward, even in English would not have done
me any good.

The Chinese would have none of it. If they had studied
their *Little Red Book* properly, such an accident would never have happened. I didn't know how Mao's *Thoughts* might
have averted what happened to me, but I assured them that it
wasn't serious. They said it was. I said I had fallen into similar
stuff before, even if only metaphorically, and that I thought
it was all rather funny. They said they didn't. I suspect they
must have had a hard time keeping themselves from breaking out in giggles, but they didn't even crack a smile. Gloom
prevailed.

Finally, I found a solution, a way for the Chinese to save
face and faith. I invoked in their defence the name of the
Great Helmsman himself. Didn't Chairman Mao once say,
I asked, that a fall in the pit is a gain in wit?

The invocation of Mao's name seemed to give the comic aspects of the incident political respectability. It was as if
my visitors suddenly had been given dispensation to relax.
First, there were small, uncertain grins. Then, when they all
looked at each other and saw that they were all grinning, they
allowed themselves to break out in laughter. We laughed, we
shook hands and they even accepted my offer of a drink of
whisky. We parted and they went away happy.

Mao's *Thoughts* had done its work once again.

Morning in Peking. The bicycles come sweeping down the avenues, thousands of them, slowly, all at about the same speed, feet pushing pedals with the flowing deliberation of shadowboxing, a hum of tires swishing on the pavement punctuated here and there by a creak of an unoiled chain or the squeak of a pedal, a stream of wheels flowing. No one races. No one darts out of the stream.

No one in Mao's China seems to be in a hurry. Not the man pulling the two-wheel cart piled high with boxes that by all the rules of physics should come tumbling down but never do. Not the woman in the flooded paddy bending over again and again to plant rice seedlings. Nor the workers tending the looms in the textile factory. Life is hard. So is work. But both are slow. It is almost as if the Chinese had adapted to their workaday lives the art of T'ai Chi, the slow-motion exercises of balance and poise that train the muscles by relaxation rather than effort. It gives the New China some of the look of the mythical Old China as though the reign of Mao had returned the Chinese to Confucian serenity, given them the opportunity to be their old selves again.

But I know better. Anyone who has seen the Chinese in other, less repressive settings than China — in Taipei, in Hong Kong, in Singapore, or, for that matter, Vancouver — knows better. By contrast with China itself, the Chinese enclaves of Southeast Asia are full of raw energy, of jostling crowds, rushing delivery men, chanting hawkers, the crazy hustle of traffic, the frenzy of the stock exchange, calculating fingers dancing lickety-split across the clickety-clacking beads of the abacus, the racket of jackhammers, of wrecking and building, everything always on the move.

The Chinese of Taiwan, Hong Kong and Singapore are in a way well suited as control groups to test the effects of the Maoist experiment. The parallels between China and its offshoots are striking. Singapore may have a democratic electoral system and the complication of racial groups other than

the Chinese, but it is run much like China by the fiat of a
single powerful figure. Its prime minister, Lee Kuan Yew,
is a patriarchal ruler, a Mao *sans* ideology. In Taiwan, instead of the Communist Party, they have the failed Chinese
alternative, the Kuomintang (National People's Party) of Sun
Yat-sen and Chiang Kai-shek. The dwindling remnants of
the Kuomintang run the island as outside occupiers, much
like the Manchus once ran China, with a heavy hand but
efficiently. In Hong Kong, the British colonial government,
though clearly the most alien of these regimes, is also the
least intrusive. The British govern the colony but do not
run it; the blind dollar does. The *fin d'empire* detachment
of the British makes Hong Kong an almost pure yardstick
of the untrammelled essence of being Chinese. The nominal
overlay of British power acts as a mere catalyst that gives
the Chinese in the colony the freedom to be uninhibitedly
themselves.

There is nothing serene about the people crowding
Kowloon's Nathan Road on Hong Kong's mainland or
the crowded tiny sweatshops in Wong Tai Sin churning
out furiously whatever the market will take this week with
nimble hands and quick minds, ever ready to turn to whatever it will take to make a living next week. Hong Kong is
a hard place that shows little mercy for the timid and the
slothful.

But if you think it is only the crass and cruel spur of
capitalism that makes this tiny economic powerhouse hustle
and bustle, then look again, look at Hong Kong not working,
just enjoying itself: the thousands of restaurants resounding
to the noise of boisterous families and the hubbub of teeming
street fairs; the rites of filial piety of *sao mu*, the sweeping of the
graves, which after the tombs have been properly decorated
with burning candles, food to keep the dead ancestors from
starving and money (frugally phony, of course) to help them
pay their way in heaven, turn into noisy family picnics by the
gravesides with the food, with typical Chinese unsentimental
common sense, retrieved from the presumably none too hungry dead; the clicking of mah-jong tiles; the gay chatter of the
young hikers on a ferry heading for a trek on Lantau Island;

the bedlam of firecrackers, crashing of gongs and clanging of bells at Chinese New Year; the smoke of smouldering joss sticks at the Buddhist temple, and, here and there, the faint, sweet whiff of opium; and, always and everywhere, the aroma of food, of Peking duck and Beggar's Chicken, stewed snake and shark's fin soup, fish stomachs and sea slugs, bear's paws and hundred-year-old (actually much more recently pickled) eggs, or perhaps only an amah's bowl of rice topped with a scrap of fish steamed with a few drops of soya sauce, a sliver of ginger and shreds of scallion; the parade of cheongsams, the tight, proudly worn, side-slit-to-the-thigh Chinese dresses that are a woman-watcher's delight; the belching businessmen who wash down their food not with tea, but with slugs of cognac drunk from water glasses; or the flashy vulgarity of the rich at the Happy Valley racecourse unabashedly showing off their good fortune.

The Chinese of Hong Kong certainly didn't learn the loudness of their enjoyment, their ribald gusto from the snooty civil servants London sent out to rule them. What drives them all is Chinese exuberance, the capacity of living life to its fullest.

The comparison between China and its offspring abroad makes it clear that the difference between them is energy. The Chinese of Hong Kong, of Taiwan, of Singapore expend energy prodigiously because it gives them the opportunity to improve their lives. People inside China conserve energy to survive. So what at first blush looked like traditional Chinese serenity turns out to be more a lethargy of resignation than a calmness of souls at peace, the result of Maoist Man being deprived of any sense of individuality or chance of spontaneity.

I watched once as the crème de la crème of Maoism, 10,000 of them, waited for hours in the Great Hall of the People for Chou En-lai to show up with a guest, Romania's President Nicolae Ceauşescu. I fidgeted, I stood up, I left the hall, had tea, came back, fumed, tried unsuccessfully to draw out some of the Chinese, talked to other miffed foreigners and went out again. But the Chinese officials stayed put in their seats, quietly, patiently, unfidgeting. In other lands there would at least have been the buzz of impatience, in most, yells or whistles of displeasure and restlessness, a loosening of collars and ties, people standing in groups chatting and grumbling, or retreating to a bar, or even just giving up and leaving. Not here. And when Chou and Ceauşescu finally did show up more than two hours behind schedule, there was not a word of apology or even explanation.

Even those most spontaneous of humans, little children, are quickly enveloped into the strait-jacket of Maoism. In a nursery school in Shanghai, a troop of tots sings and dances before a group of foreigners. "There is a gold sun in Peking," the children sing, "no, it's not the sun, it's Chairman Mao." The kids are cute. The foreign visitors are enchanted. I spot an odd hand movement the children are making as if they were pitching a ball. "What are they doing?" I ask, knowing the Chinese are not given to the overhand pitches of baseball or cricket. The reply: "They are tossing grenades at the imperialists."

Where Hong Kong is a profusion of color, of lipstick and silk, of flowers and fruit, of flickering paper lanterns and cascades of twitching neon signs, a place where the laundry that hangs from apartment balconies, on poles like flags, gives even grim tenements a colorful look, Peking is grey, without so much as a blade of grass, everything covered with a film of sandy dust brought in by winds from the Gobi desert. What color there is to be found is either the imperial red and gold of the Forbidden City, the red of communist propaganda, or the rare appearance of flowers for ritualistic occasions: huge bouquets wrapped in plastic to be handed ceremoniously to distinguished personages or paper ones waved by crowds for such great occasions as, of all things, the arrival of the Peruvian minister of fisheries. Peru, it turns out, has earned China's approval by extending the limit of its territorial waters to 200 miles and arresting American fishermen caught in this zone. For a hero like the Peruvian fisheries minister, the Maoists are even willing to forget for a day their antipathy towards skirts. Several hundred young women in colorful dresses are at Peking airport to dance for the Peruvian.

If there is no spontaneous energy or joy in Peking, there is great strength of purpose. But it is a madcap purpose, Mao's single-minded pursuit of the perfectly egalitarian society.

At Peking's Tsinghua University, the few students left — fewer than 3,000 out of the 12,000 who were enrolled at the start of the Cultural Revolution — spend half their time doing manual work in workshops to improve their credentials as upstanding proletarians and much of the other half listening to ideological lectures. When they graduate, they are likely to be nothing more than sterile ideological drones. At the Tientsin heavy-machine building factory, workers design the machinery and engineers work on the plant floor. Once the workers learn something of the engineers' trade by trial and error at great cost to plant efficiency, it will presumably be their turn to be purged for having become tainted by the bourgeois pretensions of professional competence.

Mao's Great Proletarian Cultural Revolution is to politics what the perpetual motion machine is to science: to keep it going you have to pour in more energy than you get out of it. In short, it is a hoax.

Tiananmen Square, May Day, 1971, the last time Mao Tsetung would appear on top of the gate of the Heavenly Peace from which twenty-one years earlier he had declared the triumph of communism in China. He stood there, a tiny figure, looking for all the world like a Lilliputian replica of the giant portrait of himself hanging below him.

The square was packed and churning with half a million people, thousands from Hunan cheering in that corner, a cast of hundreds from Mongolia dancing here, immense choirs everywhere singing a multitude of chants, actors declaiming propaganda through overloaded loudspeakers, acrobats twirling, dozens of different shows going on at the same time, a crowd so vast that the voices of several thousand people yelling in unison would peter out into nothingness in the noisy vastness of the square. Above it all, the thunder and crackle of fireworks, hundreds of them, exploding in all sizes, shapes and colors, casting an eerie light over this teeming anthill of worshipful humanity.

Pushing our way through the crowd from the gate to film the surging masses in the square, I looked back towards the rostrum. All I could see now of the Great Helmsman above his portrait was a slow, feeble wave of a brightly lit dot of an arm, waning power beckoning, it seemed, from the edge of the grave.

Poor Mao, the perfect revolutionary disillusioned by the imperfections of what he had wrought, thrashing around vainly to save his revolution's egalitarian purity and creating only chaos. The disciple of dialectic materialism had set himself up as a god and now, as has happened to overweening deities ever since Zeus and his divine playmates frolicked on Mount Olympus, he was ripe for the fall.

All those Mao buttons, the *Little Red Book*s, the statues everywhere would soon end up on the trash heap of history. The signs of Mao's ideological waning were slowly becoming visible.

At the Fusham pottery plant, where at the height of the Cultural Revolution they produced nothing but busts of Mao, they turned to other things. First, cautiously, they put away their Mao moulds and started making safely non-political figurines of animals. Then, emboldened, they defied Mao's ban on The Four Olds: old habits, old culture, old customs and old ideas. They turned to Chinese mythology and history and went back to producing what sold, the traditional figures of "emperors, kings, generals and beauties" that Mao passionately hated. Finally one day, the twenty-foot statue of the Great Helmsman that had guarded the entrance to the Fusham plant throughout the Cultural Revolution was taken away.

"Heaven's mandate," the Duke of Chou said 3,000 years earlier, "is not easily preserved because Heaven is hard to rely upon."

But sometimes Heaven relents.

Teng Hsiaoping grins as he stands dwarfed beside a robustly pregnant Margaret Trudeau. He knows he has created a sensation. It is October 1973, and Teng's tour of squiring Pierre Trudeau and his wife around China is his first international outing on his own since he surfaced a few months ago from six years in disgrace as a "Capitalist Roader." The Number 2 villain of the Cultural Revolution is now a vice-premier, the Number 2 in the government. Everyone wonders what it means and how far it will go.

Teng's fame — and part of the reason for his downfall in the Cultural Revolution — stems from a pronouncement the Duke of Chou would have been proud of: "I don't care whether a cat is black or white as long as it catches mice." For Mao, of course, this was heresy. In Mao's China, ideology was all. Cats that were not spotlessly red did not live long enough to get to catch mice.

And Teng very nearly didn't. His boss, Liu Shaochi, the Number 1 Capitalist Roader, was murdered. His son, Teng Bufang, was almost killed, too. He was beaten and tortured by Mao's gangster Red Guards who were trying to force him to testify against his father. When they had finished, they left Bufang lying unconscious in a room with a locked door and a conveniently open window.

Somehow, Teng Bufang ended up four floors below the open window with his back broken. Though he was denied medical treatment and should have died, Bufang survived. Eventually, Teng Hsiaoping managed to get his son transferred to the prison compound where he was being held. The father nursed his son, massaged him and bathed him in hot baths, hoping to get movement back to his legs. It didn't work. Teng Bufang was permanently crippled.

The elder Teng would remember for the rest of his days who it was that had done this terrible thing to his son: young thugs, ostensibly political idealists, taking advantage of political turmoil to wreak havoc on China's stability.

"We should never forget how cruel our enemies are," he would say two decades later of another wave of young political activists. "For them we should not have an iota of forgiveness."

By the late eighties China has changed so much it is unrecognizable. Almost everywhere cats are busy catching mice. The country has soaked up some of the energy of Hong Kong and some of its corruption, too. There is money jangling in millions of pockets and chickens in pots that once held only thin rice gruel. Mao lies buried not far from a Kentucky Fried Chicken restaurant. China has jeans and rock, luxury hotels and capitalists. The government still has its boom boxes everywhere blaring propaganda into the streets, but youngsters carry their own boom boxes around now and they certainly don't play "The East Is Red." In movie houses, instead of revolutionaries *Taking Tiger Mountain By Storm* as they did when Mao's wife, Chiang Ching, was the ruthless cultural czar of China, Rambo, the imperialist mercenary killer, guns down scores of evil-looking oriental commies and gets away with it.

Even the transcription of Chinese characters into the Latin alphabet has been changed. Peking is now known as Beijing, Canton is Guangzhou, Sian is now written as Xian and Mao Tse-tung is in the history books as Mao Zedong. Teng Hsiaoping, the survivor, has become Deng Xiaoping, the supreme leader of China, the man who freed the cats to catch mice and the newest darling of most western Sinophiles.

But when Deng tried to leash the cats again, they started chafing as cats will once they get used to hunting mice.

One day, Deng Xiaoping looked out over Tiananmen Square and saw tens of thousands of young people challenging the prevailing order, requisitioning buses as barricades, defying the party, cocking a snoot at the army and threatening the most sacred of his Four Cardinal Principles, the People's Democratic Dictatorship. The young, who knew nothing about the sufferings of their elders before the Revolution and after, were talking again of ideological purity, this time even of importing the heretical principles of bourgeois democracy. They were also complaining loudly about growing corruption among party officials. Deng himself was under fire for having had his son named chairman of the Welfare Commission for the Handicapped, a post the crippled Bufang allegedly used for his personal enrichment.

Schools, factories and offices were closing down. Once again, there was chaos in the country.

If most of the young have no remembrance, the old often have nothing but. To an octogenarian like Deng, nothing was new; in one form or another he had seen everything. He knew that if there is one thing that is constant in China, it is that it is prone to disunity and chaos. Ever since he was a child, when the last of the Manchu emperors was overthrown, China was torn by war, revolution and unrest. But he, Deng Xiaoping, was able to break that cycle to give China a decade of unparallelled peace and prosperity. In his ten years in power, the gross national product, the wealth of China, had doubled. And this was only the start. According to his plan, the national output would double again in the next twelve years. By the year 2050 — yes, he had a sixty-year plan — China would be a developed nation. A developed nation of 1.5 billion people would be not just the biggest nation on earth but quite possibly also the most powerful.

But Deng believed firmly that what he called "this unbeatable achievement" would not come about if the students in the square and their accomplices within the party got their way. He was convinced that above all China needed stability and discipline. As far as he was concerned, more freedom only meant more anarchy; that's the way it has always been in China. He was prepared, he is reported to have said several years before the events of Tiananmen, to "kill 200,000 in exchange for twenty years of stability."

So Deng Xiaoping did what Mao had done twenty years earlier when faced with the unruliness of the young. He called in the People's Liberation Army to teach the youngsters a lesson. But where the army had restored order in the late sixties by packing off the rebellious Red Guards to pig farms to reflect knee-deep in mud on their sins and errors, this time it shed the blood of the young in the sacred precincts of Tiananmen.

In a way, the students were more threatening to Deng than the Red Guards. The Guards had been believers who had gone astray and could be reformed. But the students had committed the most serious ideological sin of all: not believing, not having any ideology at all.

"They were the most selfish generation since 1949," Liu Binyan, a Chinese dissident journalist who once had been a believer, wrote afterwards. "They were cynical, contemptuous of all authority, had no hope of nor good feeling toward the Communist party. They did not think China had a future; nor did they think they had a responsibility for their country and society.

"However, precisely because they valued their own feelings and individuality so highly, they could, compared to previous generations, least tolerate the suppression of individuality, the limits on freedom."

And so, says Liu, once the students had made a free choice, "they were willing to sacrifice anything."

Wang Weilin was one of them.

You've seen Wang Weilin. You couldn't have helped but see him unless you were on the moon in June of 1989. And you are not likely to forget him. Ever.

Wang Weilin was the young man who was pictured in every newspaper and on every television screen except in China and like-minded countries, standing in front of a line of oncoming tanks in Beijing, daring the lead tank to run him over. When the tank hesitated and stopped, he climbed on it and tried to talk to the crew through chinks in its armor. Friends finally led him away.

The picture of Man against Machine fascinated us because an unarmed human being, however brave, is obviously no match for a tank. No human being can stop fifty tons of moving steel with bare hands. Much to our delight, Wang succeeded in stopping it by strength of will. He demonstrated that the monstrous machine was ultimately only as strong as the will of the humans inside and that his will was stronger than theirs.

But this particular machine represented the will of the state. The will of the state, the Chinese government's order to its army, was to crush the uprising. So when this one tank crew balked at crushing Wang Weilin, it became a symbol of what might have been. First one tank stopping, then the line behind it, then other units, the whole army and, finally, the whole system coming apart.

It had happened that way many times before. It happened to Czar Nicholas II when his soldiers refused to put down unrest in Petrograd in March 1917. It was to happen to Nicolae Ceauşescu in Romania in December 1989, when his soldiers refused orders to shoot in Timişoara. And it happened to many an autocrat in between. The soldiers of the Shah of Iran were out in the streets of Tehran for months killing demonstrators in 1979. Then one day they just quit shooting. They had had enough. For the Shah, it was over.

No machine of repression, however powerful, can survive when the people on whom it has relied to enforce its will have lost theirs. The pictures of Wang Weilin and the tanks held out the hope that the moment of change had arrived in China.

It had not. It was not that Wang's victory was an isolated incident. In the days leading up to the crackdown in Tiananmen, others had stopped army vehicles with their bodies, and many army units had refused to act against resisting civilians. But in the end, Deng and the other members of the party's Gang of the Old found army units that did not flinch at running over civilians, shooting at their own people and keeping the lid on afterwards.

The reasons they did are many. Mainly, though, the sit-down nature of the demonstrations had given the government time to organize the crackdown. The soldiers they picked were apparently mostly country boys. Their families would have done well under Deng's economic reforms. They probably cared little about politics, knew next to nothing of the students' cause and would not naturally have been sympathetic to the students — who enjoyed advantages no soldier had — or to the city slickers who supported them.

The Chinese government, of course, insists there was only one reason: the rising in Beijing was an isolated incident not in tune with the country. In any case, the tanks won. And Wang Weilin lost. Hong Kong newspapers reported he had been arrested. Other reports said friends later saw him on Chinese television among a group of those arrested as "counter-revolutionaries and political hooligans." All had their heads shaven and were reported to have been slated for execution. The government has denied executing him.

Wang Weilin was nineteen years old.

Afterwards, Deng found many excuses for what he and the army had done. The main one was that they had saved the country from counter-revolutionary rebellion. But Deng was also aware that there was more to the turmoil in Tiananmen Square than that.

"This storm," he told the soldiers who had carried out his orders, "was independent of Man's will."

A curious remark for a twentieth-century leader to make — even for a Marxist. Marxists believe in the iron law of history, that history is inexorably driven by impersonal forces unleashed by changes in the modes of production. But Deng was hardly likely to concede that the rebelling students may have been the standard-bearers of the next stage in Marx's dialectic process of history.

Deng probably had Mencius rather than Marx on his mind. The Chinese sage, a follower of Confucius, taught 2,300 years ago that popular uprisings were a test of a ruler's right to govern. If he was overthrown, it was because he was a bad ruler and Heaven had withdrawn its mandate. When he was asked about the murder of a king named Chou Xin, Mencius replied: "I have heard that a fellow called Chou was put to death, but not that a sovereign was killed."

In the Mencian view, a rebellion is automatically justified

if it is successful. By the same token, if the ruler manages to suppress the revolt, his victory is proof that he has retained the Mandate of Heaven. So Deng appears to have been only reminding the soldiers that in taming the storm they had the Will of Heaven on their side.

But Mencius also taught that there was a tougher test for rulers than just surviving the next uprising: "There is only one way to hold power and that is to hold the people. And there is only one way to hold the people's hearts and that is to provide them with what they like, and to refrain from imposing upon them what they loathe."

Loathing is the child born of the blood of Tiananmen.

CHAPTER IX

Think, in this batter'd Caravanserai
Whose portals are alternate Night and Day,
How Sultan after Sultan with his Pomp
Abode his destined Hour, and went his way.

Omar Khayyám

The admiral and the mullah were locked in a battle of politeness. I couldn't hear what they were saying because I was already seated on the admiral's plane and they were outside on the tarmac. Not that it mattered. Since I don't speak Farsi, I would not have understood a word even if I had heard them. Yet I could tell what they were saying. I could see it in their gestures, their facial expressions, their body movements. The admiral, dressed in the gold-trimmed white uniform of the Imperial Iranian Navy, was offering the bearded mullah in his dark robes and white turban seats for him and his retainers aboard his Navy plane to Teheran. Thank you for your kindness, the mullah appeared to be saying, but I could not possibly displace those poor people on your plane; they have already suffered enough. I appreciate the generosity of your reluctance, the admiral seemed to be replying, but surely your presence in Teheran would help so many more of those poor devils than just the few you would displace on the plane. They bowed, they smiled and exchanged a few more verbal flourishes until the cleric spread his hands outward in resigned acceptance. The admiral nodded to a subordinate, and, while the mullah delicately turned his back on the scene, three unhappy, protesting passengers, homeless refugees who had waited in line for hours on the sun-baked Tabas airstrip to get seats aboard the plane, were hauled off by sailors. The mullah and the admiral got aboard, and we took off.

There was one other thing that had been evident in the encounter at the airstrip: however much the admiral and the mullah had smiled, you could tell by the stiffness of their smiles and the exaggerated politeness of their gestures that they detested each other. They were, in fact, at war with each other for the future of Iran, a war whose outcome was as yet uncertain (which was probably the main reason why they were so elaborately polite), and they had come to Tabas to do political battle.

Tabas no longer existed. Four days earlier, it had been a palm-filled oasis at the edge of the vastness of Iran's Dasht-e Kavir, the Great Salt desert, an ancient caravan town of carpet weavers and date growers. Then, on the night of September 16, 1978, an earthquake flattened Tabas and killed more than half of its 13,000 people. It was over the ruins of the town and the misery of its survivors that the battle was being fought.

Shah Mohammed Reza Pahlavi, whose regime was in desperate trouble after his troops had killed hundreds of anti-government demonstrators — by some estimates as many as 3,000 — eight days earlier in Teheran's Jaleh Square, saw in the Tabas tragedy an opportunity to demonstrate that he and his army cared about his people. To make amends for Black Friday, as the massacre of Jaleh Square came to be known, the Shah sent cargo planes to Tabas with troops armed with shovels, food and field kitchens, doctors and medicine, tents and blankets. The army and the Red Lion and Sun Society, the Iranian counterpart of the Red Cross, set up a tent city for the wounded and the homeless at an airstrip on the edge of town.

But 300 metres from the army encampment, there was another camp, literally the enemy camp, a parallel rescue operation in direct competition with the government. In the tents here, instead of portraits of the Shah, there were pictures of an old man with a white beard and a dark turban scowling from beneath a bush of heavy eyebrows. His name — then unknown outside the Middle East — was Ruhollah al-Mussawi ibn Mustafa ibn Mustafa ibn Ahmad al-Mussawi al-Khomeini.

The Khomeini camp at Tabas had field kitchens and a field hospital just like the army did. While the Ayatollah's supporters had no planes, they did have trucks. The trucks brought from nearby towns a commodity that was in short supply in the government camp: water that was desperately needed in temperatures of 35 degrees and above. The army also was unable to match the competition in another vital way: the Khomeini camp had enough clergymen to pray over the thousands of dead, who had to be buried quickly in the broiling heat, and to preach their political message as they did so.

For the mullahs, it was a unique opportunity. They had been banned from all political activity by martial law. But here in Tabas they could defy the Shah's edict because they knew the government would not dare to arrest them while they were burying the dead and helping the survivors. So they used the occasion to snipe at the government. They criticized the government because it had not brought in enough bulldozers to search for the dead. When it did, they charged that the Shah's men would bulldoze the ruins of Tabas, thereby desecrating the bodies buried in them. The Shah, when he came to Tabas to be filmed being thanked by grateful survivors, was once again on the defensive. He had to promise he would do nothing about clearing the rubble of Tabas and rebuilding the town without consulting its people and their religious leaders.

Even though by now Khomeini's name was on a million lips, Iranians still knew very little about the man. His fame rested on being the Shah's most bitter and uncompromising opponent. But he had been out of the country for thirteen years.

Khomeini had been an obscure teacher in Qom, a city of mosques and religious schools, until 1963 when he organized anti-Shah demonstrations — among other places, in Jaleh Square. The protests were brutally suppressed at a cost of 3,000 lives. The Shah had Khomeini arrested. The mullah might have been executed if Ayatollah Kazem Shariat-Madari, a popular and moderate leader whom Khomeini would later destroy, had not arranged his promotion to Ayatollah, the highest rank of Shia clerics. Executing an Ayatollah, a "marja-e taqlid," a source of emulation to all Shiites, a man who had risen to the state of "ijtehad," the vision that allows him to interpret the Koran, would have been politically costly. So Khomeini was sent into exile, ending up in the holy city of Najaf in Iraq.

Khomeini continued calling for the overthrow of the Shah from abroad. For years, as Iran prospered because of the oil boom, his voice was all but unheard. But as dissatisfaction with the Shah grew because of the heavy-handedness of his regime, the cruelty of SAVAK, his secret police, the ostentatiousness of his court, the corruption of his courtiers, and the blatantly uneven distribution of Iran's fabulous wealth, Iranians were once more ready to listen to Khomeini.

The Ayatollah got his message through by ingenious use of an indispensable tool of the contemporary mosque, the audio-cassette recorder. Electronic gadgets have greatly eased the lives of muezzins, mosque callers, who, before Sony and Panasonic came along, used to have to climb to the top of their minarets five times a day to call the faithful to prayer. Now cassette players and loudspeakers do the work for them, blaring forth "La-ila-ha Il-lal-lah" (There is no God but Allah), more loudly than any muezzin ever could. The Ayatollah's supporters smuggled recordings of his fiery sermons into Iran and then made thousands of copies that were passed into every corner of the land.

Khomeini's message from outside came through more clearly than the muted and often suppressed voices of those who were battling the dictatorship at home. His slogans — "The Shah must go" and "Out with the Americans" — were more easily understood than the more complicated reforms advocated by other mullahs and opposition politicians. The more the Shah cracked down, the more appealing the Ayatollah's uncompromising message had become. By 1978, Khomeini had become the undisputed leader of what for years had been a fractious and largely ineffective opposition.

Teheran that summer of 1978 was a boom town. Its hotels were crowded with foreign businessmen. Just about every snake-oil salesman in the world had come through town trying to pick up a few crumbs from Iran's hoard of billions of petro dollars. The world's biggest corporations, even whole countries — Canada included — were trying to do the same. The money had been pouring into Iran ever since the Shah and the Saudis engineered the oil shortage of 1973 that quadrupled oil prices almost overnight. Construction cranes towered everywhere. There were extravagant new homes on the slopes of North Teheran, fancy restaurants in which mounds of caviar were washed down with vodka, boutiques selling Paris haute couture and gaudy bejewelled bric-a-brac, and honking traffic jams where not so many years ago camels had brayed.

The country was modernizing madly. But it was a spotty modernization with the old and the new often living side by side. I watched an old man once taking listless swipes at the floor at Mehrabad airport with one of those short-handled brooms that you see all over the Third World, a broom with a shaft so short that you have to bend down to use it, the type of broom that has made millions of women in the underdeveloped parts of the world prematurely stooped. Yet right around the corner I spotted a three-man crew with one of those modern industrial floor cleaners that spread foam over large swaths of flooring to be sucked up by a huge vacuum cleaner.

Here was a country whose ruler was buying vast quantities of the world's most advanced technologies when it had not got around yet to applying itself to making brooms that did

not cripple people, a country where modernization meant
that the street scribes who wrote letters and filled out forms
for the illiterate half of the population had now advanced
from pens and inkwells to typewriters, a land flowing with
oil where dried cow dung was still the principal fuel of many
a rural household. It was this disparity, this incongruity that
had created much of the tensions that were about to tear the
country apart.

The Shah was driven by the urge to catch up with the
industrial power of the West. Impatient and dissatisfied
with the backward country he had inherited, he yearned
to recapture the glories of ancient Persia by building what
he called his Great Civilization. To match the grandeur of
Cyrus, Darius and Xerxes, of Zoroaster and Omar Khayyám,
he drove the people of Iran without giving them time to catch
their breath and get used to what was happening to them. It
was transformation on a grand scale. For the Shah, everything
always had to be the largest, the newest, the best, the costliest:
twenty nuclear reactors, a vast petrochemical industry, dams,
steel mills and a huge, well-equipped military machine. He
could afford it. But Iran couldn't. When his reckless spending
program overheated the economy and created shortages and
breakdowns, he slammed on the brakes, creating a downturn
that brought heavy unemployment and bankruptcies. Farmers who had been given land under his "White Revolution"
reform program found that they could no longer afford to
farm. The Shah's reaction to problems was always tighter
control, more repression. His idea of combatting inflation
was to hire 10,000 snoops off the street to monitor prices (and
extort money on the side), fine a quarter million offending
shopkeepers and send thousands of others to jail or into exile.
It was more feverish madness than development.

Some Iranians revelled in the helter-skelter boom. But most
others were repelled. There were too many foreigners — and
not just salesmen who filled their order books and left. There
were legions of Westerners who stayed, engineers and technicians, advisers and consultants involved in everything from
getting the phones to work to making the desert bloom.
They brought their alien ways with them. The group that

most riled Iranian traditionalists was the American pilots
and mechanics who manned and maintained the Shah's and
the oil companies' fleets of helicopters. Many of the chopper
jocks were retreads from the war in Vietnam who had had
trouble settling down when they returned home. They had
gone overseas again to try to recapture the wild, wide-open
lifestyle of wartime Saigon. They imported not only their
booze but also women, many of them Vietnamese recruited
from among refugees fleeing communist rule in Vietnam.
These reincarnations of the pliant *mama-sans* of Saigon's
Tudo Street presumably helped make many Americans lost
in Isfahan feel more at home than home did. But they enraged
the Iranians.

The *nouvelle richesse* of Teheran had other weaknesses that
fed the resentments that grew into revolutionary fervor. For
one thing, to become rich was not so much a matter of energy,
ingenuity or productivity. What seemed to be required more
than anything else was a grovelling sycophancy towards the
supreme dispenser of largesse, the Shah. Newspapers were
full of pictures of him and his empress, Farah Diba, in a constantly changing array of extravagant costumes, her weighed
down by jewellery, him by his equally glitzy medals and deco-
rations. They looked for all the world like cut-out paper dolls
dressed in clip-on finery from Ali Baba's cave. The photos of
the Shah were not confined to the news columns. The newspapers carried page after page of ads, paid for by contractors,
extolling the wisdom and graciousness of His Imperial Majesty the King of Kings, Light of the Aryans, on the occasion
of a contract-signing, a ground-breaking perhaps, or the completion of some multi-million-dollar project. It was pandering
to the man's well-known vanity.

In Teheran, the measures of inequality came in topograph-
ic layers. Teheran is one of those cities where prosperity drops
with the slope of the land. The city stands on the lower slopes
of the Elburz mountain range. At the top, cool and green
from the snows melting on the peaks, the rich and powerful,
starting with the Shah in his palace. In the middle, below
the towers of hotels and office buildings, the colorful war-
rens of the bazaar. The influential *bazaaris* were not just

shopkeepers. They were traditionally also bankers, import and export traders and political power brokers. But in the Shah's scheme of things, they found themselves being increasingly shoved aside by department stores, supermarkets and huge banks, most of them owned by the Shah's relatives and friends.

At the bottom of town was the great sprawl of resentful poverty, of people who, whatever leftovers may have trickled down their way, felt not only left out but offended by the ways of those above them. What made lower Teheran particularly angry was seeing pictures of Farah in a slinky gown and the Shah lifting champagne glasses in a toast at a dinner for foreign visitors. As far as millions of Iranians were concerned, that picture said it all. It combined three popular hates: drinking, immodesty in women and foreigners.

But even worse for the Shah was the resentment of him among many of those higher up on the hill, people he needed in his camp, people whom his regime, even if they refused to acknowledge it, had helped make prosperous. They were the technocrats and professionals, younger people, many of whom the Shah had helped to go abroad to study. Apart from whatever they were taught in overseas universities about medicine, engineering or economics, the students had also picked up modern notions and freer ways. When they came back and had to take their place in the Shah's forelock-tugging system with all its inefficiencies and corruption, they chafed at the restrictions and the hypocrisy. As scornful as they were of the Shah's pretensions, though, they were equally ill at ease and even contemptuous of the obscurantist politics of the mullahs. But by 1978, most of them had come to see that the politicians they favored, men with rational and gradualist approaches to the country's problems, could not gain the support of the broad masses. So many of them rooted for Khomeini too, hoping more than believing that the fundamentalist message he preached was window dressing to please the masses. They wanted to believe that his Islamic republic would be a democracy, as Khomeini kept repeating while he was in exile. They lulled themselves into believing that this frail old man would not try to run the country and that even if he did, he would be replaced quickly by someone more modern and pragmatic.

There were a lot of people in Iran and in his entourage abroad who saw Khomeini as Iran's Mahatma Gandhi and themselves playing Jawaharlal Nehru to the Ayatollah's Gandhi role as a holy man who stays above it all. We know now, of course, that they could not have been more wrong.

He came shuffling across the road, an old, old man in a worn coat and what looked like plastic sandals, looking as though he was no longer quite of this sordid world. He ignored the crowd around him shouting, "Allah-o-Akbar" (God is great). The narrow road was crammed with conspicuously armed policemen, reporters and cameramen, curiosity seekers who had somehow made it through the police cordon and a phalanx of the old man's devoted countrymen, many with tears in their eyes.

It was December 11, 1978, and Ayatollah Khomeini was on his way to prayers on the Shia holy day of Ashura, the tenth day of the mourning month of Moharram. Shiites mark Ashura by fasting and flagellating themselves, most only with a pro forma breast-beating but many brutally with chains and knives that cut to the quick. The fasting and self-flagellation symbolize a sharing in the passion and martyrdom of the Imam Hussein, grandson of the Prophet Mohammed, son of Ali, the first Imam. Hussein, whom the Shiites regard as the Prophet's successor, was hacked to death in the year 680 on the plain of Karbala by the soldiers of Caliph Yazid, the Sunni claimant to the succession. Hussein's death culminated in the rupture in Islam between Shia and Sunni that has lasted to this day.

While far away in Teheran blood was being shed in Khomeini's name by people who were casting him in the role of Hussein and the Shah as a latter-day Yazid, the Ayatollah prayed on a rug spread on the soggy alien soil of France. He had ended up at Neauphle-le-Château, a village near Paris, in

October after the Shah, convinced that Khomeini's influence over Iranians was to a great extent due to the proximity of his refuge just across the border in Iraq, had pressured the Iraqis to expel him. At the same time, he persuaded other Muslim countries not to give the Ayatollah refuge, forcing Khomeini to seek shelter among the infidel.

For the Shah, it turned out to be a costly mistake. Far from weakening the Ayatollah's influence, his enforced stay in France had increased it. In Iraq, he was isolated, more or less under house arrest. In France, his compound at Neauphle-le-Château became a crowded place of pilgrimage for Iranians. Direct-dial communications put even his supporters in Teheran as close to him as his phone. The Ayatollah's broadsides no longer had to be laboriously smuggled into Iran. They were telephoned, recorded at the other end, and within hours they were transcribed and photocopied for distribution by the hundreds of thousands. Moreover, with that strong, brooding face, the Ayatollah became an instant media star, and the power of print and broadcast spread his fame around the world. His fame among the unbelievers, in turn, burnished his reputation at home with both his supporters and opponents.

I had been in Teheran in November and had seen how Khomeini's persona had grown to dominate Iran. Where not so long ago he had merely been the Shah's principal accuser, he had become first a possible alternative and then the Shah's all but certain successor. Millions were now answering the Ayatollah's calls to bring down the Pahlavi dynasty. A strike by oil-field workers had cut off the country's main source of revenue. Communications technicians had walked out and so had post office workers, teachers, airline pilots and civil servants. Banks were closed and so were gas stations. The strikers demanded the release of political prisoners, the disbanding of the secret police and the expulsion of foreign workers. So did the hundreds of thousands of marchers who filled the streets yelling "Marg bar Shah" (Death to the Shah). At night, when the streets were emptied by a curfew imposed by the army, the demonstrators took to balconies and rooftops to bang out the rhythm of "Marg bar Shah" with pots and garbage-can lids. The town would go to sleep to the racket of the three-beat rhythm and wake up to it the next morning.

The Shah could now count on the support of only the army, and even that appeared to be wavering. While the professional army — the army in which privates on long-term enlistments made $400 a month, a princely sum for illiterate peasant boys — stayed loyal because it had a stake in the system, many of the conscripts, who were paid $1 a day, were beginning to desert. Though they were only a small part of the army, the conscripts were the backbone of the infantry units that had been assigned the dirty work of breaking up demonstrations.

At the beginning of November, near Teheran University, I watched troops barring a boulevard as a huge column of demonstrators approached. You could hear the orders being given and the sound of guns being cocked. But where not so long ago the soldiers used to shoot to kill, this time I saw them fire only tear gas and a few shots over the demonstrators' heads. When that didn't work, the troops retreated. With the army pulled back, the demonstrators turned to rioting. Cars and buses were overturned. Windows were smashed. Government buildings, a British embassy building and offices of foreign companies were attacked. The information ministry was burned down. Banks and airline offices were sacked. But the favorite work of the rioters was torching liquor stores and movie houses, the principal purveyors of Western licentiousness. The centre of Teheran was devastated. The country was paralyzed. The government had all but ceased to exist.

It began to be clear that for the Shah, the end was near. He did what autocrats tend to do *in extremis*. He fired the civilian prime minister and handed the government over to the generals. He turned on his friends and closest collaborators, many of whom had done nothing more than follow his orders loyally, and had them arrested on charges of corruption as a sop to the mobs and a distraction from his own sins. Then he tried to negotiate his survival and that of his regime. It might even have worked. Most opposition politicians, even some of those close to Khomeini, were willing to settle for free elections and a plebiscite to decide the Shah's fate. But Khomeini was adamant. The Shah had to go.

When I returned from Iran to France, I went to Neauphle, curious to meet the man who, by the strength of his will, was managing to block any chance of a political compromise in Teheran. Normally in these situations, reporters look for a press spokesman. But in the garden of Khomeini's compound, there was a sign on the wall that said: "Ayatollah Khomeini has no spokesman." Not only no spokesman, but no deputies, no formal political organization and no program but the overthrow of the Shah and the formation of an Islamic republic, whatever that was. But he did have plenty of helpers, many of whom had their own agendas and their concepts of an Islamic republic that ranged from a clerical dictatorship to a liberal democracy using the Koran only as its moral guide.

While I was trying to figure out what to do next, I got to talking outside Khomeini's house to a bearded Iranian in thick glasses who spoke fluent English. He had done medical research at a university in Texas, he said, but now he was devoting his life to the Ayatollah's cause. There would be no problem talking to the Imam, he assured me. A little later, I met another Iranian, a burly, darkly handsome fellow who also spoke English. He had studied, he said, in Canada, at Notre Dame University in Nelson, B.C. He, too, said he could get me an interview with the Ayatollah. Wait here, he said.

When I got in to see Khomeini, my two new acquaintances were sitting on the floor beside him. The bearded man, it turned out, was there to translate the Imam's words into English; the other handled interviews in French. The Ayatollah squatted between them on the rug and gave no indication that he had noticed me. It was as if he were merely a still color photograph of himself. Only when my questions were translated was there any movement and then only of his lips and only barely. He spoke slowly and quietly, almost in a whisper, never once looking at me. But if the sound of his words was gentle, their meaning had the whip of a lash. No compromise. Never. The Shah is a criminal. He must be tried and severely punished.

As for the proposals of most of his own allies for a plebiscite, they were, Khomeini said, misguided. As far as he was concerned, there had already been a plebiscite — in the streets. "The whole nation," he said, "has made it clear publicly that the Shah must go and that his regime does not have any legitimacy. The monarchy must be replaced with an Islamic republic."

Khomeni ruled himself out as head of that republic. He said he had no political ambitions, but he declined to name anyone else as leader of the new regime or to throw his support behind any of the existing opposition parties. "There are many competent people," was all he would say.

Among the "competent people" who would take part in running the Islamic republic once the Shah was gone were the two men who sat beside him that day. The man with the beard and eyeglasses was Ibrahim Yazdi; the other man's name was Sadegh Ghotbzadeh. Both regarded Khomeini as their spiritual father. Both believed his protestations that he had no personal political ambitions and his assurances that the Islamic republic would be a modern democratic state. Both, at his bidding, would take the job of foreign minister and both would lose it in the deadly machinations of Khomeini's brand of priestly politics. Yazdi, a careful plodder, would at least come out of it alive.

The headstrong and impetuous Ghotbzadeh, a cynical idealist, lubricious ascetic, doom-ridden optimist, a man who believed in the purity of the revolution even as he recognized the moral rot in most of his fellow revolutionaries, would rebel against the man he had loved as a father and plot his overthrow as a subverter of his own cause. Within four years of that day in Neauphle-le-Château when an Iranian Islamic republic was still a dream, Ghotbzadeh was in Teheran's Evin prison, the place where the Shah's secret police used to torture and kill, the prison where Khomeini's agents came to perpetrate the same cruelties. It is said by some that when Ghotbzadeh's jailers asked Khomeini what to do about the rebel he had regarded as a son, the Imam replied: "Do what is good for Islam."

So they hauled Sadegh Ghotbzadeh before a firing squad and shot him.

If a car as much as backfires noisily, I thought, looking out on the scene, we stand a good chance of being killed. We were surrounded by hundreds of thousands of frenzied Iranians, body packed against body mile after mile, several millions of them filling broad boulevards, spilling over into side streets, yelling, crying, laughing, praying, waving, jumping, pushing, climbing, hanging on by their fingertips from precarious perches the better to see the Imam. Given the rumors that had been circulating all day that the Ayatollah's enemies were out to kill him once he arrived, I was sure it would have needed only one loud noise, any pop like a gun, to roil the crowds. The excited mass would in all likelihood have reacted by surging forward, possessed by a will to overwhelm the first manifestation it could find of its many hates. In this case, the most readily available enemy would have been us, the foreign journalists riding right behind Khomeini in his triumphal return to Teheran.

This was not some fearful fancy on my part; it was a realistic assessment. For all the joy in Teheran that day, I knew how crowds in such states of exaltation can quickly become hysterical and turn to bloodthirsty fury. I had seen it before on a much smaller scale. A crowd that one moment was in good humor would in the next be running down the street baying for blood. I saw it in Bangladesh and I have seen it in Haiti. Once, in Calcutta, at a rally of communists, after being welcomed with smiles and pats on the back, we found ourselves a few moments later desperately trying to get away as the crowd rocked our car, trying to turn it over, and hands grabbed at us through open windows. I didn't know then why the crowd turned on us — neither did our local guide — and I still don't. But I will never forget it. I certainly remembered it well that day in Teheran.

It was February 1, 1979. The Shah had left Iran two weeks earlier, fooling himself to the last by pretending he was only leaving on a vacation. He had, after all, he must have reminded himself, been forced into exile once before — in

1953 — and, with the help of the CIA, returned to power one week later. The government he left behind this time — such as it was in the chaos all around — was headed by Shahpour Bakhtiar, a social democrat with impeccable credentials of opposition to the Shah. But Bakhtiar also opposed clerical rule. He accepted the job of prime minister from the Shah hoping to save Iran from both. Though he dissolved the secret police, declared freedom of the press and broke diplomatic relations with Israel as Khomeini had demanded, it was not enough. Not for Khomeini and not for the people. It was too late for compromises. A million people marched through the streets of Teheran demanding that Bakhtiar, too, go.

Khomeini decided to force events by returning home. He landed in a chartered Air France Boeing 747 with a retinue of several hundred journalists and rode into town with this strange little army of foreigners trailing him. As we crawled, seemingly inch by inch, through this dense mass of chaotic humanity, we were seeing this one man coming home to rout by the force of his personality the two forces that still stood between him and his Islamic Revolution. The first, the Iranian army, nearly half a million strong, would quickly crumble under the hammer blows of his preaching. Beset by desertions and mutinies, the army gave up within ten days of the Ayatollah's return. The army's surrender forced Bakhtiar to flee the country.

The other force the Ayatollah still had to contend with was made up of his allies, people who shared his vision of bringing the morality of the Koran into Iranian public life but who dreamed also of freedom, democracy, social harmony and economic progress. These moderates, devout Muslims but laymen, were now the government. Their undoing would take a little longer.

"America Held Hostage," screamed the headlines in the U.S. after Iranian students had seized the U.S. embassy in Teheran and held its diplomats captive. But the headlines had it wrong. Except for fifty-three diplomats, their families and

Jimmy Carter, it was not America that was being held hostage; it was Iran. And it was the Iranians, and not the Americans, who were the affair's real losers.

The students who took over the embassy on November 4, 1979, had planned a short occupation to protest the Shah's admission to the U.S. for medical treatment. Their main target, though, was not so much the U.S. as Iran's Provisional Revolutionary Government. Politics in Iran is a bit like those automated phone-answering services that require you to "push one" to get the instructions that will give you access to whatever information it is that you want. Fear and hatred of foreigners have been the "one" button of Iranian politics for centuries. Arabs, Russians and the British had all played that role in recent times. Now it was the turn of the Americans.

The students were inspired by hard-line mullahs who believed the provisional government had betrayed the Islamic purity of the revolution. In a way, they were right. Prime Minister Mehdi Bazargan and the moderates in his cabinet were struggling to control the excesses of the revolution: the ideological stridency of the mullahs, the casual murderous ways of the revolutionary courts, the storm-trooper behavior of the Pazdaran, the revolutionary guards, and the snooping and meddling of the komitehs, neighborhood committees that behaved as tyrannically towards their neighbors as had those in Mao's China or Stalin's Russia. Bazargan was also embarked on a much more dangerous mission: trying to normalize Iran's relations with the U.S. The day the U.S. embassy was seized, he was in Algiers negotiating with the Carter administration.

The expected short sit-in to undercut what remained of Bazargan's authority got out of hand and became a long siege for one simple reason: Khomeini. One word from him and it would have been over. Instead, he gave the occupation his blessings. He took it over and used it for his own purposes.

Khomeini had returned home to Qom after the revolution. Ostensibly, he had left most of the running of the country to others, just as he had said he would in Neauphle-le-Château. But the politicians in Teheran soon discovered that they could not get anything done without making constant pilgrimages to Qom to get the Imam's assent. Even at that, Khomeini grew ever more distrustful of the politicians and even of many of the mullahs. He saw every step towards restoring tranquillity and normality as an attempt to derail his Islamic revolution. It became clear that he would not let himself be relegated to the role of a revered relic, that he wanted to rule, not reign. The takeover of the U.S. embassy, now called the Nest of Spies, would become the Ayatollah's road to absolute power.

Khomeini quickly managed to get the Americans hopping to his tune. And he kept stirring up the crisis to keep it alive. One week. One month. On and on, day by day, week by week, month after month. First, Washington went through the let's-be-reasonable stage: Let's not get excited, we can talk this thing through. Then, bluster: If you won't play the game by our rules, we'll take your marbles away. They froze Iran's assets in the U.S. Next, the panic stage: the search for intermediaries; freelance mediators grandstanding in Teheran; secret meetings in Europe; emissaries you wouldn't buy a used car from dangling phantom carrots. And the White House biting, hoping against hope to hear a crunch. Whenever the glimmer of a solution did appear, Khomeini would step in and veto it.

By now more than a year had gone, and it was election year in the U.S. Jimmy Carter, ridiculed and pilloried, confined his campaign for re-election to the safety of his own backyard, the White House Rose Garden. Finally, he called the U.S. cavalry to the rescue. Or rather the Delta Force, a commando unit with a Rambo reputation. And failed yet again. Eight American servicemen died in the Iranian desert in a botched attempt to rescue the hostages.

After that came resignation and Carter's mortification at the polls — and the countdown to Ronald Reagan's inauguration. Khomeini savored his triumph over Carter to the last. He made sure the hostages were not released until the moment Carter had ceased to be president, not a second sooner.

For the Americans, it was over. They welcomed their hostages back as heroes, gave them a ticker-tape parade in New

York, a party at the White House and declared the affair a victory and over.

In Iran, it was not so simple. Iran would never be the same again.

The scene on Takht-e Djamshid Street was pure theatre of the absurd. On stage outside the Nest of Spies were the extras, the crowds that every time a TV camera showed up would start yelling, "Marg bar Amrika" (Death to America). There were fists waving in front of the lens, close-ups of fierce grimaces, U.S. flags trampled, then burned. Day after day, politics as theatre.

The stars of the show — the American hostages and their captors — were hidden off-stage behind the graffiti-laden wall of the embassy compound. Every once in awhile, a messenger — a student or a mullah — would emerge from behind the scenes to give the plot direction: a threat one day, a tantalizing hint of solutions the next. Whenever the captors felt that enthusiasm for the Islamic revolution and anti-American indignation were waning among Iranians or the Americans were showing signs of slipping off the hook, they would stir the pot a little by giving journalists a peek behind the scenes: pictures of the hostages enjoying a few Christmas goodies given to them by their compassionate captors, a news conference inside the embassy at which they announced the release of women and blacks among the hostages as a goodwill gesture, or shredded documents whose tiny bits had been painstakingly put together to reveal a supposed American conspiracy which usually implicated, it just so happened, some luckless Iranian on the mullahs' latest hate list.

The media were also an important part of the cast and scenario. We knew it and we said so. Every time I stood before a camera in front of the embassy with a chorus of noisy demonstrators crowding over my shoulder as I tried to explain what was happening, I was aware that I was being used as a messenger. In ancient Greek drama they called the actor who played a similar role to mine, the role of filling in the gaps in what the chorus was saying, "ypokrites," a word that has passed down to us as hypocrite.

The Iranians were using TV's instant communication capability as a weapon against the West. They had turned the industrialized world's technological strength against it by using the media, above all American journalists, to conduct negotiations with Washington and pass on their anti-American messages to the rest of the world. The satellite transmission room of Iranian TV was crowded every evening. While I was trying to feed my report to Toronto, ABC's Peter Jennings would be sitting on a stool in another corner of the control room chatting "live" to Ted Koppel in Washington. We, too, were the enemy — our hotel was also called the Nest of Spies — but we were useful enemies and therefore were tolerated, even cultivated. We had no trouble getting interviews and information from the students and their mentors. But it was always their information, their line. Slowly all opposing views within the country were being strangled.

The carefully orchestrated show was effective not just in roiling American public opinion and politics. In Iran, it served to destroy reputations, shake governments and, above all, radicalize the population. The radical students at the embassy set the political tone for the country. Moderate politicians of every stripe were suspect because moderation requires compromise, greys rather than just black and white. In Khomeini's Iran, there was to be no room for shading of any kind.

Bazargan resigned. So did Ibrahim Yazdi, my interlocutor in Neauphle. Sadegh Ghotbzadeh would quit a few months later. Abolhassan Bani Sadr, a Neauphle graduate who became president, would be forced to flee for his life into exile. Being a mullah was no safeguard either. Not even being an Ayatollah. The Grand Ayatollah, Kazem Shariat-Madari, who had once saved Khomeini from execution, would end his days a broken man under house arrest. Minister after minister either quit or fell because Khomeini undercut their authority and played off one faction against another. The political infighting turned to plots, purges, arrests, executions

and assassinations. The result: paralysis and chaos. And a war
that devastated the country.

Khomeini had been provoking Iraq's leader, Saddam
Hussein, for months by calling for his overthrow. It was
part of the Ayatollah's campaign to export his revolution.
In September 1980, seeing his enemy weakened by political
turmoil, Hussein invaded Iran. Khomeini could have ended
the war on favorable terms several times in the first two years,
because, despite initial setbacks, the strength of Iran's much
greater manpower had begun to turn the tide. But he would
not settle for anything short of the fall of Hussein. So the war
continued for nearly eight years.

Iran suffered considerably more than Iraq because it used
masses of men to fight Iraq's tanks and planes. Eventually,
Iran had to throw its children — boys of thirteen — into
battle. Yet hundreds of thousands of Iranians volunteered
and fought, driven by their faith in the Ayatollah's promise
of heavenly rewards for those who fell as martyrs.

The Iranians found themselves increasingly isolated. The
exporting of Khomeini's revolution through terrorism had
earned them many enemies, enemies who went out of their
way to help Iraq. In the end, with the possibility of defeat
looming, Khomeini was forced to back down and accept a
cease-fire. "Taking this decision was more deadly than drinking hemlock," he said. "To me, it would be more bearable to
accept death and martyrdom."

With the end of the war, it appeared that a new era was
dawning, that the country could turn from the rigidities of
the Islamic revolution to reconstruction and overcome its
frustrations and discontents. There were small but significant signs of a turn towards a semblance of normalcy. Chess,
which had been banned because it was, after all, the game of
shahs, was allowed again. Diplomatic relations with Canada,
which had been broken after the Canadian Caper in which
Ambassador Ken Taylor and his staff sheltered six American
diplomats and smuggled them out of the country, were re-es-
tablished. Overtures were made to other countries. The trend
seemed to signal a waning of the Ayatollah's rigid orthodoxy.

But Khomeini was not about to let Iran backslide. Once

again he needed a crisis to propel him back to the top. This time he pulled from his ample sleeve a surprise, a thunderbolt that would galvanize the faithful not only of Iran but throughout Islam. And appall the rest of the world. He issued a *fatwa*, a religious edict: "The author of the *The Satanic Verses* book, which is against Islam, the Prophet and the Koran, and all those involved in its publication who were aware of its content, are sentenced to death."

Once more the crowds were out in the streets of Iran yelling for blood. This time it was, "Marg bar Salman Rushdie." And not only in Iran. And not just the Shiites. This time Khomeini had crossed Islam's great divide to reach out to his old enemies, the followers of the Caliph Yazid, the Sunnis.

It is said that Khomeini did not bother to read *The Satanic Verses* before condemning its author to death. He should have, and not only for the sake of fairness. He should have read it because he might even have agreed with much of it.

Rushdie's book is not about Islam or about Satan. It is about the ache of alienation in the modern world. It is about Salman Rushdie, the boy from Bombay, and the cost of his journey to fame and fortune in London. It is about everyone who has ever felt the pain of dislocation and the guilt of having abandoned his roots. That surely includes most of the Muslims of the Diaspora in Britain, Canada and elsewhere who demonstrated against Rushdie and wanted him dead. The book is not only about Muslims either; it is also about Joe Schlesinger, the Jewish boy from Bratislava, and the loss of his roots. I recognized myself in Saladin Chamcha, one of the two heroes of the story, when as a boy he is suddenly transported from India to school in England and finds himself facing a breakfast kipper on his plate. He does not know how to eat it. Every time he tries, he gets a mouthful of bones. No one offers to help him. Although he is on the edge of tears, he stubbornly persists. Eating that fish becomes a matter of pride, of showing the English that they can't get him down, his first step in coming to terms with this new, strange country.

For Saladin Chamcha, it was a kipper. For me, it was a bike. I had never ridden one before I came to England and while I was learning, I fell and skinned my knee. I got up, knee throbbing and eyes smarting from barely suppressed tears, looked at the blood and said to the boys standing around me, "It's nothing." At least that's what I thought I had said. What they heard was more like "Eat ease no sing," and for the next few days I was pursued by chants imitating the inadequacies of my English. Eat ease no sing. No sing, no sing, no sing. I, too, resolved to "show them." And I did. Not that anyone seemed to notice when I soon started coming in first in spelling tests. Never mind, at least I had showed myself. I may not have been able to pronounce the words properly, but, by God, I learned how to spell them.

I no longer have to worry about pronouncing words the way others do. My idiosyncratic accent has become my professional trademark, distinguishing my voice from all those voices on the tube that tend to sound alike whether they're reciting the news or selling laxatives. Saladin took a different, in fact quite opposite, approach, but it also brought him into broadcasting. He did it by learning to do perfect imitations of accents. Not just English accents. All accents. And not just the speech of humans either. In TV commercials his voice was the voice of condiment bottles and packages of potato chips pleading to be bought.

But it was not Saladin's constant tug-of-war between his Bombay and London identities, his pathetic attempts to be anything but what he was, that aroused the wrath of Khomeini. It was the religious torments of the other protagonist of the book, Gibreel Farishta (Gabriel Angel). Gibreel is a Bombay movie star who is tortured by a sudden loss of faith. He tries to prove to himself the non-existence of God by breaking the laws of Islam, by stuffing his face with forbidden pork.

Defiance does him no good. The God he knows does not exist is still there inside him, hiding in his subconscious. The duel between faith and atheism, between Gibreel's need to believe and his inability to do so is played out in his dreams. His disturbed dream world parallels the world of the Prophet Mohammed. But it is a sacrilegiously distorted vision that causes the hidden believer in him insufferable anguish. It has a brothel whose inmates bear the names of the wives of Mohammed, and its Prophet agrees for a time to honor three pagan deities in addition to Allah. What is more, the three are goddesses. Not just pagan but female to boot!

Gibreel would not have been at all surprised that his dreams drove the Muslim world to fury. After all, they tortured him even more. So cruelly tormented was he by his dreams that by the end of the book he is driven mad, commits murder and kills himself. The punishment for Gibreel's blasphemies — the sentence Khomeini pronounced on Rushdie — has already been meted out: by Gibreel on Gibreel!

Gibreel is driven mad because he cannot stand not believing and punishes himself because he cannot forgive himself for the guilt of his faith-shaking doubts. By day, awake, the man is gross, his life indecent. But inside him is that irreducible kernel of faith, the vestige of the inheritance of generations that lived by its rules, the essence of that thing we call culture that cannot be denied.

Saladin suffers too, from the contradictions of cultural exile. He desperately wants to be a part of England yet finds himself constantly rebuffed. When he switches from being a disembodied voice on the telly to appearing before the camera, he is fitted with wigs, masks and false noses to hide his wrong-colored otherness. His veddy English wife leaves him. After being slapped around by British immigration officers, finding himself transformed for awhile into a goatish demon with horns and hooves, and being felled by a heart attack, Saladin returns to Bombay, apparently to stay and start life afresh.

For Saladin Chamcha, redemption. For Gibreel Farishta, punishment. Their stories are surely morality tales that any clergyman might well recite as a warning of the pitfalls that await those who have the hubris to believe that in this modern age of relativism and rationalism they can discard the faith and culture of their fathers with ease and impunity. Gibreel and Saladin are the kind of characters a mullah might hold up as deterrent examples. The Saladin lecture: Let yourself be seduced by the glittering corruption of godless Western ways and you shall suffer the pain of humiliation and rejection, the loneliness of the loss of your identity. Only by returning among your own can you find redemption and peace of mind. The Gibreel lesson: Abandoning the teachings of the Koran and living in godlessness leads to nightmares of blasphemy, and blasphemy to death and the torments of hell. Not believing is neither an excuse nor a solution.

But Khomeini chose to preach a different lesson. In the last year of his life, he used it to lay claim to the moral leadership of all Islam.

The Ayatollah left Teheran as he had come. In a gigantic outburst of emotion. Despite all the hundreds of thousands who had died in the war, the hundreds of thousands more who had been wounded, crippled and made homeless, despite the impoverishment of the country with one out of every three workers jobless and debt the country's main product, despite all the sacrifices by tens of millions that had gone in vain and the promises that had soured, despite the uncertainties, pessimism and cynicism about the future, when Khomeini died June 3, 1989, Iran was swept by a storm of grief.

As it had been when he returned from exile ten years earlier, Teheran was once again flooded with crushing crowds. Only this time the millions were wailing and beating themselves in sorrow. They literally wouldn't let their Imam go. So many wanted to touch the body in the open coffin that in a surge they overturned the litter, spilling his half-naked corpse to the ground. Eight people were killed in the crush, hundreds more injured.

When Stalin died, the Soviet Union was also consumed by grief despite all the tyrant had done to it. In great part, of course, it was orchestrated. But even those who hated him and were glad to see him dead knew that Stalin had done for Russia what the czars only dreamed of, that out of his reign of terror he had transformed the country — poor, backward Russia — into a superpower that was respected as well as hated and feared the world over. When Mao died, the

Chinese were aware that, for all the pain of his latter-day vainglorious ideological adventurism, he had enabled China, for the first time since the British shoved drugs down their throats in the Opium War more than a hundred years earlier, to stand united on its own feet.

That's what Khomeini had done, too. For more than 200 years, since the days of Nadir Shah, the last of a long line of conquering Persian rulers, foreigners — the British and the Americans, the Turks and the Russians, the Uzbeks, Georgians and Afghans — had been gnawing on the carcass of Persia almost at will. Khomeini managed to stop them. He expelled the Americans, fended off the Russians and repelled an Arab invasion. His revolution reached deep into the Arab world and beyond. He made the world notice Iran.

But unlike Stalin and Mao, unlike Hitler and Mussolini, unlike any reformer, revolutionary or dictator of the twentieth century, Khomeini did not embrace any of the modern visions, not fascism or other form of corporatism, not communism or socialism, not liberal pluralism or even military dictatorship. He created a throwback: a theocracy. Not even the Vatican is ruled as closely by religious writ as was Khomeini's Iran. Islam has always prided itself on providing more than just a code for personal conduct, on being a system with rules for all aspects of human existence. But Muslim rulers, like Christian kings, used religion judiciously to further their secular aims and ambitions. Saudi Arabia is also an Islamic state but Saudi kings have not given their clerics the keys to the kingdom.

For Khomeini, the secular was totally subordinated to religion. None of the reverses and tragedies that marked his ten years in power changed his mind. In his last will and testament, he lashed out against those who "claim clumsily and explicitly that the laws of Islam, which were recorded 1,400 years ago, cannot be used to administer countries of the contemporary world." The laws of Islam, he argued, did not "grow old with the passage of time"; they still had the power "to lead mankind to the desired status of evolution." With their frenzied grief, their mass adulation, Iranians demonstrated that as a nation they agreed with the path Khomeini had chosen for them. And so did the leadership he had left behind. The power vacuum, the political infighting, the danger of a breakdown of the regime that so many outsiders had expected once the supreme arbiter was gone never happened. The leaders quickly closed ranks and went on as before. There has been no Iranian Gorbachev or Deng to dismantle the master's handiwork. The emphasis may have changed a little. There is less lightning and thunder about piety and morality from on high, a little more willingness to talk to the rest of the world. But the main outlines of Khomeini's revolution remain unchanged.

Iran, by all accounts, is now a quieter place than when I first went there a dozen years ago. There may not be more happiness. There certainly is not more to eat. But for all the damage and all the suffering Khomeini brought Iran, he left it with one major accomplishment. He rid the country of a crippling malaise that has been ravaging so much of the Third World. Its symptoms: the resentment of being dependent on stronger powers, the loss of self-confidence, the rage at being patronized by foreigners, the helplessness of having your country's fate decided by outsiders, the corrosive self-hate that comes from aping their mores and from the loss of pride, tradition and customs. Its outcome: the drift or paralysis of resignation that, when it becomes intolerable, boils over into violence.

The disease — call it the post-colonial syndrome or neo-colonial angst — struck Iran more heavily than most developing countries because of the glaring contrast between Iranians' pride in their glorious history and the indecent haste with which the Shah galloped towards turning the country into an imitation of some cheap Western Ruritanian model of ersatz imperial glory. But opting out by retreating into the past may turn out to be a poison rather than a cure.

The Ayatollah Khomeini restored the pride of the Persians by marching them back into history. As he lies in his grave at Beheshti-e Zahra cemetery surrounded for miles around by the dead of the revolution he started and the war his hate fed, his soul will have all eternity to ponder whether it was worth the price. The Iranians he left behind don't have that much time. Sooner or later, they will have to start marching forward again. Into the twenty-first century, with religion or without.

CHAPTER X

In Salvador, death still patrols.
The blood of dead peasants
has not dried, time does not dry it,
rain does not erase it from the roads.

Pablo Neruda
Song of Protest

It is the ugliest cathedral in the world. It squats in the centre
of San Salvador, an unfinished block of concrete weighed
down by two chunky towers and a heavy dome as if the
workers who were building it had left for lunch one day and
had not come back. More than a decade after work on the
church stopped, construction rubble still lay piled against its
walls. The windows were either gaping holes or covered with
green corrugated plastic that bathed the church with a sallow
light worthy of nothing more than a warehouse. Behind the
altar a plywood wall hid the unfinished chancel. Outside,
rusty steel trusses protruded where gargoyles and statues were
to have stood. Ends of steel rods stuck out in every direction
like dirty wisps of fuzz. From across the plaza, where the
statues of Christopher Columbus and Queen Isabella of Spain

254

keep watch, the cathedral looked as though it were in need of a shave.

The cathedral stands there in the Plaza Barrios, naked and graceless, as Man's reproach to God. The history of El Salvador and much of the rest of Central America is so filled with shame and pain that if God is indeed almighty, the Metropolitan Cathedral of San Salvador is a reproach well earned. El Salvador is one of those places — as were the death camps of Nazi Germany, the killing fields of Cambodia, the gulags of Stalin's Russia and the starvation zones of Ethiopia — where it becomes impossible to believe that a good God would have wanted such a world.

El Salvador is a country debauched by the Spanish conquistadores in the sixteenth century, brutalized by the army sworn to defend it and raped by its ruling class of avaricious coffee growers in the nineteenth and twentieth centuries, and betrayed for much of its history by the one institution in which the suffering peasants placed their faith and trust, the church.

So it is proper that the cathedral of San Salvador, the seat of the archbishop-primate of the country, should be devoid of grace. There is little in their past or present to inspire Salvadorans to raise spires soaring to the heavens in gratitude for the gift of divine favor. They have no reason to celebrate the sweetness of life with the exuberance of stained-glass windows. History has deprived them of the skills and creative imagination to build arches whose grace might sing the Lord's praise. There is no Pietà here: only dolls of saints with waxy, vacuous faces framed by heavy hanks of lanky black hair. There is in the cathedral of San Salvador hardly a trace of the glorious cultures of the Mayas, Aztecs and Spaniards from whom the people of El Salvador are descended.

And yet mark this: the cathedral of San Salvador is a holy place. Its unfinished state is not a mark of abandonment. On the contrary, it was an act of commitment that has become for the San Salvadoran church a badge of honor. Work on the cathedral was stopped in the mid-seventies by Archbishop Luis Chávez y Gonzalez. "The time has come," he said, "to stop building churches and start building the Church." He ordered that the money collected to build the cathedral be used to help landless peasants. The efforts of the long-suffering peasantry to organize were being brutally suppressed by the military dictatorship of the day. The archbishop's gesture was for the Salvadoran church an act of redemption and a re-affirmation of a truth that it had for centuries ignored and then all but forgotten: that the glory of God is better served by helping the poor and protecting the persecuted than by building temples to proclaim it.

The San Salvador cathedral is also more sacred and venerable than many an older and more splendid church because it is a place sanctified with the blood of innocents. Twice — in May 1979 and March 1980 — peaceful demonstrators were slaughtered on its steps by the heirs of the marauding conquistadores: the forces of law and order and the killers of the rightist death squads, the extra-curricular hobby clubs of the Salvadoran army.

Above all, though, the cathedral of San Salvador has become a place of pilgrimage and veneration because of a man who lies buried there: Archbishop Oscar Arnulfo Romero, the primate of El Salvador, murdered in 1980 by a death-squad executioner. His tomb is covered with dozens of small plaques, all inscribed with variations of the same message: "Gratitude to Monsignor Oscar Arnulfo Romero, pastor, prophet and martyr, for a miracle granted."

The tragic tale of Oscar Romero is the story of Thomas à Becket in modern dress. Like Becket, Romero was installed as archbishop because his patrons, vexed with his obstreperous predecessor, had good reason to expect him to be more accommodating to the needs of the state. Like Becket, Romero died because he surprised and provoked the state by using the power of his office and of his church to defy it. Like Becket, he was murdered at the altar by killers acting to please a chief demanding, as did Henry II of England, to be rid of "this meddlesome priest."

But Becket and Romero came to martyrdom from opposite directions. Where Becket was a man of the world, skillful in the affairs of state, Romero was chosen because he was not.

Becket enraged his friend, King Henry, by challenging his authority in a jurisdictional dispute between the ecclesiastical courts and those of the king; theirs was in essence a struggle for power between the mighty. Romero defied the military rulers of El Salvador in defence of the poor and powerless. What drove Becket was intellectual devotion to the duty he had been handed and only reluctantly accepted when Henry had him appointed Archbishop of Canterbury. What changed Romero was outrage of the heart.

Romero was appointed to the San Salvador archdiocese in 1976 after the government succeeded in convincing the Vatican to retire Chávez, the archbishop who had halted work on the cathedral. The army had grown irritated with Chávez for his hostile pastoral letters and for his support of the Jesuits in encouraging peasants to join a union, the Christian Federation of Salvadoran Peasants. Jesuits helped organize an unprecedented action: a strike at a sugar mill at Aguilares, forty kilometres north of the capital.

The regime of Colonel Arturo Molina saw in Romero, the conservative bishop of Santiago de Maria in Usulutan, a solution to its problem of controlling pesky radical priests. Romero's biographer, Father Plácido Erdozaín, recalls how the bishop looked to him when he came to San Salvador to take up his post as primate: "Churchy, lover of rules and clerical discipline, friend of liturgical laws, he was convinced that 'the most important thing is prayer and personal conversion.' "

The realities of El Salvador changed Romero. A few months after he took office, there was a massacre of demonstrators protesting electoral fraud. Then the army attacked Aguilares and turned a church there into a barracks for its soldiers. Several priests were murdered. Romero denounced the violence. But the turning point for him was apparently the death of Ernesto Barrera, a priest killed while fighting alongside the guerrillas of the Popular Liberation Front. Barrera's death shocked Romero into a profound change that, for a man who believed in the power of prayer rather than action, must have been soul-shattering. For the first time he spoke in favor of violence against the government: "When a dictatorship seriously violates human rights and attacks the common good of the nation, when it becomes unbearable and closes all channels of dialogue, of understanding, of rationality, when this happens, the church speaks of the legitimate right of insurrectional violence."

The passive pietist had become a passionate advocate of activist radicalism. And he knew the price of defying the army. "If they kill me," he said in an interview in early 1980, "I will rise again in the Salvadoran people."

Romero took the final step in a sermon on March 23, 1980. From the pulpit of his cathedral, he told the soldiers of El Salvador, "No soldier is obliged to obey an order contrary to the law of God. It is time that you come to your senses and obey your conscience rather than follow sinful commands." To the army that was treason.

The next day Oscar Romero was murdered at the altar of the chapel of the Divine Providence hospital. He was killed by a single bullet in the heart as he celebrated mass. The killer escaped.

Romero died for his faith, a faith not of some desiccated pious orthodoxy, but a church of compassion, a church of understanding, a church preparing to come to terms with the realities of the twentieth century in the Third World. To most Salvadorans, Archbishop Romero is already a saint. And he will have to become a saint one day for the Church of Rome if it is to have any hope of a future in Central America.

El Salvador and Nicaragua are intertwined in my mind. Both are seas of poverty dotted with tiny inlands of riches. In both, for most of their history, a few rich families owned just about everything and ran most of the rest. Both have suffered from murderous militaries, bloody revolutions and repression. Both countries live off coffee, cotton and sugar. On every table in both you will find the same *gallo pinto*, the painted rooster, the mixture of rice and beans that is the staff of life in Central America. What I saw in one would often remind me of something I had seen in the other.

The church of San Sebastián, a small market town in Salvador, looked to me very much like the church across the street from the house in which Augusto Sandino, the father of Nicaragua's revolution, was born in the little town of Niquinohomo. In both churches you can see the heritage of Spain. In both you will find the quiet devoutness of the remnants of an Indian culture resigned to the idea that life is pain. In one, I saw a funeral; in the other, a wedding, and both were equally sombre. The mourners in San Sebastián were too used to seeing their loved ones and neighbors being killed in other people's battles to lament openly. They sat there quietly, numbed by grief, submissive to fate, murmuring their responses. In Niquinohomo, the couple standing before the priest at the altar was the only sign that this was a wedding and not a wake. There was no joy, not a smile, only a quiet, dignified solemnity, an awareness, it seemed to me, that in the lives of *campesinos*, marriage is not so much a matter of romance as a sober-minded arrangement to share the rigors of life and alleviate its sufferings.

For all their similarities, the El Salvador and Nicaragua I watched through the eighties were in most important respects the very opposites of each other. In El Salvador, after all, it was the extreme right that had the upper hand; in Nicaragua, the revolutionary left was in charge. Yet despite this discrepancy, the two countries were in fact embarked on the same enterprise. They were groping for a way out of the trap of poverty and cruel injustice that history had imposed on them. In both countries, there were not only rebels in the hills contesting power, there were also governments in their capitals trying to change the flow of history.

In El Salvador that attempt was led by José Napoléon Duarte. Duarte is now dead and discredited, his rule as president a failure. He is remembered, if he is remembered at all, more as the cause of many of El Salvador's problems than as a leader who tried to resolve them.

Duarte's way out for El Salvador was Christian Democracy, the fusion of the contending pulls within Catholicism between the yearning for social justice and pluralist reform and its penchant for tradition and stability. His hero was Konrad Adenauer, West Germany's first chancellor and the founder of its post-World War II democracy. He kept a bust of Adenauer on his desk in the presidential palace. Duarte saw parallels between the German chancellor's career and his own. Adenauer had been arrested by the Nazis and ousted from his post as mayor of Cologne but came back and rebuilt his country out of the ruins of the Nazi defeat. Duarte, a former mayor of San Salvador, had won the presidency in 1972 but the army stole the election, arrested, beat and tortured him and then packed him off into exile.

In 1980 Duarte, too, got a chance to rebuild his country. Just as Adenauer was forced to manoeuvre between the Allies and what remained of the largely Nazi bureaucracy he had to work with, so did Duarte intend to manoeuvre between the Americans, the Salvadoran military and the leftist guerrillas, hoping to play them off against each other to transform the country into a democracy.

It didn't work out that way. With Ronald Reagan in the White House, the Americans had no great interest in restraining the old murderous ways of the Salvadoran army. Provided the soldiers killed communists, Washington did not much care who else was killed, as long as they did not murder Americans. Even when they did kill Americans, the U.S. could not bring itself to use its full power to crack down on the officer corps. The Salvadoran colonels soon learned that they could ignore Duarte, that they could use him as a democratic front, that they could handle the Americans and keep the spigot of U.S. aid open by being somewhat more discriminate in their killing.

Duarte's tragedy is that of a good man who in opposition suffered for his principles and, once in power, thought he could achieve what he believed in through accommodation with his enemies on the right and ended with his ideals buried under a mountain of corrupt compromises. By the time he died of cancer in 1990, the Christian Democratic option for true reform in El Salvador had all but died too.

In Nicaragua, they took the opposite path, the way of revolutionary collectivism and failed as well.

We were driving north from Managua on the Pan-American highway when I spotted a procession of children marching alongside the road. They were all carrying little chairs turned upside down on their heads. The chairs were obviously homemade, flimsy things hammered together from odd bits of wood. As light as the chairs were, some of the smaller kids staggered under the load. It was eight in the morning, and the children were obviously heading for school.

We stopped, and I followed them to see what kind of school it was that made its students bring their own chairs. What I found was the proud and yet pathetic essence of the Sandinismo. There were two buildings, really huts of the kind that are mostly just a tin roof supported by posts, with walls that have more door and window openings — without doors or windows — than wall. Inside, a dirt floor, a blackboard and a chair and desk for the teacher. Nothing else. Not even a single book. Yet when the huts filled with children and their chairs, their noise and their laughter, it was a school, a real school. Words began to fill the blackboard and the sound of words, the sounds of learning drifted out.

Outside, a young woman was giving a phys. ed. class. She looked awkward because she was wearing high heels. She struggled so hard to keep her spikes from sinking and sticking in the soil as she jumped up and down that it made her look like a fly flapping about trying to free itself from a strip of flypaper. For her, it seemed, high heels were too important a symbol of sophistication — or were they perhaps a credential of having risen from the ranks of campesinos to authority? — to be discarded for mere comfort and efficiency.

It may not have been a school you would have wanted to send your kids to, nor I mine, but it was an important school, an impressive achievement of the Sandinista revolution, a school where there had been no school before. The Sandinistas were rightfully proud of such schools and of their campaign to teach adult illiterates to read and even to write a little; of the clinics that they managed to open with the help of

Cuban doctors and nurses where there had been no medical care before; and of the land — confiscated sometimes illegally, often arbitrarily and sometimes capriciously — that they handed to co-operatives of landless peasants to till.

It was the little, primitive schools, the equally primitive clinics and the co-op farms with only the most rudimentary equipment that made me feel when I first came to Managua in 1983 from San Salvador as I had felt when I'd arrived in Peking a dozen years earlier from Calcutta. The poverty in all these places was staggering. But in Daniel Ortega's Nicaragua, as in Mao's China, one had the feeling that the regime at least was trying to alleviate poverty. Nicaraguans may not have been eating much better because of the Sandinista revolution but, like the Chinese in the early days of Mao, they had been given hope.

Unlike China and the Soviet Union, Ortega's Nicaragua was not a communist dictatorship. There was quite a bit of communism in the Sandinista system, and there were quite a few elements of dictatorship. But throughout the rule of the Sandinistas, there were substantial sectors of private enterprise operating in Nicaragua; they were barely tolerated but they were there. And while the Sandinistas maintained an extensive and sometimes heavy-handed security apparatus and had many other copycat features of Moscow-style control, dissent was grudgingly condoned, even though opposition was routinely harassed. The Sandinistas contended that these were only wartime measures, that considering that their enemies were waging a war against them, they were being restrained. Their opponents, of course, argued that whatever restraint the Sandinistas did show was only the result of pressure from the contras and the United States.

In any case, Nicaragua never suffered the dark silence of Maoist China or Stalinist Russia. There was never any shortage of people willing, even eager, to criticize the regime openly. In many respects the Sandinistas behaved as if they still believed — as the Soviet and Chinese aparatchiks so obviously did not — in the need for justice and humanity. In others, they exhibited the classic symptoms of the arrogance of unbridled power.

The contrast between El Salvador and Nicaragua was overwhelming. Hunger and undernourishment were conspicuous in Salvador. What little there was of land reform was undermined by official neglect, even sabotage, and by the intimidation of the death squads. Violent death was everywhere.

The worst of it was that the reign of terror was random.

The death squads did not kill just leftist activists. They killed the poor. They killed the priests and nuns. They killed unionists and journalists. They killed Catholics because they were Catholic, and they killed Protestants because they were not. To the death squads, everyone except their own was a communist. Often it seemed that they were killing just for kicks.

El Salvador was a spooky place. In a burst of gallows humor, foreign correspondents, who were constantly being threatened by the extreme right, had T-shirts made up bearing the inscription, *Periodista! No dispare!* (Journalist! Don't shoot!). We didn't wear them out in the field, of course; they would have been an irresistible invitation to some soldier or cop to take a pot shot at us. It was bad enough as it was. In a single weekend in March 1989, three journalists were killed in separate incidents. Two were shot in the back at army roadblocks. The third, a Dutchman, was hit during a battle, presumably accidentally in crossfire. Then, while his colleagues were taking him to a hospital, an army helicopter machine-gunned their vehicle although it bore clear press markings.

It was a relief to go from sinister San Salvador to dreary Managua.

There was ruthless violence in Nicaragua, too. But it was confined mostly to the contra war, and the war was being waged along the underpopulated mountain chain that runs across Nicaragua on a slant from north to south and divides the country between a Hispanic Pacific region with rich soil and a swamp-infested east populated mostly by Miskito Indians and English-speaking Caribbean blacks.

When I first came to Nicaragua, the contra war was young, and all the fighting was taking place close to the Honduran border. As the war went on, it spread through the mountains to the centre of the country, not only south from Honduras but also northwards from the Costa Rican border. The Salvadoran rebels, too, had their strongholds in the mountains. But they were active almost everywhere in the country, cutting roads and power supplies, attacking large army buses, staging raids right in the heart of the capital. The contras, by contrast, never managed to break out of the mountains into the Pacific plain where most Nicaraguans live. Theirs was mostly a hit-and-run war. Their victims, as in the Salvadoran war, were mostly civilians, and they never managed to occupy any significant chunk of Nicaraguan territory.

While potential targets such as military posts and bridges had to be heavily guarded in El Salvador and were routinely attacked, most of Nicaragua outside the mountain war zone seemed almost on a peace footing. Even the Sandinista government compound in Managua, a place that in any guerrilla war would count as a prime target, seemed less heavily protected than is Buckingham Palace.

The one measure of contra penetration I always watched for when we travelled to the war zone was the bridge at Sebaco, a hundred kilometres north of Managua. There was an important road junction just beyond the bridge. Nicaragua's main north-south road, the Pan-American Highway to Honduras, curved off to the left; the road to Matagalpa, the main city of northern Nicaragua, branched off to the right. There was no other paved road to serve the area. If the Sebaco bridge had ever been cut, the North would have been effectively cut off from Managua, giving the contras a lot more manoeuvring room.

In El Salvador, a bridge like the one at Sebaco would have been heavily guarded. There would have been gun emplacements and obstacles to slow the traffic. Despite such precautions, the bridge would likely have been blown, replaced and attacked yet again. But the Sebaco bridge was never attacked despite the fact that, except for a military post just south of it, it was all but unguarded. The bridge at Sebaco stood there as a sign of the contras' military impotence.

That does not mean that the contras were politically ineffective. Nor that they were merely what the Sandinistas tried to make them out to be: supporters of the former Somoza dictatorship, former members of the Somoza national guard, puppets of the Americans and mercenaries. There was a disingenuousness about the Sandinista propaganda that fooled no one more than it did the Sandinistas themselves. Right to the end, the Sandinistas had difficulty accepting that they may have alienated Nicaraguans, not just *Somocistas* and not only the rich of Managua and of the large estates, but ordinary *campesinos*. The contras had grass-roots support from the very beginning and nowhere more than in the hill country where the Sandinista revolution itself was nurtured.

I got a demonstration of the appeal of the contras early in the war in 1983. All night through the border hills a Sandinista army detachment had chased a contra group that had crossed from Honduras. When we met up with the soldiers early in the morning, they were coming back carrying with them the bodies of five contras. The soldiers insisted the dead men were *guardistas*, members of the Somoza National Guard, but they looked much too young. The Sandinistas knew that, too; they knew their names and their ages and that they all came from the nearby village of El Limon and had only recently left home to join the contras. So the Sandinistas put the bodies on the back of a truck and took them to El Limon. They paraded the bodies around the square as a loudspeaker called on the villagers to come out and take a look at them. The grisly show was a warning of what would happen to the young men of El Limon if they continued joining the contras.

There are many reasons why the contras enjoyed more support in the hills than on the plains. In the first place, mountain men everywhere — from Scotland to Kurdistan — are more prone to challenge authority than lowlanders. The difficulties of hilly terrain make it easier for them to sustain a rebellion. Farms in the hills are also poorer and therefore more likely to be worked by the people who own them than in the lowlands. The small coffee growers in the north of Nicaragua and the cattle ranchers in the hills of the central provinces of Boaco and Chontales were conservative, and they resented Sandinista efforts to deprive them of their land by grouping them into co-operatives.

If the contras could not have operated in Boaco and Chontales without being re-supplied by CIA airdrops, neither could they have survived there without the support of the local population. That was a factor that the Sandinistas preferred to ignore. They insisted that the contras had no popular support. However, if you looked closer, much of the contra war was less a conflict between left and right or an offspring of the Cold War but rather, as so much else in Nicaraguan history, a war of clans, of family against family.

El Robledal is a Sandinista farm co-operative. But don't let that fool you. El Robledal is essentially a family farm. Just about every one of its 150 people is a Galeano. The president of the co-op is Alcide Galeano. The school — this one has solid walls, doors and window shutters because it gets a good deal colder in the northern hills than in the lowlands — is named after Oscar Danilo Galeano. In El Robledal, the double surnames of Spanish usage are either Galeano Something — for those whose fathers were Galeanos — or Something Galeano — for the offspring of Galeano mothers. El Robledal is so inbred that there are even quite a few Galeano Galeanos.

The Galeanos of El Robledal are good Sandinistas, because it was the Sandinista government that gave them their land and also the means of keeping it: guns. So when the call went out from Sandinista headquarters during the election campaign of 1990 for a show of support for Daniel Ortega during a rally he would hold in Estelí, El Robledal responded enthusiastically. The Galeanos knew that Estelí, their provincial capital, was in danger of falling into the hands of the allies of their contra enemies, the UNO coalition of Violeta

Chamorro. If Estelí City fell, so might Estelí Province, which would be awkward even if *el Frente*, the Sandinista Front, still stayed in power in Managua as everyone in the know knew it would. So they all set out on trucks for the bone-shaking ride along the dirt rollercoaster that serves as El Robledal's road to Estelí. Well, actually not quite all the people of El Robledal; just those who traditionally counted in such things, the men.

The men of El Robledal left behind not only their women and their children but also their guns. They were told they would not need guns in Estelí; the power of the Sandinista revolution would protect them from the UNO-contras.

When the men of El Robledal returned after the rally, they found a surprise. A band of twenty contras had raided the co-op while they were in town. The rebels tore up all the voter registration cards they could find and stole the co-op's cash reserve of 29 million cordobas (about $400 at the time) and all its guns. Before pulling out, the contras told the co-op's women to tell their men that if they voted for the Sandinistas it would cost them dearly.

For all the damage the contras had done, they had not hurt any of the women and children. For good reason. The contras were not exactly strangers. They were neighbors. They came from La Rinconada, a settlement just a few kilometres down the road. Many of them, including their commander, the man they called *Pantera* (the Panther), were also Galeanos. Galeano men may kill Galeano men but they do not kill each other's women and children.

The men of El Robledal decided that they would have to replace the stolen guns if they were to feel safe as the election neared. On Sunday, March 18, a week before election day, five Galeanos set out on horses for the nearest Sandinista army post to try to get new guns. In country as rough and primitive as the mountains of Estelí province, you can't phone ahead to say you need guns or send an order for so-and-so-many guns by telex or FAX. You just go and hope for the best. But when the Galeanos got to the army post, the soldiers told them they had no spare guns. So the five men set out to return home empty-handed.

The person who must have alerted the contras about the arms trip — possibly the same person who tipped them off about the men of El Robledal going off to attend the Ortega Rally — could not have known the Galeanos would be returning gunless. To the contras, getting new arms that easily must have seemed like too good an opportunity to miss.

The emissaries from El Robledal were only a couple of kilometres from home when they rounded a corner and ran into the contra ambush. They didn't have a chance. Four were killed on the spot; the fifth died later.

By the time we got there, vultures were feasting on the dead horses. And in El Robledal, there were four new widows and eleven new orphans.

What the Galeanos are to farming in their obscure little corner of the northern hills, the Chamorro clan is to newspapering in the capital. There are three newspapers in Nicaragua. All are run by Chamorros. Violeta Barrios de Chamorro, the matriarch of the clan, owns *La Prensa*, and her daughter Cristina runs it. Doña Violeta's brother-in-law, Xavier Chamorro, is publisher of the pro-Sandinista *El Nuevo Diario*, and her younger son, Carlos Fernando, is the editor of the Sandinista party daily *Barricada*.

Throughout the rule of the Sandinistas, *La Prensa* was the most powerful anti-Sandinista voice in the country. Neither it nor its Sandinista competitors let family ties stand in the way of their political battles. All three are mainly propaganda sheets. What gives the Chamorros that extra edge of editorial certitude and an air of righteousness is that they seem to believe that, as Chamorros, they always know what is best for Nicaragua. The Chamorros have always had that sense of assuredness — a Chamorro was the country's first president — and the upset election of Doña Violeta in 1990 as the country's fifth Chamorro president can only have reinforced that conviction.

The saga of the Chamorros may be more glamorous than the stories of other families in Nicaragua. But they are only a part of an intertwined oligarchy of clans. Doña Violeta herself is an offspring of the Barrios family, which has been as powerful and, if anything, even richer than the Chamorros. The Chamorros and the Barrios, the Lacayos, Argüellos and Cuadras are used to running things, no matter who is in power. The Number Two in the Sandinista army is a Cuadra. An Argüello is the president of the National Assembly. Doña Violeta's daughter Claudia was the Sandinista ambassador to Madrid and a close ally of Daniel Ortega. The other daughter, Cristina of *La Prensa*, is married to Antonio Lacayo, who serves as chief-of-staff to his mother-in-law. Lacayo's sister in turn is married to Alfredo César, who was once part of the Sandinista government, then switched to become the contras' political director and by 1990 was performing much the same function for President Chamorro.

New people are always trying to muscle in on the oligarchy. In 1849, the first Chamorro president had a man named Somoza hanged because Somoza had tried to take the presidency away from him. (Somoza's life apparently might have been spared had he not also committed the much more serious crime of stealing Chamorro's mistress.) Usually, though, the newcomers to power were co-opted and absorbed into the family compact. But that process broke down when another Somoza made a grab for the presidency and succeeded.

Anastasio Somoza was the man the Americans left in charge of the Nicaraguan National Guard when they pulled out their marines in 1933. "Somoza may be a son of a bitch," President Franklin Roosevelt said, "but he's our son of a bitch." Never was U.S. policy towards Central America stated more succinctly. For Nicaraguans, history has always been a choice between being on Washington's leash and tasting its lash.

Within four years of the departure of the U.S. troops, Anastasio Somoza had made himself president and dictator. The Somozas — Anastasio's two sons succeeded him — angered the oligarchy because they were greedier, crueller and more corrupt than the usual upstart dictators. The old families resented the Somozas because they ran the country as if it were their own private estate. In the late seventies, the editor of *La Prensa*, Doña Violeta's husband,

Pedro Joaquín Chamorro, became convinced that Anastasio Somoza, Jr., had to go. Chamorro allied himself with a group of young leftist guerrillas, called Sandinistas, who had been fighting a lonely and none too effective war against Somoza for years.

Somoza had Chamorro imprisoned, exiled and, finally, on January 10, 1978, assassinated. The murder set off a furore. Forty thousand people attended Chamorro's funeral. Buildings associated with the Somoza regime's corruption were attacked by mobs and burned. Pedro Joaquín Chamorro became the national martyr whose name galvanized and united the opposition. Still, it took eighteen months of sustained fighting by the Sandinistas to oust Somoza.

When it was over, the Sandinistas agreed to share power with their allies. Pedro Joaquín's widow became a member of the ruling junta along with Daniel Ortega. But the coalition quickly broke down. Violeta Chamorro and others resigned, charging that the Sandinistas were turning the country into a Marxist dictatorship. The Sandinistas were now left running the country on their own.

Shortly thereafter, Ronald Reagan came to the White House and started his proxy war against Nicaragua. Washington was once more trying to force its own sons-of-a-bitch on Nicaragua.

In El Salvador, the war grinds on. Nothing has been resolved, not politically, not militarily. Nothing symbolizes better the lack of movement in El Salvador than the fact that more than ten years after Archbishop Romero was murdered, the case is still unresolved. Solving it and prosecuting and convicting the murderers would have been a powerful signal that the days of the murder squads are gone. The failure to solve the case helped bring the extreme right back to power and with it a resurgence of the death squads.

To this day, no one has been tried for Romero's murder although there is credible evidence about who killed him. Unless there is a radical change of government and the power of the army is broken, no one ever will be. The Salvadoran Supreme Court effectively closed the case in December 1988 by ruling that a crucial witness in the case could not be arrested because the delay of eight years "completely undermines the credibility of his testimony." That ruling means that any new evidence or testimony by other witnesses would be thrown out on the same grounds even though there is no Salvadoran law that limits the validity of testimony.

The decision by the Supreme Court, dominated by judges of the extreme right, was just another in a long line of scandalous court actions shielding death-squad murderers. In El Salvador, justice has become rare; it has been cowed in most cases into looking the other way.

Of the 70,000 people killed since the civil war started a decade ago, human rights' monitors estimate most were civilians murdered for political reasons. Some of these assassinations were perpetrated by rebels of the left. But most of the murders — more than 40,000 of them, according to the estimates of the Roman Catholic church's legal aid office in San Salvador — were assassinations and massacres committed by the army, the police and the death squads, most of whose members are serving or former members of the army.

Yet all through the eighties, not a single army officer, active or retired, was convicted of a death-squad murder. The only people jailed were a few ordinary soldiers convicted of the murders of Americans. These convictions were obtained only after heavy pressure from the U.S. embassy. But not even the Americans, who bankroll the army, could reach the higher-ups behind the killings. It was not until 1990 that several officers, one of them a colonel, were arrested and charged with the murder of six prominent Salvadoran Jesuit priests. These arrests took place only because of the heavy pressure put on the Salvadoran government by the U.S. Congress and the American Catholic Church.

The Romero case was the most important of all the thousands of assassinations of the high and the humble in El Salvador, not only because of the standing of the victim but also because of the prominence of the prime suspect: Roberto d'Aubuisson, the founder of the extreme rightist Republican

Nationalist Alliance (ARENA) party, defeated presidential candidate, deputy in the National Assembly and, at one time, the assembly's president. The base of d'Aubuisson's political career and power was his role as the apparent *padrino* (godfather) of the death squads.

D'Aubuisson, a former army major, was accused not of firing the bullet that killed the archbishop but of organizing the murder. Shortly after the killing, his original accusers were among the highest in the land: President Duarte and Robert White, the U.S. ambassador to El Salvador at the time. But theirs were accusations, not evidence.

The evidence linking d'Aubuisson to the killing came much later. It was not until 1987 that investigators were able to bring Amado Antonio Garay before a magistrate. He testified that on the day of the archbishop's murder, on orders of his employer, Alvaro Saraiva, a cashiered Salvadoran air force officer who was d'Aubuisson's protégé, he had picked up a bearded man he did not know and had driven him to the hospital chapel. Sitting in the back seat of the car, the man fired his gun through the door of the chapel.

Garay also testified that he was present when Saraiva reported on the success of the Romero killing to d'Aubuisson. Investigators said he later also identified the gunman in his car as Hector Antonio Regalado, a dentist whom d'Aubuisson had retained as his chief of security when he was president of the national assembly. Regalado was alleged to have been a death-squad hit man, who, among other things, was accused of having used a Boy Scout troop to do his killing for him and then had the ten teenage Scouts of Santiago de Maria murdered to keep them from talking.

Garay passed several lie detector tests, and his testimony was checked out by investigators. As a result, the Salvadoran government asked for the extradition of Saraiva from Miami, where he had been living illegally. U.S. authorities arrested the former captain and ordered him extradited.

That is where the Salvadoran right stepped in to keep Saraiva from testifying. Not only did the rightists manage to get a Supreme Court ruling that the Salvadoran extradition request to the U.S. was illegal; they also used their majority in the National Assembly to fire the attorney-general, who had been handling the Romero case. As for d'Aubuisson, no matter how strong Saraiva's evidence against him might have been, the predilection of the Salvadoran legal system to see no evil in members of the officer caste would almost certainly have spared him from ever having to go to court to defend himself. But the actions of the Supreme Court and the Assembly did save him from an embarrassment that would have killed his political career and devastated his party's fortunes.

Once again, Roberto d'Aubuisson had demonstrated his power. The major — to the Americans in San Salvador he was just Major Bob — was not only the most feared man in El Salvador, he was also to many a hero, the potential savior of his country.

March 1982. Following the little major campaigning was a wild ride. We were jammed in the back of a small red pickup truck with four of his bodyguards brandishing their automatic arms. In a car just behind us, the car we were filming and the guards were supposedly protecting, rode the major himself. Every few minutes, in a particularly enthusiastic burst of gun-waving at someone or something by the roadside, a gun butt would poke me in the ribs. It was all for propaganda, disembodied arms jutting out of car windows throwing leaflets at curious gapers, speeding bumpily along the Pan-American Highway through San Miguel Province, daring the rebels, who could and did cut off the highway daily at will, to come out and get us.

D'Aubuisson campaigned where others dared not, in the little towns surrounded by guerrilla strongholds, where Duarte's face was seen only on television in closely guarded halls filled with carefully picked supporters, towns in which the army and police took a few cautious steps into the countryside during the day but holed up for safety in the plaza at night. D'Aubuisson's cavalcade, meanwhile, made it a point to be seen in the worst of places.

The major's message was simple and brutal: The killing

could be ended only by more killing more quickly. His symbols: the gun and the watermelon.

Everywhere he went there would be a watermelon with a machete beside it waiting for him on the podium. When he got going, when he was in full oratorical flight denouncing Duarte and his Christian Democrats for their failure to win the war, he would lift the machete, point it at the melon and say, "The Christian Democrats are like this melon." Swish. Down came the machete slicing through the melon. "This is what Duarte is: green on the outside, red on the inside." Towards the end of the campaign, his message was so well known that he no longer needed the machete. The melon was pre-cut for him and all he had to do was to hold up half of it and the crowd would yell, "Green on the outside, red inside."

Green was the color of Duarte's Christian Democrats, the color of land redistribution reform, which was popular with almost everyone except the large landowners who had lost much of their land to the peasantry and therefore backed and financed d'Aubuisson, his party and, in many cases, the death squads. The red stood for traitors, not just Duarte and the leftist rebels fighting in the hills but also union leaders, teachers and churchmen. And the Americans, too, for being squeamish. And, of course, foreign journalists.

The army could not win the war, d'Aubuisson argued, because its hands were tied by the Duarte government and the Americans. If he were to win the election, he insisted, the war would be over quickly. He would hold up three fingers and say, "*Tres meses*" (three months). He kept repeating the promise everywhere he went. He did not go into details about how he would win the war in three months. He didn't have to. All he would say was that he would let the army do its job unhampered. His audiences understood. They knew the Salvadoran army and its history.

Tres meses was shorthand for *La Matanza* (The Massacre), an army operation in 1932 in which thousands died. It started with a communist-led uprising of peasants. The army put it down quickly and brutally, leaving hundreds dead. But worse was yet to come. After the uprising was over, the army

and paramilitary forces scoured the countryside systemati-
cally killing peasants, most of them Indians. Estimates of
the number of *campesinos* killed in the *Matanza* vary from
10,000 to 30,000 in a country with a population of a million and a half. The most authoritative source — if for no
other reason than his surname — was Alfredo Schlesinger,
a Honduran journalist who covered the killings and favored
the government side; he set the death toll at 25,000. In any
case, it was the biggest massacre since 1523–24, when Pedro
de Alvarado and Martin Estete, two of the cruellest of the
conquistadores, subdued what is now El Salvador. What the
conquistadores started, the army in a sense finished in 1932.

The *Matanza* marked the end of a separate Indian culture
in El Salvador. The Indians were forced to abandon the last
vestiges of their Maya, Cuzcatlan and Pipil heritage: their
language and their distinctive dress. The *Matanza* also consolidated the hold of the oligarchy of large coffee growers.

In the fascinating ways of history, you could trace the ori-
gins of El Salvador's present troubles back to the day in 1883
when Adolf von Baeyer, a German chemist, managed to un-
ravel the mystery of the chemical structure of indigo, a dye-
stuff made from plants. That led to the manufacture of synthetic dyes and the end of the indigo-growing industry in El
Salvador and elsewhere.

Indigo had until then been the mainstay of the Salvadoran
export economy. There had been worries about El Salvador's
over-reliance on indigo, and coffee had been brought in in
the 1850s in an effort to diversify. But there was a difference
between the two commodities. Whereas indigo was grown
on small subsistence farms, often communally owned, coffee was grown in El Salvador on *fincas*, large estates with
their own processing plants. With the collapse of indigo, the
coffee industry took over and consolidated itself into an oligarchy dominated by fourteen families. The unequal system
of land tenure and the manipulation of the coffee growers
to make sure that a large work force would always be available cheaply led to chronic unrest. Quelling it became the
Salvadoran army's main mission, and stopping land reform and unionization of farm workers the principal aim of

government. *La Matanza* was the logical culmination of that process.

For four decades, memories of the *Matanza* kept the Salvadoran work force docile. By 1982, though, the *Matanza* had taken on a new meaning. To the new leftist rebels, the uprising fifty years earlier was an inspiration. They named their umbrella organization the Farabundo Martí National Liberation Front, after Augustín Farabundo Martí, the leader of the 1932 rebellion. On the right, the most notorious of the death squads carried the name of General Maximiliano Hernández Martínez, the military ruler who carried out the *Matanza*.

To many of the voters who flocked to d'Aubuisson's rallies, especially those in the small towns where life had been most immediately disrupted by the war, the idea of some new form of *Matanza* was appealing. The people in small market towns did not have much but they had something: a house, a shop, perhaps a market stall consisting of nothing more than a blanket on the ground, a job even if that job was scavenging. But now the guerrillas from the hills were knocking out bridges, blowing up power pylons, halting traffic on roads and burning trucks. The produce from the countryside on which the town depended stopped coming. So did the customers from the small villages who used to come to buy their supplies. On top of that, there were the burdens of the army quartering its troops in town and refugees flooding in from the war-ravaged villages. Sometimes, too, the guerrillas would attack the town directly, burning the town hall perhaps or killing a *padrino* who provided jobs.

D'Aubuisson's message of ending the war quickly appealed to these people. What was more, he was personally appealing, young and articulate. His robust military rhetoric appealed to the men, and the smile that always crinkled his face attracted the women. When he rode into a town in a cavalcade of armed men with machine guns cocked and held at the ready, and then strode to the podium with his pistol conspicuously tucked into his pants, there was no mistaking that the man stood for a crude, brutally tough attack not only on the guerrillas but on just about every institution in the country that brought some measure of social justice and alleviation of poverty.

Yet, though his reputation and popularity rested on his brutal approach to problems and his penchant for violence, d'Aubuisson always denied he had anything to do with the death squads and, most particularly, with the murder of Archbishop Romero. In public, he denied the charges with anger. In interviews with American reporters, he usually reproached them in a sorrowful manner for how they had let themselves be taken in by communist propaganda. Once in awhile, when there was nothing much at stake, when he was not making a speech at a rally, not talking to American congressmen, he laughed it all off. That is what he did that day in 1982 in eastern Salvador when I asked him whether he had ordered the archbishop killed.

After racing around the countryside most of the day, d'Aubuisson invited us to join him while he was taking a break in a quiet garden. It was a relaxed affair, more a chat than an interview, as much lazy laughter and sipping of cold beer and Cokes in the afternoon heat as talking politics. Whenever I could get a word in to ask him about his role in the death squads, he would wink at his bodyguards and then deny he had anything to do with the killings. Not only denied it but had fun doing so. When I asked him about the Romero killing, he replied with the same "catch me if you can" insouciance that Gary Hart later used while running for the U.S. presidency to fend off questions about his extra-marital flings. The bodyguards laughed as if the idea of their leader being involved in murder was just too ridiculous to contemplate. But while d'Aubuisson dismissed the accusations against him as politically motivated falsehoods, he did not condemn the killers. They were, he said, patriotic men who had become outraged by the betrayal of the country they saw all around them.

He was very confident that afternoon that he would win. He was wrong. And yet in a way he was also right.

There are few things as exhilarating as watching democracy struggling to be born through an election. Watching people vote who had never done it before, watching them crowd the polls, seeing the hardships and, frequently, the intimidation that they have had to overcome restores your faith in democracy, not necessarily in its workings after the elections are over, but in the strength of the human hunger for the free expression of the communal will.

In the last few years, the list of democracies a-borning has become long. In Chile and Czechoslovakia. Poland and Brazil. East Germany and Namibia. In Argentina and, oh so imperfectly, in Romania. In Nicaragua and even, painfully, in the Soviet Union. What was unbelievable at first has become commonplace. And yet . . .

In the Nicaraguan election campaign of 1989 — the one in which the Sandinistas were upset — the Sandinistas had an unusual poster that showed two pairs of bare young legs standing up close against each other, toe to toe. One set of legs, with a bracelet around one ankle, was on tiptoes, reaching up. Beyond the top of the frame the couple were obviously locked in an unseen embrace. The caption said, "It's always best the first time. More honest. Vote Sandinista." It was a silly poster, particularly since the Sandinistas had staged and won an election in 1984 that they claimed had been free and fair despite an opposition boycott. It must have struck any voter looking at the poster that if the 1989 vote was the first time for anyone, it was a first for the opposition, not the Sandinistas. Beyond that, though, the poster had a certain ring of truth. First elections are very much like first love affairs.

There is the excitement, the sweetness of it, the feeling that no one else has ever gone through in quite the same way what you are going through. If you are a realist, you may be aware that tomorrow could bring disillusionment. But, please, not yet, not now.

Just as you would never tell the young enraptured by the first stirrings of love that what they are feeling is the result of a mundane hormonal reaction, don't try to tell the Nicaraguans or the East Germans that the events that brought them free elections in 1990 were merely autonomous manifestations of certain systemic weaknesses of the Marxist–Leninist order. In the blush of nascent democratic politics, nations feel as unique, as enthusiastic, as ready to defy convention as couples in the throes of first love. And just as prone to disappointment and vulnerable to tragedy.

Long before *glasnost* swept Eastern Europe, long before the generals of South America started giving way to the ballot box, the Salvadoran election of 1982 showed the power of the suppressed yearning for democratic expression. And its pitfalls.

On election day, March 28, 1982, I was at a polling station in San Salvador where a line of several hundred people was waiting for the polls to open. Suddenly, a burst of gunfire. I watched as everyone dropped to the ground while the army fought off an attack by guerrillas trying to fulfil their threat to disrupt the elections. You would have expected that once the firing stopped, the civilians who lay pinned to the ground as the bullets flew over them would try to get away from the danger zone as quickly as they could. Wrong. They got up, dusted themselves off, re-formed the line and waited patiently for their turn to vote, ignoring the bodies of two dead guerrillas a few metres away.

What I saw in the capital was occurring in many other places in the country. In Apopa, just north of San Salvador, the guerrillas swept down from the hills and took the town. It took several hours for the army to dislodge them. In the meantime, the voters waited patiently and, once the guerrillas had retreated, they went back to vote. In San Salvador, the lines at most polling stations stretched several blocks, and people waited in the hot sun for hours. In the countryside, they walked for miles, often through territory controlled by the guerrillas. It was an impressive demonstration of the Salvadorans' will to have a say in the political process and of their faith that voting, something of which they had little experience, would somehow improve their lives.

Nothing, of course, is ever quite that simple. The guerrilla campaign to stop people from voting was matched by pressure from the government urging them to vote. In small

towns, there were threats from the police and town halls of
fines and other reprisals. For many, the question of voting
became a quandary. Once voters had cast their ballots, one
of their thumbs was rolled in an ink pad to make sure they
couldn't vote again. The ink was invisible to the naked eye;
a special infra-red flashlight was needed to detect it. The
idea was to protect voters from retribution by the guerrillas.
But many voters saw that the system would not necessarily
always work as it was supposed to. "With my luck," one man
complained to me, "if I don't vote, the cops will get me; if I
do, I'll run into rebels who have one of these funny flashlights
and they will take it out on me that I did vote."

In some places, it was the threats of the guerrillas that were
more potent; in others, the power of the police was greater.
It didn't seem to make much difference. The guerrillas were
unable to intimidate the mass of voters by their show of force;
they would have had to massacre quite a few of them to make
their threats effective and that would have been politically
counter-productive. If, on the other hand, enough people had
taken advantage of the guerrilla attacks and confusion as an
excuse not to vote, the police would have had an equally hard
time going through with their threats to go after all of them.

The turnout was heavy and, except for the hard core of
rebel support that did boycott the election, the voters' will
prevailed. José Napoléon Duarte and his Christian Democrats won. Roberto d'Aubuisson lost. He lost the legislative
elections of 1982 — even though, with the support of splinter
parties, ARENA controlled the assembly — and he lost the
presidential elections of 1984. His opponents, the Americans and even some of his more moderate supporters were
relieved. It had been a close escape. If he had won, Washington would have had to distance itself from the wild major's
government. The U.S. Congress would have almost certainly
cut off the hundreds of millions of dollars in aid that, besides
keeping the war going, was also making many Salvadoran
officers and businessmen rich.

But the exhilaration of free elections soon wore off. Like
love, democracy can turn sour. The Salvadorans learned that
quickly in El Salvador as the army returned to business as

usual, as Duarte wasted his mandate, as the Americans undermined him by continuing to put anti-communism ahead of
everything, justice and democracy included.

Nicaraguan President Daniel Ortega on a white horse riding
like a conqueror. Daniel Ortega's name on T-shirts, tens of
thousands of them. Daniel Ortega on TV in a music video.
Images of Daniel here and Daniel there cut to the urgent
beat of voices singing, Daniel, Daniel, Daniel. There are also
Daniel caps, so many of them that even the contras in the
hills have taken to wearing them. Hey, why not? They're free
and they keep the sun out of the eyes. Want a Daniel pen,
comrade?

Ortega is standing on the back of a truck that is moving slowly through the streets of Masaya. A discordant brass
band and a siren announce the candidate's coming. Today
Daniel is kissing babies. And not just kissing them. Click,
goes the instant camera beside Daniel as a child is passed up
to him. Another baby, another click. It's a production line,
two cameras working in relay. Baby up, click, baby down,
sixty seconds and here, comrade, is your cute child's photo
with Daniel. Vote for Daniel! Next baby please!

Daniel Ortega, the erstwhile earnest revolutionary who used
to wear drab uniforms and thick eyeglasses, who looked and
sounded like a Caspar Milquetoast version of Fidel Castro,
has changed into tight jeans, colorful shirts and contact lenses.
Instead of sheltering behind a rostrum at rallies with a microphone blotting out most of his face, instead of losing himself
in the comforting camouflage of a phalanx of flunkeys, Ortega
now prances about on the platform at rallies like a rock star,
alone, just him and his wireless mike bathed in the stardust
of lights.

That's what the Sandinista revolution has come down
to in 1990: marketing Daniel. No more marathon-length
Castroesque revolutionary harangues; the revolution is now
being sold like soap powder. "*Todo sera mejor*" — everything will be better — say the posters, the T-shirts, the TV

messages, the Daniel caps and Daniel's speeches. Viva New and Improved *Sandinismo*! Buy it now while supplies last!

But *todo sera mejor* was a double-edged sword. Given the terrible condition of Nicaragua's economy, the slogan just begged for the retort that things certainly couldn't get any worse. The Nicaraguan currency was all but worthless. Where not so many years before the thousand-cordoba note was the highest denomination, there was now a two-hundred-thousand bill, and everyone knew a million-cordoba note would be needed quickly if Nicaraguans were to be spared carrying around heavy bagfuls of money. The Soviet aid that had kept the economy afloat had been cut to a trickle, and just about the only thing that kept the country going were the dollars sent by Nicaraguan exiles in North America to their families.

Still, the Sandinistas had every expectation of winning the election. They had called it because winning it would give them the undisputed legitimacy that would once and for all defang their remaining enemies in Washington. And they were sure they would win. After all, they had won the war against the contras. The only question was how and when the contras would be disbanded. They realized they were in trouble over the economy, but they were confident that they could make people understand that the mess was not their fault, that it was the result of the war and of the trade embargo imposed by the United States. Now that the war was over, they could go on with the job of rebuilding and soon *todo sera mejor*.

The government also felt confident because the opposition was split into fourteen parties and seemed disorganized. Its presidential candidate, Violeta Chamorro, was considered weak, nothing much more than a nostalgic symbol, the widow of a glorious ghost. She was even further handicapped when she broke a knee in an accident and was forced to campaign from a wheelchair. She always appeared in white, white dress and white hat, riding on a white vehicle that looked like those popemobiles that John Paul II uses on his world tours. Indeed, that's what she looked like, a handsome elderly woman playing pope, the gentle messenger of peace.

But once they had loaded Doña Violeta laboriously off her popemobile on to the platform, once they had adjusted the microphone to wheelchair height, there was nothing gentle about her message. She was white and her cause virtuous, and the Sandinistas were all black, bloody dictators and economic incompetents.

Yes, she said, the war had been terrible, but it was the Sandinistas who had caused it, by their ideological intransigence, by their dictatorial arrogance, by betraying the ideals that her martyred husband had stood for. Yes, the war and the U.S. embargo had damaged the economy, but Sandinista incompetence and hare-brained schemes had put it well on the way to ruin before the war, even though the U.S. and various international organizations had pumped hundreds of millions of dollars into the country. And now that the war was over, the Sandinistas were still maintaining a huge army and the draft, to say nothing of the enormously costly apparatus of police and bureaucrats, to maintain themselves in power. As for the anti-Somoza revolution and land reform, they didn't belong to the Sandinista party; it had just kidnapped them.

While Chamorro hobbled on crutches, Ortega strutted. He was acclaimed at rallies as *nuestro gallo* (our rooster) with much cock-a-doodle-dooing from the crowd. Violeta, by inference, was *la gallina,* the lowly hen, a not very enviable role in a society as macho-oriented as Nicaragua. Daniel's supporters boasted that his rallies were always bigger than hers. They preferred to ignore that when he held a rally, the entire state bus and trucking system was at his disposal to bring in supporters. When she held one, many regularly scheduled public buses stopped running, and transportation companies refused to lease vehicles to her organization.

All the polls said the Sandinistas would win; it was only a question of by how much.

Astoundingly, *la gallina* won. Overwhelmingly, by fifty-five percent to forty. Masaya, the birthplace of the Sandinista revolution, went for Violeta. Whole Sandinista army units voted for UNO, Chamorro's coalition. Most Nicaraguans didn't believe that Ortega could make things better. They

went to his rallies as they had been required to do for a
decade and when interviewed by pollsters, many of them
dutifully recited what they had always been expected to say
under the Sandinistas. But when they got a chance to vote
freely, they put an end to the Sandinista revolution.

Elections are to democracy what weddings are to marriage. In
democracy as in marriage, you have to work at it or lose it.

Doña Violeta worked at it right from the start. When Daniel
Ortega, dejected by his devastating defeat, came to her house
the day after the election to congratulate her, she put her arms
around him and kissed him. It was certainly not a kiss of
love, nor even necessarily one of reconciliation. But neither
was it just a polite, empty gesture. It was rather a kiss of
accommodation that was to set the tone for her presidency.

The kiss was the start of a delicate balancing act. Chamorro
had won political power, but the Sandinistas still had the
guns; taking control of the guns away from them would be
no simple matter. Her coalition had a majority in the national
assembly but it was a collection of quarrelling parties. By far
the biggest single party in parliament, the Sandinistas were in
a good position to harass her government and frustrate her
programs.

To get the Sandinistas to loosen their hold on the army and
the police, she had to assure them that the contras, who were
once again feeling feisty because of her victory, would disarm.
To get the contras to go home, she had to convince them that
she had the power to protect them from the Sandinistas.

She put her balancing act in motion by embracing not only
Daniel Ortega but also his brother, Humberto, the Sandinista
minister of defence. She took on the defence ministry post
herself, but left Humberto Ortega in his post as commander
of the army. General Ortega, in turn, quit the Sandinista
party to signal that he and the Sandinista army would from
now on serve as purely professional soldiers.

Chamorro's fractious allies were outraged. She had turned
the job of chief gamekeeper over to the chief poacher. But it

worked. Within two months of her inauguration almost all of the contras in the country had been disarmed. And the Sandinista army, which had been by far the most powerful army in Central America, had been cut down by General Ortega — acting on Chamorro's orders — to less than half of the troop strength it had at the start of the year.

The problems of Nicaragua are still enormous, and Chamorro's manoeuvring room and capacity to solve them are limited. But the country has taken the first steps towards a precarious democracy. And peace, albeit a stormy one, has finally come to Nicaragua.

In El Salvador, in the meantime, peace and compromise still seem beyond reach. Roberto d'Aubuisson may have been defeated, but his work had not been wasted. By scaring everyone, he had become the benchmark. He himself may have been unacceptable, but by just being there, always on the edge of power, he had made everybody to the left of him — and that covered ninety-nine percent of the political spectrum — politically acceptable.

When d'Aubuisson's ARENA party finally did capture the presidency in 1989, it was not led by the major but by Alfredo Cristiani, a nice, unflappable sort of chap whom everyone calls Freddy.

Freddy is a bona fide Salvadoran rightist who does not sound like one. He is a wealthy businessman, a coffee planter, tall and handsome. Freddy speaks good English, not the heavily accented English that Duarte brought back from Notre Dame University in Indiana, but an English that speaks of pricey American prep schools or a good nanny. You could invite Freddy to tea at the White House and you could be sure he would know which fork to use and that he would not leave bloodstains on the napkins.

Cristiani campaigning was no Major Bob. Where d'Aubuisson was jovial and friendly even if threatening, Freddy was reserved and conciliatory. Where the major embraced women everywhere he went, I saw Cristiani recoil when a couple of weighty market women tried to put their matronly arms around him. He was obviously not used to the press of plebian flesh.

Cristiani won mainly because the Christian Democrats were in disarray and split. But he also won because he was not d'Aubuisson and yet had d'Aubuisson's people behind him. To the ARENA people, Freddy was their best chance of getting power and they were confident they could control him; others in Salvadoran politics and the Americans were afraid they might be right.

The verdict on Cristiani is mixed. He has repeatedly made peace overtures to the rebels and managed to get them to the negotiating table. He has not hesitated to combat them by unleashing the army against the civilian population of San Salvador. It was in the aftermath of the fighting in the capital in the autumn of 1989 that soldiers murdered the six Jesuit priests. Cristiani forced the army to arrest a colonel and two lieutenants. But he was not able to keep the army from hindering the investigation and sheltering the higher-ups who all but surely had a hand in the case. He is constantly in danger of being undercut by ARENA's extremist wing and the army. If he is not the peacemaker nor the man who put the death squads out of business, neither is he the creature of its killers. Washington can live comfortably with such a man. Freddy doesn't threaten; he soothes.

But the soothing sounds of peace are still being drowned out in El Salvador. The killing goes on. The army still shields its killers. The murderers of Archbishop Romero can sleep easily. Their hour of accounting is still far off.

CHAPTER XI

Men took on together an illusory past.
Only one thing was missing — the street had no other side.
Hard to believe Buenos Aires had any beginning.
I feel it to be as eternal as air and water.

Jorge Luis Borges
The Mythical Founding of Buenos Aires

The smell of mothballs hangs over Eva Perón's tomb. It is
May 7, 1989, and the remnants of her ardent army of admirers
have come to celebrate Evita's seventieth birthday. The first
chill of the Buenos Aires autumn, a balmy 15 degrees to the
rest of the world, has made the aging, cold-prone ladies of the
women's wing of the Perónist Party bundle up in coats just
taken out of the southern hemisphere's summer storage. As
the women stand praying, crying, kissing Evita's plaque on
her family's tomb, the slightly sickening aroma of naphtha-
lene envelops this small corner of La Recoleta cemetery as if
a surrogate for the smell of death.

The smell is trapped by the narrowness of the alley in which
the tomb stands. La Recoleta is not so much a graveyard
where bodies are returned, dust to dust, to the earth and

worms. This is a necropolis, a veritable city of the dead with streets and little houses in which the dead reside, resting in their coffins as if in bed. Most of the people brought to rest here didn't have far to go. La Recoleta is a rich man's playground both inside the cemetery and outside it. At the front entrance, chic cafés, fashionable stores and luxurious apartment buildings stretch across the rich Barrio Norte — Evita used to arouse crowds by threatening to burn down the Barrio Norte — to the splendid old mansions of Palermo Chico. Behind the cemetery, a playground for those seeking more earthy pleasures: a red-light district.

The cemetery, too, caters to various tastes and purses. There are modest row tombs, more ambitious semi-detached ones guarded by statues of mournful angels and elaborately vulgar mausoleums built like small castles or cathedrals. These are solid homes made of stone. To keep up with the times, many of the more recent ones have picture windows displaying ornate coffins, some covered with burial cloths that, by the look of them, must be changed regularly, like bed linen. Others have curtains to give their inhabitants privacy. There are also split-level models. The founders of the clan lie in the foreground. The caskets of their immediate offspring perch on a small balcony behind them. Many of these vaults also have stairs leading to basements into which subsequent generations are herded much like kids shooed into the family room to keep them out of the old folks' hair. La Recoleta might have made even Narcissus come to terms with death. But then Argentina is an exceedingly narcissistic country.

The tomb of Eva Duarte de Perón, though, has no picture window. Her casket is hidden behind two sets of metal bars and for good reason. Evita's embalmed corpse has led an insecure existence. It was lost for a long time, kidnapped, it turned out, by a general to spite her husband. When it was found in Italy, Juan Perón brought the remains to Madrid, where he was in exile at the time. After his return to power in 1973, Evita, by now one of history's best-travelled corpses, finally came home to the safety of the Duarte family tomb.

Ever since, Evita's grave has been the shrine of Perónism, and she the prime symbol of the movement her husband had founded. Without her, Juan Perón lost his touch. Three years after her death in 1952, he was overthrown by the military. By the time he returned from exile eighteen years later to become president for a third time, he was seventy-eight and semi-senile. In the year of life left to him, his government and his reputation unravelled. After his death, he was succeeded as president by his third wife, Isabelita, a dancer. She got her start towards the presidential palace by attracting the general's attention when he was in exile in Panama City in the late fifties by doing her number at the Happy Land cabaret in a skimpy dress made of ostrich feathers. It took Isabelita only two years to fritter away what was left of Perónist credibility. Most Argentinians were relieved when the army casually kidnapped her in 1976 and toppled her regime.

Where the remembrance of Juan Perón had become tainted by failure, the memory of Evita remained pure to millions of Argentinians because she had died young, beautiful and at the height of Perónista power. She had entertained the masses with her sumptuous lifestyle of elaborate gowns and dazzling jewellery. Even when she was dying, wasting away from cancer, she did it dramatically, like the consumptive heroine of a nineteenth-century melodrama. Like Mimi in *La Bohème*, Evita remained at centre stage to the last.

Juan Perón provided the strong-arm ideology of the regime, Evita its exhibitionist spirit. He looked after the repression, the plunder, the manipulation of the army, the mobilization of labor union power. Where Juan used his power to take from the rich and the public treasury, Evita spent extravagantly not only on herself but also on the poor. She sat in a large palace built like a Greek temple and held audiences at which she haphazardly handed out gifts large and small to thousands of people.

If Juan personified the state, Evita embodied the social welfare system. The Argentinians may not have had an unemployment insurance system, but they had Evita. To millions, she became Lady Bountiful, who had risen from the poor, who knew the pain of *los descamisados* (the shirtless ones) and shared their bitter envy of the rich. From upstart actress who traded on her sexuality, awkward provincial in snobbish Buenos Aires, autocrat mixing ruthless shrewdness, carefree generosity and extravagant exhibitionism, she was turned into a folk saint whose blonde replica was everywhere. As Argentina went downhill after she died, ever down as successor after successor vainly tried to match the Peróns' popularity by continuing their spendthrift policies until they had bankrupted the country, the spirit of Evita loomed larger, and her populist aura continues to burn brightly to this day.

Now, two days before the seventieth anniversary of her birth, a week before elections that will put another Perónista into the Casa Rosada, the Pink House, from whose balcony Evita and the general used to enfold the adulation of the crowds, the faithful crush past me down the narrow alley to her tomb, trampling elaborate wreaths. As I watch the old and the elderly, women mostly, and listen to their stories, I tell myself that this is the past on parade. One woman talks about a scholarship she got after Evita heard her story of hardship; another remembers never having had a pair of shoes until the Peróns came to power when she was eleven. "For us, Evita was everything," she says. What I am seeing, what I am hearing, it seems to me, is a tearful mustering out of the generation of the forties and the fifties.

The few young faces in the crown look curious, some even puzzled by the outbursts of emotionalism around them. Modern Perónism, post-Perón Perónism is no longer supposed to be the authoritarian movement of mystical faith that it was under the general and Evita. It prides itself on new, more pragmatic leaders, *renovadores*, or reformers, who want to carry on the populist tradition of old-style Perónism but in a democratic and more down-to-earth fashion. The modernizers see the new Perónism as the counterpart of European Social Democratic movements and of the British Labour party. Where Perón's role model used to be Benito Mussolini, theirs is Felipe Gonzalez, the cool, non-ideological Socialist prime minister of Spain. To them, the worshipful adoration of Evita is an embarrassing throwback to an obscurantist past.

All of a sudden, bustling and shoving. A wedge of young, muscular men shoulders its way down the alley bearing aloft a huge wreath. Behind the phalanx, a burly man in a black leather coat. There's a stir, and the elderly make room for Saul Ubaldini, the general secretary of the CGT, the Perónist Confederation of Labor, Argentina's main union organization. As the leader of more than four million union members, Ubaldini is the most powerful Perónist in the country.

Ubaldini lays his wreath, crosses himself several times and starts speaking. But he is not speaking to the crowd, not looking at the people. He is addressing himself directly to the corpse inside the tomb. "Evita," he declaims with a catch in his voice, "you are alive in the Argentinian people and, as always, you are the revolutionary flame of peace."

By the time he has finished imploring her, assuring her of Perónism's bright future, the crowd reacts as if Evita were indeed still with them. *"Evita presente,"* they yell. Evita is here. *"Viva Perón, viva Perón."*

As the mass of people, energized by Ubaldini and the younger contingent that swarms behind him, surges past Evita's tomb, tears glistening, they break into song, the old anthem of Perónism, *"Los muchachos Perónistas"* — the Perónist Boys. *"Perón, Perón, qué grande sos!"* they sing, *"Mi general, cuanto vales!"* Perón, Perón, how great you are, my general, how worthy!

Perónism present has gazed reverently into its discredited hokum past and has found its future there.

Buenos Aires is a beautiful city. It has the feel of Europe to it. It has broad boulevards, generous *fin-de-siècle* architecture that bespeaks money and optimism, shopping arcades reminiscent of Italian galerias, ornate cafés built for that most European of pleasures, lingering and dallying over a cup rather than just drinking up and rushing out. Schoolboys can still be seen here parading in English school caps and naked knees as reminders of Britain's once powerful sway. The park of Palermo is every bit as splendid as the Bois de Boulogne in Paris, and the opera house, the Teatro Colón, would not

look out of place on the Ring in Vienna. Here a sound of
London, a replica of Big Ben striking; there a glimpse of a
Madrid boulevard or a panorama of Barcelona.

Yet Buenos Aires is a sad place. Sad not just because it is
going downhill — which it is at a rapid pace — but most of
all because it never got to fulfil its promise. It is falling down
before it ever got finished. It is like a young bride who was
stood up at the altar and half a century later still wears the
tattered, discolored remains of her wedding dress.

So much promise. Argentina had everything: lots of land,
natural riches, wheat and meat, a clement climate, intelligent
and diligent people. A hundred years ago, Argentina was considered a land of opportunity as promising as North America.
In the early part of this century, when the French wanted to
say that someone was filthy rich, they would say he was *riche
comme un Argentin.*" The future seemed limitless. And then,
about forty years ago, the future became nothing but a re-run
of failures past.

Now even Argentinians see themselves as having dropped
from El Dorado into the Third World. How they got there is a
terrifying story — and a warning to other countries — of how
a country can have it all and still blow it.

Everybody has a different explanation of why it happened.
The best is a story that Argentinians like to tell about themselves. God, so the story goes, gave the land that is now
Argentina everything he had in his store of riches. He gave it
so much that the angels were moved to protest that the future
inhabitants of the country would have an unfair advantage
over all the other peoples of the world. "Don't worry," God
told the angels, "I will even things out. I shall populate this
land with Argentinians."

As in most other countries, some of Argentina's woes are
imports. But its biggest problems are strictly homemade.

The Argentinians started off on the wrong foot right from
the beginning. Too much land went to too few people. Argentina had no homestead laws to help newcomers. Instead of
being given land and citizenship, immigrants were exploited
as sharecroppers. With no political rights and no stake in the
land, they became a source of instability. Too few people

came to Argentina to settle; they came mostly to exploit it, to make a fortune and leave.

Argentina was also late in industrializing. Powerful landowners blocked protection for nascent industries, leaving the country dependent on foreigners for manufactured goods and capital. That left Argentina for a long time without the middle class that helped other countries achieve political stability. As a result, politics was a class struggle between rich landowners and merchants on one side and an impoverished proletariat on the other. When the fight was not about class, it was between Buenos Aires, the *entrepôt* of middlemen, and the producers in the rest of the country. With no national consensus among civilians, the army became the supreme arbiter of power, the destabilizing stabilizer. The presidency was turned into a preserve of generals.

"This is a country which was formed by generals," Perón once said, "liberated by generals, led by generals and today claimed by generals."

The generals were not content — as the pure patriots they claimed to be — just to rule as wisely as they could and retire on their military pensions. In the nineteenth century, they made their fortunes in land grabs. In the twentieth, the armed forces took over whole industries until, in the 1970s, officers ran just about everything. Whole industries were divvied up equally among the three services. But the soldiers didn't mount their coups on their own. Every time they overthrew a government, it was with the backing of some important segment of civilian society.

The result of a century of abuse was an unbalanced, divided society and constant social, political and economic unrest. Argentinians never learned to live together in peace and harmony, they never learned the art of compromise and the habits of tolerance. Coup followed coup. Every new regime would try to redress the wrongs and ineptitudes of the previous administration until it crashed under the weight of its own misdeeds and incompetence. Democratic governments elected by the urban masses were overturned by military regimes fronting for the landowning oligarchy that was forced out by a populist dictatorship, which in a few years was replaced by another military regime, which after awhile would be ousted by a different faction of the army. Then back to civilian rule. Until the next time.

The vicious game of musical chairs at the top corrupted all layers of society. Tax evasion on a grand scale became a way of life even as Argentinians demanded — and got — more government services and ever higher subsidies. Uncertainty became the only certainty. Disillusionment led to protest and the ineffectuality of peaceful protest to riots, guerrilla warfare and terrorism. Terrorism of the left was matched by terrorism of the right. Sometimes the two joined forces on the back side of the ideological moon in whose darkness the extremes of the political spectrum get to embrace each other's sick despair.

Eventually, as it had done with so much else in Argentina, the army took over the terrorism business and re-fashioned it on a bigger scale than anything the civilian amateurs ever inflicted. The military was turned into a machine of intimidation and inquisition, of torture and murder. People were not arrested; they were kidnapped. And they certainly were not tried; they just disappeared. *Los desaparecidos*, the disappeared ones, were men and women, young mostly, lawyers, writers, workers, students, journalists, in fact, anybody. The homely Ford Falcon became a universally feared instrument of police terror. The Fords would cruise the streets without licence plates and everyone knew that the absence of registration plates was in itself a licence, a licence to kill, and that these ever-so-ordinary cars were machines of prey that could swoop anywhere and carry off their quarry without leaving a trace. Nine thousand people "disappeared" during the military tyranny of the late seventies, and yet, with the exception of a few brave souls who protested, most of the country took the horror in its stride.

The generals also went on a spending spree. With no one to say them nay, they spent billions on submarines and frigates, planes and helicopters, and other toys. Civilians, too, joined the binge, tucking away in foreign bank accounts billions borrowed from abroad. By the late eighties, repayment had fallen so far behind accumulating interest charges that the debt grew out of control and became a cancer. With accumulated interest, Argentina now owed far more than it had originally borrowed. Argentinians blamed their predicament on the greed of foreigners. But even as their government was going broke, even as industry and commerce were being starved of investment funds, there would have been enough money to repay most of the debt if Argentinians only had enough confidence in their country to repatriate the money they had sent abroad and to bring the dollars they held at home out of hiding.

Argentina was bankrupt; Argentinians were not. Most of them still lived relatively well. The country was so richly endowed that they were able to live off the proverbial fat of the land for decades. Even now there is still a lot of glitter and cash in the Barrio Norte, and the few true slums are inhabited largely by Paraguayan immigrants.

Argentinans just got used to living with runaway inflation. The most important rule for coping with money that loses value every hour is to spend it quickly or change it into other currencies. And to watch those ever multiplying zeroes on banknotes. It's easy to mistake six zeroes for five or to be confused by a note that was printed a few years ago as a 10,000 bill but has recently been re-issued with a barely distinguishable over-print that says it's now worth a million. Hyper-inflation keeps merchants and store clerks hopping, changing prices to keep ahead of inflation or perish. Customers try to beat them to it by hitting stores before they get a chance to change their price tickets.

Runaway inflation is worst for wage earners. Though salaries and wages are indexed, the pay increases are mostly tied to last month's inflation rate. Since salaries are paid at the end of the month, they are always running a month behind on the inflation scale. Even when allowances are made for the current month's likely inflation, it doesn't help much because that in itself will push inflation even higher.

The only sure way of beating inflation is to find a way of earning a living in foreign currencies. As the local currency loses value, it becomes marginal for anything but routine expenses: food, utility bills, gasoline, clothing, restaurant meals. The prices of large-ticket items, such as cars and apartments, are expressed in U.S. dollars. No one wants to be stuck with huge quantities of money whose value shrinks by the minute.

In Argentina, there are two economies: one in australs, the other in dollars. The dollar people, business people and professionals mostly, are still living well even if precariously. The austral people are being pauperized. The worst hit are the middle class — the teachers, the small shopkeepers, people who have no strong union behind them — and the poorest of the poor. There is now hunger in the land of plenty. Argentinians are at least realizing — or at least they say they are — that not even the bounty of the land can shield them any longer from the effects of their recklessness.

The decline of Argentina's currency is a measure of the country's impoverishment. During the early Perón years, the treasury was overflowing with gold earned by providing a famished, war-torn Europe with food. The peso stood at five per U.S. dollar. Ten years later it was twenty to the dollar; fifteen years after that, 1,000. It was 10,000 (actually a million but the central bank handily had knocked off two zeros to make the peso seem stronger) when the Falklands war started in 1982, 30,000 when the war ended a couple of months later. Several more zeroes were knocked off, but it didn't help. Inflation accelerated to sixty percent a year, then zoomed to sixty percent a month and beyond. The peso had to be abandoned and was replaced by the austral.

When it was born in 1985, the austral, relieved of the peso's surfeit of zeroes, was worth roughly one dollar. Within four years, the austral, too, was on the ropes, losing more than ninety-five percent of its value in four months. The mint just could not keep up with the demand for new notes. The printing machines were breaking down from the strain of rolling night and day. For awhile, the mint even ran out of paper.

By now, though, nothing could stop the paper flood. From parity with the U.S. dollar in 1985, the austral sank so fast that by the end of 1989 it took nearly 4,000 to buy a dollar. And it went on falling.

"*El que no salta es un Inglés*," the crowd yelled over and over. If you don't jump, you're an Englishman. Since no one wanted to be an Englishman, thousands of Argentinians bounced up and down as they yelled, making the Plaza de Mayo look like a giant jumping jack contest. The chant was a leftover from the World Cup of 1978 when Argentina won the world soccer championship by beating the Netherlands. Millions of Argentinian fans bounced and bobbed then because they did not want to be taken for Dutchmen.

But now it was 1982, and what Argentina was involved in with the English was no game. It was war, the war over the Falkland Islands. But masses of Argentinians in Buenos Aires behaved as if the war were only sport by another name. The same huge pep rallies that had supported Argentina's soccer squad now cheered on Argentinian soldiers. Only now the jumping rite had become more ominous. People who didn't jump were threatened and sometimes attacked. I was spat upon.

The Falkland fighting and soccer ran on parallel tracks. The World Cup championships were on again, and the front pages of newspapers were split between the two wars. When Argentina was playing its first football match, people stayed glued to their TV sets and all but forgot that their troops in the Malvinas, as the Falklands are called in Spanish, were retreating. It was Argentina's 0–1 loss to Belgium in the opener, rather than any news from the front, that started the process of disillusionment that overwhelmed the country with the defeat of its forces at Port Stanley.

At the beginning, even most opponents of the military regime joined in cheering the Malvinas invasion. At the Teatro Colón, when the hero of *Tosca* was executed, he fell to the ground clutching an Argentinian flag, even though in the plot he is an Italian liberal fighting a dictatorship. The church, the unions, the Communists, the Perónists, most of the Radical party and many literary lions lined up on the side of the regime.

"Opponents to the regime like myself," wrote Ernesto Sábato, a famous novelist, "are fighting for our dignity, fighting to extricate the last vestiges of colonialism. Don't be mistaken, Europe, it is not a dictatorship that is fighting for the Malvinas; it is the whole nation."

That was precisely one of the main reasons that led the dictatorship to invade the Malvinas in the first place. Only a few days before the invasion, thousands had converged on the Plaza de Mayo in front of the presidential palace to demonstrate against the regime of President Leopoldo Galtieri. The rally was broken up with brutality. Dozens were injured, hundreds were jailed. The regime seemed in trouble.

After the invasion on April 2, there were more and bigger demonstrations in front of the Casa Rosada. This time, though, they were in praise of General Galtieri. He would stand on the balcony, much better looking than Perón, better tailored, too, very photogenic with his wavy silver hair, holding up his arms, deluged by cheers. The villain of yesterday had become the hero of the day. The invasion had done for the regime what it had not managed to do in six years in power: it had unified the country. If Galtieri had won, he would have been a bigger hero than Juan and Evita Perón ever were, probably the biggest Argentinian hero since José de San Martín crossed the Andes and defeated the Spanish in 1817.

The Malvinas were a national preoccupation, one of those issues that by any measure other than nationalist emotion may be marginal but are central to national self-respect. Argentina claims the islands as the successor to Spain. The Spanish bought them from the French at a time when there was already a British settlement in the islands. Whatever the merits of Argentina's claim to the Malvinas, it is certainly weaker than, let's say, Spain's claim to Gibraltar or China's claim to Hong Kong. Yet though Spain and China could easily have overrun these enclaves, they have refrained from using force.

Argentina's government was incapable of waiting. Its economy was facing ruin. Its reputation was at a low and falling. The generals thought they could outbluff the British. Even if they couldn't, no matter; they had all those new shiny toys they had recently bought and they couldn't wait to use them. So the

Argentinian armed forces, which had not fought a war against anyone other than their own people for more than one hundred years, took on one of the world's foremost warrior countries. And lost.

Another rally in front of the Casa Rosada. This time, a different chant: *"Galtieri, hijo de puta."* Galtieri, son of a whore. It is June 15, 1982, eleven weeks since the Argentinian flag was unfurled over the Falklands. Last night, the Argentinians surrendered at Port Stanley, and rage is now reigning in the Plaza de Mayo. Galtieri wisely stays inside.

Having cheered their hearts out because they believed that the greatness and unity that had eluded Argentina for so long were now in their grasp, Argentinians have turned on the generals. They feel cheated because they have been deceived by the military and, most of all, because they have been made to look like fools in the eyes of the world. The soldiers have to go.

The soldiers went, meekly. From now on, democracy, not imposed order and discipline, is to be the panacea. Argentinians elected Raul Alfonsín president in 1983. Alfonsín seemed to be a good choice, a man who had the guts to oppose the dictatorship and to come out against the Falkland War when doing so was considered almost treason, a man who talked plain common sense.

But Alfonsín failed, too. Once more inflation was running out of control. And so were the unions. Once more the armed forces, which only so recently had slunk off in disgrace, were feeling their oats and staging coups. Like children playing cowboys and Indians, the soldiers put on their war paint every now and then, came out of their barracks and rumbled around a bit in their armored personnel carriers, complaining that their honor had been hurt, their budgets cut or their generals jailed. After a brief confrontation with loyalist troops, the show of pique was over; a few officers were arrested and the rest returned to barracks until the next time. The rebels, who always somehow managed to get out of jail either by escaping or being amnestied, even formed a political movement of sorts. They called themselves *carapintadas*, the painted faces.

By 1988, even some of Alfonsín's strongest admirers were critical of him. They believed he had been so preoccupied with turning the country into a democracy that he had neglected everything else, that he hadn't cracked down when he should have because he was trying to create unity, not division. His opponents maintained that his preoccupation was not with democracy but with keeping his Radicals in power as the permanent party of government. The following year, the Radicals were defeated in elections. What was even more humiliating to Alfonsín was that the economy was falling apart so quickly that he was forced to quit before his term was over.

Once again it was the Perónistas' turn. No general this time. No general's lady, either. A ladies' man instead. With Victorian mutton-chop sideburns. Carlos Saul Menem became the world's first pin-up president. During the campaign he appeared in a magazine photo posing languidly, dressed in only black-and-white shorts, lying on a bed covered with white lace, his midriff tire showing despite a sucked-in belly, cuddling a shaggy dog. The dog's coloring even matched Menem's shorts!

Once elected president, though, the playboy candidate turned serious. He started out with a tough reform program. For a few months, it even worked, and Menem became the new Argentinian wonder. Then, as they always have, Argentinian realities caught up with him. Hyper-inflation came back, the soldiers started talking about painting their faces again and Saul Ubaldini and his Perónist unions went on strike against a Perónist president. Everything was back to normal: down.

For all their failings as a nation, as individuals Argentinians tend to be clear-eyed and tough survivors.

"I've lived better times, worse times," says a song, *Aquí*

estoy (Here I am), made popular in the mid-eighties by the singer Nacha Guevara. "I've watched winters pass, seen dictators die. . . . only God knows what I've been through. . . . and yet here I am."

Aquí estoy, says the Argentinian. And that he is.

Once upon a time (1982–83) there was an Argentinian president by the name of General Reynaldo Bignone, who summed up his country's problems succinctly, not with an answer but with a question: "What is wrong with us Argentinians?"

The answer he was looking for can't have been the one most Argentinians already know: that as a people they have been disunited, undisciplined, undemocratic, unruly, self-absorbed, authoritarian, impatient, improvident, intolerant and stubborn. (And resentful of foreigners who said so.) What the general really wanted to know was why Argentinians, who are not evil and certainly not stupid, got to be the way they are and why they can't seem to change.

There is no one answer. A lot of Argentinians blame the Peróns. But Argentina was set upon its path before the Peróns; they just accelerated the pace. Others argue that it is the short intervals of democracy that ruin the country; too much permissiveness and too many corrupt politicians, they say. But democracy has hardly had a fair run in Argentina. Many, of course, blame the soldiers and rightly so. But usually when the soldiers take power, they are mobbed by cheering civilians. For all their differences in blame-laying, almost all Argentinians are agreed that, whatever they may have done wrong as a nation, foreigners — the Spanish, the British and the Americans — bear the largest share of responsibility for their troubles. They are not impressed by the fact that quite a few other countries have had to deal with the same pressures from these imperial powers and didn't end up in the Argentinian dead-end.

As for foreigners, they are mostly mystified. V.S. Naipaul, a writer who made his living performing exploratory surgery on countries, confessed that Argentina had him baffled. "The failure of Argentina," he wrote, "is one of the mysteries of our time."

There may be no solution to the mystery, but there are clues. The main one is that Argentinians, despite their conspicuous nationalism, do not seem to be all that comfortable being who they are where they are. They tended for a long time to think of themselves more as Europeans than South Americans. Argentina was the place where they made their money; once they made it, Europe was where they enjoyed it. This, of course, is the classical disease of colonial societies. Canada once suffered from it, too; so did the U.S. But in Argentina it has largely lasted to this day.

Argentinians aren't comfortable being stranded at the end of the Americas. They don't much like the neighborhood. Their neighbors are either too Indian or too black for their tastes. What they are looking for is approval by the Europeans. In part, that's what the Falklands War was about. The Argentinians have always admired and yet resented the British. In a way, it was not Spain that was their mother country, their admired model; it was England. Britain, which had been Argentina's best customer and biggest supplier, became its stepmother. In that sense, the Falklands War was modern Argentina's war of independence. Victory would have proved that Argentinians were better, or at least as good, as the English. Instead, the British whipped them. That left Argentinians feeling that they still were a second-rate nation, a colonial society, but a colony without a mother country.

Orphans, petulant orphans — that's what the Argentinians are like. As so many orphans resentful at having been abandoned, they throw tantrums every now and then to show their resentment.

But don't cry for Argentina. The Argentinians could still have had it all if only, as a nation, they had not refused to grow up.

CHAPTER XII

I so want to believe the time has come at last
to call murder by its proper name of
Murder!
Knavery, albeit crowned with laurels,
would be knavery once more,
lies once more lies as in days of yore.
And brandished pistols would no more open
innocent doors.

Jaroslav Seifert
Prague Castle
translated by A.G. Brain

Prague, November 1989. You did not join the crowd. You dove into it as you would into water. And once in, you realized after the first shock of being immersed in a sea of people that the press of bodies would keep you afloat, that you could safely surrender yourself to its streams and eddies. This was not a crowd that would carry you crashing into danger, one of those angry, trampling mobs I had seen so often elsewhere. Here in Prague on this cold November night, a warm and gentle sea of happiness enveloped me.

"*Svobodu, svobodu, svobodu.*" The chant of "freedom, freedom, freedom," starts somewhere near the statue of King Wenceslas, the patron saint of Bohemia, and comes crashing down Wenceslas Square, breaking in waves against the buildings and reverberating back over our heads.

Then a more insistent sound, the sound of surprise and of the pleasure of recognition. "Marta, long live Marta," the crowd chants as the vague image of a woman appears silhouetted in the bright lights of a balcony above us. As the last loud "Marta" fades away, a hush and then Marta's voice.

"*At mír dál zůstává toutou krajinou.*" May peace rest with this land.

There is no other sound. Just Marta Kubišová's voice over the loudspeakers, a voice not heard in public for two decades, ever since Marta and her song were stilled by the wreckers of the Prague Spring. Now she and her prayer are back.

> May malice, envy, hate, fear and strife pass away,
> Let them pass away.

It is a slow melody. Every word is carved out sharply. Malice. Envy. Hate. Fear. Strife. The words are not spat out in anger. The tone is of sorrow, even of forgiveness.

> Now that the lost rule of your destiny
> Is coming back to you,
> Coming back, my people,
> Let this, my prayer, speak
> To hearts not blighted,
> As buds by frost, by evil times.

In the square, tears and stillness. Lips move to the words but no sound comes from them. Tens of thousands of hands rise in the V-for-Victory salute. The white, red and blue flags of Czechoslovakia that were being waved about with such exuberance now droop and flutter weakly to a gentle breeze.

Marta's prayer is an echo of Czech history, of the words of the seventeenth-century Moravian churchman, philosopher and educator, Jan Amos Comenius. When the song ends, the square is so still I can hear the people around me breathing almost as one a sigh of emotional release. Then, as if woken from a trance, the crowd erupts. Marta. Marta. Long live Marta.

I had never heard of Marta and her song before. I had been cut off from Czechoslovakia for nearly forty years so completely that in many ways I knew less about what had happened to the Czechs than I knew about the fortunes of the Chinese and certainly much less about the fate of the Slovaks than about the tribulations of the Salvadorans. But here in this square that I knew so well, the decades rolled back as I stood among these people savoring the unaccustomed sweet taste of freedom and of community, as I listened again to the familiar language that like any language spoken only by a small nation is a private code. A lingua franca like English may be the key to the world. A language like Czech protects those few who share its secrets against the encroachments of a threatening world. Sharing it makes you family and, standing in Wenceslas Square, I felt its pull.

It seemed only yesterday that Stalin had so vaingloriously celebrated his seventieth birthday and I had left. Today, I was back to see his ghost being buried. For most of the people around me, the intervening years of misery I had managed to escape were their whole lifetime. Except for the brief sparks of the Prague Spring, they had known nothing else. For me, the Prague Autumn revolution of 1989 was a punctuation mark, an end to the exile's ache of estrangement I had felt the last time I had visited Prague. For the people of Czechoslovakia, it was the beginning of a new life.

I was in Paris when the news came from Prague that a peaceful student demonstration there had been brutally broken up by police. Dozens of students had been injured and one was reported to have been killed.

I had come to France to cover a dinner of the leaders of the European Economic Community hosted by President François Mitterand. The meal at the Elysée Palace was more than just the routine state dinner. Mitterand's guests had flown in from all over Europe to affirm their determination not to let the storm that was sweeping through eastern Europe shake apart the process of west European integration. What worried them was that West Germany would turn away from its allies towards East Germany and beyond. They could feel the ground shaking, the four decades of stability and balance in Europe falling apart. They wanted to tie Bonn firmly to the European Community before it was too late.

The news of the demise of Stalin's empire was peppering the map of Europe with new question marks. It raised the spectre of a resurrected united Germany destabilizing the continent and dominating it. The *Drang nach Osten*, the Push to the East that Hitler could not achieve with his armies, a reunited Germany could accomplish by sheer economic power, much as Japan succeeded with its Toyotas and Sonys beyond the dreams of the Japanese generals and the bosses of the *zaibatsu*, the great industrial conglomerates of Japan, who had tried to impose their Co-Prosperity Sphere on Asia by force.

West German eyes had already turned east with fascination. "*Wir sind ein Volk*," they chanted in East and West. We are one nation. But Volk is more than just a nation or a people. It is one of those multi-layered German terms that have at times shifted from the literal through the mystic to downright batty meanings involving the "essence" of a people and its communion with its natural surroundings. The Volkish school of German nationalism culminated with disastrous consequences in Hitler's slogan, "*Ein Volk, ein Reich, ein Führer*," one nation, one empire, one leader.

Nazism had been dead for more than forty years now. But in many Germans, the crumbling of the Berlin Wall rekindled the yearning for a rebirth of the Volk and its dreams of greatness. For some, it raised visions of Silesia and East Prussia, now part of Poland and the Soviet Union, being returned one day to the Vaterland, of Germany as the source and protector of prosperity and stability in the East. It was a vision that raised shudders not only in Moscow, Prague and Warsaw but also in Paris, London and Brussels. It would take time getting used again to the idea of a Great Germany dominating the centre of the continent. The way things were going, there would be very little time. A new Europe was emerging at a gallop.

The Berlin Wall had fallen a week earlier, undermined by *pestroika* in the Soviet Union, the creation of a Polish government dominated by the Solidarity movement, the self-cannibalization of the Communist Party in Hungary and the flood of East Germans who were expressing their disgust with their regime by fleeing to West Germany. The rot in communism had broken to the surface even in Bulgaria, which right to the last had remained Moscow's tamest satellite. Czechoslovakia would inevitably be next.

And now there had been a student demonstration in Prague on a date — November 17 — that evoked instant recognition in everyone who knew anything about Czechoslovak history. Half a century earlier, on November 17, 1939, the students of Prague had staged a demonstration against the German occupation. The Nazis predictably reacted with force, killing a student named Jan Opletal.

There has been so much killing in Europe in this century that by the rules of such things the murder of a group of people by police or soldiers is usually remembered only by obscure plaques or by a street named after the date of the event which gets lost among all the other streets marked with the dates of revolutions, liberations and slaughters that make the map of many a city look like a crazy-quilt calendar. But killing one person creates a martyr. Opletal became such a martyr. He had a street named after him, right off Wenceslas Square, and became the patron of the student movement.

What normally would have been a routine remembrance of a Nazi crime, the kind of anti-fascist occasion the communists used to exploit expertly to burnish their image as fighters against Nazism, turned instead into a challenge to the regime's existence. The date and the circumstances of the death combined into one of those historical replays that bring with them the momentum of an all but unstoppable emotional force.

Any regime halfway responsive to the sensitivities of the occasion would have pulled in its horns. But tired and discredited regimes, whether it be the rule of the Shah, czar, caudillo or commissar, by the time they are ripe for their fall, have lost the ability to make rational judgments or practise restraint. At the end, it no longer matters who gave the order, or, for that matter, what order was given. Inevitably, the order will have been ill-considered and its execution botched. And so it was on November 17, 1989, in Prague.

The memorial ceremony for Opletal that Friday became the biggest protest demonstration Prague had seen in twenty years. Several thousand students marched to Wenceslas Square shouting for an end to communist rule. When the police moved in, they didn't disperse the protesters as they normally did by hauling a few away and herding the rest into side streets. This time the white-helmeted riot police were joined by anti-terrorist troops in red berets. They weren't interested in just dispersing the demonstrators; they were there to teach them a lesson. They closed off the demonstrators' escape routes and trapped them on Narodní Avenue, a main shopping area. Then they set about clubbing, bludgeoning and kicking the youngsters and continued beating them even after they fell to the ground bleeding. It was, according to witnesses, a deliberate attempt to stop the growing protest movement with terror. Skulls were cracked, arms and legs were broken, spines and kidneys damaged.

It was above all the report of a new martyr that fanned the flames of defiance. The government frantically denied that anyone had been killed, and arrested a dissident for spreading false rumors. The government was right — there was no new Opletal — but it had arrested the wrong person. It turned out later — too late for the communist regime — that the death of the student had been faked. Not by the opposition, but by members of the regime itself. In a manoeuvre both Kafka and Svejk would have appreciated, elements of the secret police apparently engineered the beatings and faked the death. The "martyred" student was a policeman who rose from the dead once his body had been taken to the morgue. The plotters had counted on the news of another Opletal provoking mass demonstrations. They hoped to use the unrest to save the communist hold on power by ousting party leader Miloš

Jakeš and replacing him with more acceptable "reformers."
But it was too late for a controlled coup d'état. The arsonists
were consumed by the fire they had started.

On Saturday, there were two thousand demonstrators in
Wenceslas Square shouting for freedom. The next day, students roamed Narodní Avenue, building makeshift shrines
by laying flowers and lighting candles wherever bloodstains
marked the places where their friends had been beaten on
Friday. That Sunday night there were ten thousand people in
the square chanting, "No more violence, no more violence."
The police watched, but did nothing.

Up to now the students had been alone. But in two days
they had managed to do what the dissidents of Charter 77
and other groups had not been able to do in a dozen years:
they galvanized the opposition into uniting and grabbed the
attention of the country's conformist elite, the writers who had
knuckled under to be allowed to publish, the artists who were
ideologically tame enough to have their works exhibited, and
actors and singers who instead of having to wash windows to
make a living were paid to perform safe classics or stale puff
pieces, people whom the regime had courted and coddled in
exchange for their docility. Theatres, including the hallowed
National Theatre, closed in sympathy with the students' strike
and their demand that the perpetrators of Friday's police
violence be punished. Art galleries and museums were shut
too. At the beginning of the weekend, Václav Havel, the
dissident playwright, had left Prague to avoid arrest. By
Sunday night, he was back to lead the Civic Forum, a hastily
formed umbrella organization of the opposition. The Forum
combined the old dissidents with the newcomers, the hitherto
tame intellectuals and artists, and the students, most of whom
were also among the most favored of the regime.

By Monday, when I arrived in Prague, Wenceslas Square
was packed with people. There were now, by official count,
200,000 of them, too many to disperse with clubs. It would
have taken gunfire, a massacre to stop them. Not so long ago,
the communist leadership would not have been daunted at
the prospect of large-scale bloodshed. But now it flinched,
and the police abandoned the centre of town. The crowds

roamed the avenues and the Old Town with its narrow streets calling for free elections, an end to police violence and the resignation of Miloš Jakeš.

By now the base of the statue of St. Wenceslas, where for twenty years Czechs were forbidden to lay as much as a flower, was covered with bouquets, wreaths and with hundreds of flickering candles. Mounds of molten wax were rising by the hour. And the Good King himself was draped with flags, hand-written placards calling for the government's resignation and pictures of Alexander Dubček, the ousted leader of the Prague Spring, and of Tomáš Masaryk, the founder of the country. Wenceslas Square belonged to the opposition. The protest movement was spreading. High schools were joining the university students' strike. And there had been demonstrations in Bratislava, the capital of Slovakia. The students called for a nation-wide two-hour general strike for the following Monday to force political changes.

For all that, the struggle hardly seemed won yet. Even in Wenceslas Square, there were those who had not yet committed themselves. There were really two crowds. In the centre of the square, young people, waving flags and placards, singing and chanting. Along the sidewalks a much more dense crowd, moving, not standing, thousands streaming up and down the square. These were older people, lots of couples, some even with small children, a sure sign that they no longer expected any trouble. They looked as though they had come to see what was happening, to gauge rather than join. Some had little flags, which they waved from time to time, some stopped and applauded. But for the most, they just kept moving, looking almost as if they were window-shopping. Even in the centre of the square among the committed, there was a conspicuous absence. There were almost no factory workers, miners, farmers, the manual workers the opposition movement would need to assure itself of victory.

In fact, the signs of enthusiasm for reform petered out quickly beyond Wenceslas Square. The factories in the outlying districts of the city worked normally, and everywhere people went about their business.

In Kladno, a mining and steel-making city twenty-five

kilometres west of Prague that the communists liked to call Red Kladno, the reaction varied between suspicion and indifference. At the Poldi steel mill, workers streamed out at the shift change past students who had come to try to recruit them to their cause. "We are your children," one of the students yelled. "They beat your children with clubs. Support us." It was an argument that worked well among the white-collar workers on the avenues of central Prague. But not here at the plant gate in grimy Kladno. In what was supposedly a classless society, class still mattered greatly. For all the party propaganda about the egalitarianism of Czechoslovakia's socialist society, steelworkers and students, blue collar and white collar saw the world very differently.

The few Kladno workers who did stop to listen to the students — they were mostly the younger ones — shrugged their shoulders. "What do you want us to do, strike and live as miserably as the Poles?" one of them wanted to know. "It's all very well for you to strike," another told the students, "you can always catch up with your work, but if we go on strike we lose that money forever." Indeed, before the shift change, the plant manager had warned the workers over loudspeakers not to strike because a work stoppage would jeopardize their year-end production bonus.

There was more than the year-end bonus or two hours' pay at stake for the workers. The Poldi plant, like the mines around it, was outdated and inefficient. Any economic reform that was to have a chance of success would have to close many such plants, and those that were modernized would inevitably require fewer workers. Ergo, reform meant lost jobs. And lower wages, too. The steelworkers and coal miners were among the best paid people in the country. Just about the only people who earned more were party bigwigs, sports aces and stars of stage and film. And black marketeers. A worker at the steel furnace made twice the average wage, and a miner could make twice as much working at the coal face as a doctor did in a hospital. That, they knew, would change under reform. But it would change less if the communists stayed in power than it would with that new lot in Prague who were talking about bringing in the efficiencies of the market system. The workers of the smokestack industries knew what that meant. The press had told them all about the steel plants and coal mines that had been closed in the capitalist world, in the Ruhr in Germany, in Alsace–Lorraine in France, in the coal fields of Wales and shipyards of Scotland. The dole, not coal or steel, was king there now.

Besides, the party apparatus of intimidation was still active, from the plant manager in Kladno who threatened cutting off pay bonuses to the many busybodies who acted as the party's watchdogs. In Prague itself, the party used the People's Militia, its own private army, to seal off factories and chase away students who wanted to talk to the workers.

In Kladno, while filming on the street, we were stopped four times by people who thought they had the right to order us about. At one plant gate, a woman with the red armband of a guard came rushing out of the gatehouse. She wanted to know who had given us permission to film and demanded to see our papers. She was outraged when I asked to see her documents first. When we turned our camera on her, she quickly retreated to call the police. When two police officers showed up, they, too, reacted strongly when my cameraman, Michel Dumond, turned his camera on them. One of them lunged for the camera and Dumond. But when I yelled at him, "Remember, no more violence," he pulled back instantly, because he obviously recognized the Prague students' slogan and its implications. He made a show of checking our papers but both of them left quickly, evidently relieved not to have got themselves involved in something that might rebound on them. They must have heard of the trouble some of their colleagues in Prague had got themselves into.

Still, word of what was happening in Prague was spreading only slowly. That was one of the main reasons the country outside the big cities was all but untouched by the events in the capital. The media were still controlled by the government. The opposition had little opportunity to get its message across. Students would stop cars on the roads leading out of the capital and hand drivers stacks of pamphlets for distribution in the countryside. Even when the Prague editions of the national newspapers started telling some of the truth — because everyone in Prague could see what was happening and to hush it up would have lost the papers the last shreds of credibility — out-of-town editions were still heavily censored.

It was touch and go for the opposition. If it gave the communists time to recover from their disarray, they would close ranks and slowly re-establish control, posing, of course, as reformers. The dissidents' campaign had to break out of Wenceslas Square. And quickly. It had to spread beyond Prague, Bratislava and Brno, the capital of Moravia. It had to reach the working class and recruit it to its cause. It had to convince the country that it was more than just a movement of students, a crusade of kids, or only a phenomenon of the streets, a mob of malcontents.

It also desperately needed exposure on television. It was television — the scenes of East Germans streaming west, of the Wall coming down, of Hungarians and Poles enjoying freedoms Czechs didn't have — that had sparked the Prague revolt. TV had become the most important tool of revolution. The battle for the control of the airwaves could be seen right on the screen. Sometimes there would be relatively frank coverage of the rallies, sometimes none. Or television would broadcast live from the square, only to switch, in the middle of things, back to music from the studio.

Above all, the opposition had to demonstrate that it was an alternative to the regime and that it had capable leaders who could command the nation's respect. But where Poland had Lech Walesa, who had been seasoned by years of open struggle against the regime there, Czechoslovakia had Alexander Dubček, who for two decades had sat on the sidelines. As the leader of the Prague Spring, Dubček was a powerful symbol of what might have been, but by now he was a frail man of sixty-eight, very much wrapped up in memories of what had been. Besides, people remembered that he went into the darkness of Brezhnevian repression with barely a whimper.

If Dubček and his former foreign minister, Jiří Hájek, were too old, most of the younger dissidents were all but unknown. Václav Havel was widely known, mostly because he had been so frequently reviled in the communist media.

Almost no one had ever read anything he had written, and few knew anything about what he had to say. He also seemed to have little charisma. He was small, a loner who harrumphed continually as he spoke, energetic but somewhat shy, rumpled, always dressed in an open-collared shirt, sweater and jeans in a country where no politician, not even the leaders of the horny-handed proletariat, ever appeared in anything but suit and tie.

What Havel had going for him, though, was that people knew he was a writer and that he had been in and out of jail. Being jailed by the communists so often meant that he had not given in, that he was a man of principle. Writers with moral strength were revered in Czechoslovakia, especially philosophers. Philosophers from Comenius to Masaryk were considered the conscience of the nation. And Havel was as much a philosopher as he was a playwright. Even those who cared not a whit about poetry, plays or politics, even the apathetic Ugly Czech, could admire Havel as someone who had stood up to the communists and had continued giving them hell. He was unsullied by the compromises, large and small, that everyone — ninety-nine percent of Czechs and Slovaks — had made to survive. Václav Havel was a genuine hero.

But Havel had no mass organization. The students, who did, had no leader capable of uniting the country and knew it. On Sunday evening, he and they got together. Out of this meeting rose the Civic Forum, an alliance of the various splintered opposition groups that had provided the original inspiration to resistance, the students who had the numbers and the enthusiasm to get the revolution started, the intellectuals and artists who had bolted the regime's cultural corral, and politicians from the Socialist and Catholic People's party who, after years of toadying to the communists in a phony coalition front, had now trimmed their sails to the winds of change.

On Monday, while huge crowds of demonstrators were still milling leaderless in the streets, Havel called a news conference to announce the formation of the Forum. It was held in his apartment. Outside the building, the secret police was still on guard. The writ of the

Civic Forum did not yet extend beyond Havel's living room.

Those who would take on the leadership of a revolution of the streets need to rise above street level. They need a podium or, preferably, a balcony high enough for all to see. In this age, they also need a sound system so that the masses can hear. On Tuesday, Václav Havel, who for years had fought his fight all but alone, finally got his podium.

He stood on a balcony high above Wenceslas Square, bathed in waves of cheering. From below, he was barely visible; the brightness of the badly placed lights on the balcony almost obliterated him. You could see his arms held up for silence and they still cheered. The Czechs, who had been without heroes for so long, had found their hero. When he spoke — no harrumphing now — he had more than just words of encouragement for them. He announced that a Forum delegation had met with the communist prime minister, who had promised that the government would not impose martial law to stop the demonstrations and strikes. The regime, which the previous day had proclaimed its determination never to compromise with the protesters, was in retreat. Havel and his band of jailbirds had become the regime's last hope of peace.

But the prime minster spoke only for the government, not the party. And the party was not quite ready to give up. Jakeš went on TV on Tuesday night to warn about "boundaries that should not be overstepped." The next day, he secretly ordered that a force of several thousand members of the People's Militia be brought to Prague. But the hard-liners' grip was slipping. In the politburo, those advocating cracking down on the demonstrators were not able to muster a majority. Only a fraction of the militia force showed up in Prague, and those who did stayed only for a few hours and then went home. The party's most faithful had lost faith.

From 2,000 demonstrators on Sunday to a quarter of a million by Wednesday. For the first time, factory workers in considerable numbers began showing up in Wenceslas Square. They were mostly from industries such as electronics, which were likely to survive the shake-out of reform without great pain. But such plants represented only a fraction of the country's factories. Workers from heavy industry, the backbone of the Communist Party, were still absent. Havel appealed to them to come join the struggle. *Decent* communists, he said, would be welcome. The allegiance of these workers had become the key to the outcome of the struggle.

On Thursday, a last-ditch effort by the party to rally the workers. Miroslav Štěpán, the Prague party boss who was being blamed for ordering Friday's police attack on the students, spoke to workers at a heavy-machinery works on the outskirts of the city. He tried to belittle the student protest movement: "Why should we let a bunch of children tell us what to do?" The reaction was jeers and chants of "Resign, resign!" The workers, too, were lost.

On Friday, with 300,000 people packing Wenceslas Square and its side streets, the party gave in. Miloš Jakeš resigned. When the news broke, people danced in the streets. An unknown nonentity, who would only last a month, was named to replace Jakeš. Štěpán could no longer be party secretary, but he was still on the new politburo pulling the strings. The party, however, was no longer in control of its destiny.

By Saturday, Wenceslas Square having become too small, the daily demonstration was moved to Letná, a large plain where once a huge statue of Stalin stood, dominating the city. More than half a million people came to listen to Havel and Dubček demand the resignation of the new politburo. The reshuffle, they said, was only a trick to keep the hard-liners in power.

On Sunday, the party caved in once again. The politburo was purged of its last hard-liners. Three politburos in three days. Among those purged: Miroslav Štěpán. He, rather than Jakeš, now became the chief villain. Even communists heaped abuse on him. Communist journalists remember Štěpán's reaction when police used violence the previous winter to break up a demonstration: "Those shitheads and loudmouths had it coming to them." Within a month, the man who was to have been the new reform leader, the Gorbachev of Prague, was in jail on charges of criminal abuse of power.

On Monday, the day of the strike, just about the whole country stopped work for two hours. It was not so much a strike as a celebration. At the stroke of noon, church bells tolled, sirens hooted, horns tooted, whistles blew, people sang, clapped, jangled keys, banged anything they had at hand. There was a long way to go yet, more purges and crises, new faces in old jobs, old problems and new ones, too. But it was over.

It had been a remarkable achievement, a triumph of organization without any apparent organization other than spur-of-the-moment arrangements, an orgy of self-discipline. Normally it takes a small army of organizers working for days if not weeks to prepare for a rally of several hundred thousand people; it takes a mobilization of transport and phalanxes of police to channel it. In Prague, there was neither time, nor special buses and trains; nor any sign of the police after they tried and failed to stop the initial rallies. Yet the protests in Wenceslas Square always started on time. Half an hour before the scheduled time, the square was empty. At the appointed hour, it was full. No brawls, not even scuffles. Fifteen minutes after the Czech and Slovak anthems had been sung to end the meeting, the square was empty.

"Ten years, ten months, ten weeks, ten days," they chanted in Prague. It had taken Solidarity ten years to get power in Poland. In Hungary, it had taken ten months to overturn the old regime; in East Germany, ten weeks; in Czechoslovakia, ten days.

The laurel crown had at least been wrested from knavery's brow.

Berlin, June 1990. At Checkpoint Charlie, the main east-west crossing, you can buy your bit of the Berlin Wall mounted on wood, embedded in plastic or *au naturel*. Or, if you should feel energetic, you could rent a hammer and chisel from one of the hustlers who hang around the checkpoint and chip your own bit of history out of the remains of the Wall. Don't hurry, there is still plenty of it left. Besides, seven months after the fall of the Wall, the enthusiasm for this particular bit of history is fast fading in Berlin under the hammer blows of new realities.

The will for unification still runs strong but it is being tempered daily by irritation and fear of dislocation. There are more than 200,000 unemployed in East Germany, and thousands more are losing their jobs every day to the new demands of efficiency and profitability. Many of those who still have jobs are working shorter hours and getting less pay. To most East Germans who at first saw only the glitter of western consumerism coming their way, the price of their freedom is beginning to look dear. To many West Germans, too. They worry about what the integration of the two Germanys is going to cost them in higher taxes, inflation or a lower mark. They are irritated with the East Germans who came flooding west, because they have to compete with them for housing and jobs. They are equally irritated with those who stayed in the east, because they have to subsidize them. They have taken to badmouthing easterners as loafers who never learned to work properly as Germans should. At the same time, though, they worry that the East Germans might not be as lazy as they were made out to be, that they may take jobs away from West Germans by being willing to work just as hard for less money.

When Trabants, the slow and stinky East German cars, started coming west last year, they were cute curiosities and butts of good-natured jokes. Now they are considered nuisances that clog the roads. West German drivers in their much more powerful cars swear and honk at them. East Germans, in turn, are resentful of their swaggering wealthy western cousins. Many see the sleek, smug West German businessmen swarming through East Germany in their Mercedes as carpetbaggers. With freedom, the eastern part of the country now also has more crime because the discredited cops have lost their authority. In East Berlin, neo-Nazi skinheads regularly take advantage of the new freedom by attacking anyone they consider leftist with clubs, baseball bats and iron bars.

As if their own problems were not enough, Germans on both sides of the Wall are feeling the troubles of the rest of the former Communist bloc pressing down on them. In East Berlin, Romanian children whose families have fled the post-revolutionary uncertainties of their homeland beg in the streets. Hundreds of homeless Bulgarian émigrés camp out at railway stations. In their barracks throughout East Germany, Soviet soldiers are fretting about going home. They no longer feel needed and certainly not wanted in East Germany, but there is no room for them in the Soviet Union, no apartments, few jobs and little food. Once they were the proud defenders of the front lines of the communist world. Now they are the detritus of a crumbling empire stranded in a country that has nothing but contempt for them.

In West Berlin, people complain about being invaded by Poles. Every morning, hundreds of tourist buses filled with Poles roll into the city. The bus people descend on discount stores to stock up on goods unavailable in Poland. By afternoon, the store shelves are empty. By nightfall, the buses are gone, leaving behind on the splendid avenues of the Tiergarten park a mess of abandoned boxes, crates and grocery carts. In wealthy West Berlin, the Poles are seen as nuisances rather than as unfortunate victims of shortages and poverty at home. But the Germans had a plan for getting rid of the Poles. When the border-crossings between East and West were abolished at the end of June, when Checkpoint Charlie was torn down, they sent their border guards — both the East German ones who used to shoot their own countrymen when they tried to flee across the Wall and the West German ones who faced them — to the new united Germany's eastern border to join in keeping out the hungry Polish hordes.

There is yet another band of foreigners moving into Berlin. They are business people drawn by the promise of new opportunities and journalists who have come to cover the drama of the re-emergence of a united Germany. I am one of them. Having watched the disintegration of Mitteleuropa as a boy, I shall be spending the next few years witnessing the pangs of its rebirth. History, I hope, will do better this time. It has to. It certainly could not do any worse.

Václav Havel named what happened in Prague *nežná revoluce*, the Gentle Revolution. In Czech, that is what it is still called. But the term — and also what it implied — got lost in translation into English. One of Havel's interpreters called it the Velvet Revolution and the term stuck. Ugh! I hate the expression. It demeans what happened in Czechoslovakia.

To me, velvet is a tacky material. It can be made out of anything, nylon, rayon, acetate or any other cheap synthetic material. You can make it out of silk, too, but you'd only be wasting your money. You would still just end up with a sleazy piece of cloth, smooth to the touch, to be sure, but a material of cheap pretension, of fake gentility. Velvet always seems to be hiding something. Think of the Velvet Glove. You surely would not want to wear one unless it were to hide its companion cliché, the Iron Fist.

Velvet came to equal gentle because it is considered soft. But velvet is smooth rather than soft. It can, in fact, be quite stiff, built up on a cotton backing into the kind of material that is used for ball gowns, big puffed sleeves, rustling skirts as big as tents and low décolletages. Maybe that's why the Velvet Revolution caught on: it had the whiff of sex. (Some marketing whiz is bound to come along soon with a *Prague Velvet* product, perhaps a brand of slivovitz, a perfume or a rock polka.)

The Gentle Revolution lost out to the velvet one because it did not sound macho enough; it was too wimpy. But calling it the Velvet Revolution misses the point of the events in Prague. Velvet's smoothness implies ease, a revolution that just glided effortlessly to success. Gentleness in a revolution is a different matter. It talks of humanity, restraint, civility and decency. And that is exactly what the Prague Revolution was about. That is what made it unique. That is what made it important.

Not once in Prague while the reign of despotism was falling apart did I see its rebelling subjects resort to violence. The only act of violence I heard of was the shattering of a few window panes at the home of a communist official in Slovakia. Nor were there any threats of violence. Not once, among all those chants and slogans at those mass demonstrations did I hear anyone yell, "Kill them!" Punish them, yes, but not hang them, beat them, throw them out of their homes, take it out on their kids, let them suffer as we did.

When Ladislav Adamec, the *fin de régime* communist prime minister, came to an opposition rally to ask the demonstrators to call off the general strike, half a million voices welcomed him with a chant of "Thank you, thank you." When he had had his say, when he had made his argument that the strike was no longer necessary because the government was listening to their demands, they booed him. But first they thanked him for bothering to come to talk to them.

When people fainted or had heart attacks in the crush of Wenceslas Square, the crowds, without anyone pushing or yelling or ordering people about, made way for the ambulances where there seemed no room to make way. No police, no parade marshals, just several hundred thousand people who apparently cared for their neighbors. Considering that it was a time of crisis and revolution, of excitement and passion, the Prague demonstrators were the most disciplined and gentle crowd I had ever seen.

It wasn't just form; there was also content. From Havel going out of his way to make room for *decent* communists in his Gentle Revolution to the musicians who had been banned and persecuted by the communists naming their first post-revolutionary concert "A Concert for Decent People," the Czechs put a much needed word back into the political lexicon: decency, ordinary human decency. Decency had for too long been missing from politics and diplomacy. Everyone was too busy chasing after higher, more important goals — progress, prosperity, peace, or just power — to pay attention to plain decency, that banal amalgam of common courtesy, compasssion and consideration for others, of moderation and generosity.

"The concepts of love, friendship, mercy, humility or forgiveness have lost their depths and dimension," Havel said after he was elected president of Czechoslovakia. "For many of us they represent only some sort of psychological curiosity or they appear as long-lost wanderers from faraway times, somewhat ludicrous in the era of computers and space ships." He was talking to his countrymen but what he said was equally applicable to much of the rest of the world.

It occurred to me in Prague that I had found a common thread to all the tragedies and calamities I had witnessed. From Hitler to Stalin. From Mao to the Shah and Khomeini. From the American misadventure in Vietnam to the generals in Argentina and the colonels in El Salvador. That common factor was the breakdown of decency. Once decency goes, the descent towards inhumanity begins.

Nazi Germany is a case in point. The debate about the guilt of Germans for Hitler's crimes usually revolves around the question of how much they knew about what was going on. Most of them may indeed not have known about the ovens of Auschwitz — or been able to do much about them even if they had wanted to — but they did know, and knew it right from the start, that Nazism was based on bullying and hate. If the Germans of the thirties had had any decency as a society, Hitler would never have come to power. It was the abandonment of common decencies that started the process that led to Auschwitz.

No one has been more prone to abandon standards of human decency than the utopians who set out to save humanity. The messianic goals of communism — the perfecting of human nature into a classless egalitarian society and the withering away of the state — got lost among the deadly indecencies of the dictatorship of the proletariat. Communism's dedication to the pursuit of indecent means killed its decent ends.

But even decent means can lead to indecent ends. Without decency, that most decent form of government, democracy, becomes nothing more than a tyranny of the majority. The indecencies of democracies are not usually overt brutalities; they are most often the result of indifference, the turning of a blind eye to the exploitation of the powerless, the plight of the poor or the persecution of minorities.

There are those who argue that in politics, decency is just a palliative to relieve bourgeois guilt, and that in economics it is only an obstacle to market efficiency. Balderdash!

Decency is and has been a pragmatic tool of politics in all successful democracies. If it had not been for the decency factor built into liberal democracies and their free-market economies, the streets of western Europe and North America would long ago have been awash with crowds yelling "Down with capitalism."

The crowds that shouted "Down with communism" all over eastern Europe in 1989 did not yell "Up with capitalism." The Americans may proclaim that the events in eastern Europe signify the victory of their style of capitalism and of the American way of life, but the example the eastern Europeans were looking at with longing was not the American one. Their models were Sweden and Austria. Yes, they wanted the freedoms and the cornucopia of plenty that Americans enjoy. But they also wanted comprehensive social amenities: a universal health-care system, generous family allowances, guaranteed vacations, a widespread child daycare system and, above all, full employment. That's what the communists had promised to deliver and never did and, as everybody knew by now, never could. In short, the east Europeans wanted the western welfare state. If capitalism was the way to achieve it, so be it.

Not even the capitalist West is infatuated with the virtues of capitalism *per se* ; most people prefer to speak instead of the opportunities of free enterprise and the efficiency of free markets. Indeed, except for a few isolated hardy places such as Hong Kong, classic laissez-faire capitalism is almost as dead as communism. The mechanisms of the capitalist free market are still in place but they have been made palatable by being swathed in protective layers of decency, everything from child labor laws through controls of the excesses of the market to subsidies of communal needs. Even the private capital sector enjoys the protection of the welfare state through market regulation, tax breaks and outright subsidies.

The irony of the acceptance of the capitalist welfare state by so much of the communist world is that it comes at a time when the structure of welfare measures is under assault in the West. Welfare programs are widely seen as having grown to the point where they cost too much, drag down the economy and encourage sloth. There is nothing wrong, of course, with reform that cuts waste and excess. But what has been happening in many Western countries is that the cutbacks in welfare programs have hit hardest those who need them most. Programs that were designed for the decent purpose of reducing poverty have been turned into middle-class entitlements that cushion the comfortable.

The United States, in particular, has been guilty of cutting off those who need welfare services most while preserving and even expanding such middle-class support systems as social security. School lunch programs have been cut while that greatest of subsidies to the middle classes, the tax deductibility of home mortgage interest payments, has been left intact. Aid to poor pregnant women has been reduced while huge corporate farms are being subsidized. As a minority — and a largely non-voting one at that — the poor in America have become the victims of the middle-class majority's indifference. In the meantime, the share of the U.S. national income pie going to the richest one percent of Americans nearly doubled in the eighties. Soaking the rich has been replaced with socking it to the poor.

At a time when the failings of the welfare system are being blamed on the left, it is all but forgotten that it was originally a creation of the right. The father of compulsory, state-sponsored insurance for workers against sickness, accident and old age was none other than that great conservative, Otto von Bismarck, the Iron Chancellor of Germany's Second Reich. The old Prussian fox did it, of course, the better to ward off socialism. But Bismarckian Socialism, as it was sometimes facetiously called, managed to give industrial capitalism a human face. By imposing a measure of decency on dog-eat-dog nineteenth-century capitalism, Bismarck helped save the system from itself. Much of the rest of the industrialized Western world had to wait for another shock, the Great Depression of the 1930s, to implement the social insurance systems that gave workers the security to cope with the vagaries of free market economies. Thus the welfare state made the world safe for capitalism, and the efficiencies of capitalism, in turn, allowed the West to be able to afford the welfare state.

Now, a hundred years after Bismarck, liberal capitalism has triumphed. Bolstered by the stability and security provided by democracy and its safety net of welfare measures, it has given North America and western Europe forty years of almost uninterrupted expansion. Its conspicuous success in fostering the rise of an affluent consumer society became the measure of communism's failure and sounded its death knell. Communism, which conquered a hungry and war-weary Russia with Lenin's cry of "bread and peace," was defeated by a new hunger: for liberty, VCRs and jeans.

Now comes liberal democracy's real test. It must show that it is capable of doing more than just letting the people of the impoverished former communist empire eat cake. It must allow the decencies of pluralism, of government by consent, by laws, compromise and tolerance to flourish.

"History," someone once said, "is a nightmare from which I am trying to awake." Most of the history of this century certainly has been a nightmare. As the century closes, there are signs that the nightmare is receding. There are even voices in Washington and elsewhere that argue that history is finished, that liberal democracy coupled with enlightened capitalism is the ultimate winner in the ideological struggle of centuries, that, with communism and fascism vanquished, history will no longer be the succession of great upheavals it has always been but only a fine-tuning of the freedoms that mankind has already achieved. But I know that the storms of history are far from being finished with us yet. The clouds are already gathering.

December 14, 1989. For more than three weeks I have been immersed in the regeneration of Czechoslovakia, the rebirth of its freedom, the revival of its cultural heritage. But there is one part of that heritage — mine as well as Czechoslovakia's — that cannot be restored. It lies in what used to be the Old Jewish Town, whose synagogues and cemetery have been preserved as archaeological artifacts. This is my last day in Prague, and I have come to the cemetery to say goodbye to what is left of my roots.

The headstones here are more than just memorials to those whose names they carry; they are markers of a civilization that existed in these parts for more than a thousand years and is now all but gone. There were Jews in Bohemia when St. Wenceslas was spreading Christianity among his subjects early in the tenth century. Half a century ago, there were more than 300,000 of them in Czechoslovakia. Now only a mostly aging and dying handful is left.

Because for centuries Jews could not be buried anywhere else in Prague, they were buried here, one generation on top of the other, it is said twelve layers deep, until now the graveyard sits high above street level with the gravestones of successive generations floating on top like bottles bobbing on the sea carrying messages from some long-ago shipwrecked tribe of Robinson Crusoes. The stones stand as jumbled as history, some inclined towards each other as if engaged in eternal conversation, others so tilted they look as though they might keel over at any moment from the burdens of age and grief.

Here lie some of my ancestors, Lord knows how many. Over there is the grave of the celebrated Maharal of Prague, Rabbi Judah Loew. According to family accounts, the rabbi was one of my ancestors (my paternal grandmother was a Loew). Rabbi Loew (1512–1609) was known for all sorts of achievements — he was a mathematician and philosopher as well as a talmudist — but he became most famous for what he certainly was not, as the creator of the Prague Golem and hence a precursor of Frankenstein and modern robot makers. In Jewish folklore, a *golem* was a figure of clay or wood that a *ba'al shem*, a Master of the Name of the mystic Kaballah, brought to life by putting into its mouth a paper bearing the magical transcription of God's secret name. We all have our *golems*, mythical figures that make the hardships and disappointments of life easier to bear, whether they be part of our daydreams that bring us what we cannot have, or leprechauns who will lead us to a pot of gold, or Robin Hood exacting revenge for injustice. While clay-footed *golems* could hardly have competed in spriteliness with elves, they do seem to have been more useful. There are light-hearted medieval stories about *golems* being created merely to be servants for busy rabbis. But the

Prague Golem was created for a more serious purpose. Rabbi Loew, according to the legend, created his *golem* to protect the people of the Prague ghetto.

The late sixteenth century was a dangerous time in Central Europe. Protestants were fighting Catholics for control of Bohemia, and the embattled Catholic rulers were more inclined than ever to vent their wrath on the Jews. So a supernatural creature of great strength stepping in where God was loath to act would have been a welcome relief to ease the pain of helplessness. Indeed, the Prague Golem's strength is supposed to have discouraged potential attackers. But then something went wrong. According to the story, one Friday afternoon Rabbi Loew forgot to retrieve the magic piece of paper from the *golem*'s mouth as he usually did every week so that the creature could rest on the Sabbath. The next day the *golem* ran amok. By the time Rabbi Loew was called from the synagogue, the *golem* had done much damage and injury. At first, the rabbi apparently tried to pacify it. But when it defied him and started to roar, Loew reached into its open mouth and plucked out the magic chit. The *golem* collapsed instantly, shattering into small pieces.

Quite a few people still come to Rabbi Loew's grave. You can tell by the stones that Jews lay on graves as Christians put flowers on theirs. There's a pile of pebbles on top of the rabbi's headstone and little stones lying in small piles all around the grave. With so few Jews left here, most of the stones must have been deposited by people like me who came from afar, who returned to this place to remember what was and to mourn what came to pass.

For me, this graveyard — not accursed Auschwitz, nor Bratislava where just about everything Jewish was razed — will always be my parents' resting place. This is as close as I will ever get to their graves. This earth that was once flesh is all that remains here of the community from which I came; the rest, the survivors like me, are mostly to be found everywhere but here. This graveyard is the only thing in this country that will be mine forever. The rest of the city, the country, the people, the language, the poetry and music that still resound in my ears, will always be dear to me but they are no longer mine. My roots are too many and too tangled; they feel more at home in the looser multicultural soil of Canada.

When my father said goodbye to his sons nearly fifty years ago, he asked the Almighty to let them grow up to be just and decent men. I would hope that he would not have been too disappointed with us now. But I also know that the justness and decency of individuals, as important as they are, are not enough. To be able to live just and decent lives, men and women need just and decent societies. The evils of a cruelly unjust and obscenely indecent society killed my parents. These same evils killed millions of others and poisoned the lives of many millions more then, before and since.

But half a century after these evils drove me out, I was back to witness virtue and truth prevail in Prague. Not absolutely perhaps. Certainly not forever. But freedom is back, and justness and decency are getting a new chance in central Europe and elsewhere. In Prague, people no longer need *golems* to ease the despair of helplessness. Nor do I, nor mine.

INDEX

ABC (American Broadcasting
  Company), 204, 245
Abe (chief, Associated Press,
  Prague), 88, 91
Adamec, Ladislav, 321
Adenauer, Konrad, 260
Aguilares (El Salvador), 257
Alfonsín, Raul, 299-300
Alvarado, Pedro de, 275
An Loc (Vietnam), 158-59, 168-75
Apopa (El Salvador), 279
AP (Associated Press), xi, 88-93,
  196
Archer, Bill, 122-23
Arendt, Hannah, 58
Argentina, 12, 287-302
Argüello family, 269
Arroux, Gerard see Hébert, Gerard
ARVN (Army of the Republic of
  Vietnam), 164-69
Asaf (room-mate, Prague), 95-96
Auschwitz, ix, 46-50, 53-57, 109,
  322
Austria, 94, 98-99, 323

Baeyer, Adolf von, 275
Bakhtiar, Shahpour, 241
Barrera, Ernesto, 257-58
Barricada (Nicaragua), 268

Barrio Norte, 288, 295
Barrios family, 269
Bazargan, Prime Minister Mehdi,
  242, 245
BBC (British Broadcasting
  Corporation), vii-viii, 39
Begin, Menachem, 151
Beheshti-e Zahra, 252
Beijing see Peking
Benes, President Eduard, 10, 75,
  84-85
Beran, Archbishop Josef, 89
Bergen-Belsen, 54
Berlin (Germany), 317-19
Berlin Wall, 306-307
Berton, Pierre, 12, 121, 124
Beveridge, Sir William, 40
Bhutto, Zulfikar Ali, 25
Bien Hoa (Vietnam), 172
Bignone, General Reynaldo, 301
Birney, Earle, 121
Bismarck, Otto von, 324
Blake, Martin, 17-18
Boaco (Nicaragua), 266
"Body, the Thing and Reality in
  Contemporary Art, The", 109
Bohemia, 78, 326
Book of Laughter and Forgetting,
  The, 156

Boyd, Bill, 125
Bradley, General Omar, 63
Bratislava (Slovakia), 3-5, 70-73, 310, 313
Brezhnev, Leonid, 151, 208
British Columbia, 116-124
British Committee for Refugees from Czechoslovakia, 18, 20-21
Brno (Moravia), 313
Buchwald, Art, 129
Buenos Aires, xii, 12, 287, 290-92
Busch, Wilhelm, 9

Calero, Adolofo, 11
Calley, Lieutenant William, 185
Cambodia, 143-45, 166-67, 180
Capone, Al, 109
Carney, Pat, 121
Carter, President Jimmy, 147, 151, 242, 243
Casa Rosada (Pink House), 290, 298-99
Cat in the Hat, The, 8
CBC (Canadian Broadcasting Corporation), 131-32, 147, 153, 195, 202-204
National, The, 132
TV News, 132, 153
CBS (Columbia Broadcasting System), 202-205
Ceausescu, Nicolae, 216-17, 224
César, Alfredo, 269
České Velenice (Bohemia), 96-97
Chadwick, Trevor, 18-23
Chalatenango (El Salvador), 134
Chamberlain, Neville, 6, 11-12, 30
Chamorro, Carlos Fernando, 268
Chamorro, Claudia, 269
Chamorro, Cristina, 268-69
Chamorro, Pedro Joaquín, 270
Chamorro, Pedro Joaquín, widow of, 270
Chamorro, Violeta Barrios de, 267, 268-70, 282-85
Chamorro, Xavier, 268

Chatangsey, Colonel Norodom, 143-44
Chávez y Gonzalez, Archbishop Luis, 255-57
Checkpoint Charlie (Berlin), 317
Chiang Ching, 221
China, xiii, 193-226
China Travel Agency, 196
Chontales (Nicaragua), 266
Chou En-lai, 151, 200-202, 204-205, 209, 216-17
Churchill, Winston, 40
Cobra, 157
Collins, Ralph, 210
Cologne (Germany), 50
Comenius, Jan Amos, 304, 314
Communist Manifesto, The, 182
Costa Rica, 263
Cristiani, Alfredo, 285-86
Cronkite, Walter, 204
ČTK (Czechoslovak news agency), 88
Cuadra family, 269
Cunningham, Bill, 161
Czechoslovak Communist Party, 99
Czechoslovak State School in Britain, 34-42
Czechoslovakia, x-xi, 5-7, 10-14, 16, 99-115, 303-305, 325-28

Dacca (East Pakistan), 25-27
Daladier, Edouard, 6
Dasht-e Kavir (Great Salt desert), 228
d'Aubuisson, Roberto, 271-77, 280, 285
al-Daylami, Mihyar, xiv
de Beauvoir, Simone, 126
de Gaulle, Charles, 74, 125, 151
Deng Xiaoping, 151, 208, 220-26
DePoe, Norman, 121
d'Estaing, Valéry Giscard, 151
Dick (Associated Press, Prague), 91
Dien Bien Phu, 181

Dientsbier, Jiří, 105
Dixon, Don, 147
Djilas, Milovan, 208
Dönitz, Grand Admiral Karl, 62
Downes, Fred, 184
Duarte family, 288
Duarte, José Napoléon, 135, 259-
    60, 272-74, 280
Dubček, Alexander, 82-83, 100,
    105, 107, 310, 313, 316
Dumond, Michel, 168, 170, 312

Eichmann, Adolf, 58
Eisenhower, General Dwight, viii,
    62
El Limon (Nicaragua), 265
El Nuevo Diario (Nicaragua), 268
El Robledal (Nicaragua), 266-68
El Salvador, 59-60, 133-41, 152,
    254-80, 285-86
Erdozain, Father Placido, 257
Escobar, Estela, 59-60
Escobar, Ricardo, 59-60
Estelí (City) (Nicaragua), 266
Estete, Martin, 275
Eugénie, Empress, 177
Evin prison (Teheran), 239

Falkland Islands, xii, 296-99, 302
Fanling, 203
Farah Diba, Empress of Iran, 156,
    233
Fleet Street, 128
Flynn, Errol, 160
Flynn, Sean, 160-61, 174
Fonda, Jane, 186
Ford, President Gerald, 151
Forster, E.M., 191
Fotheringham, Allan, 122

Galeano, Alcide, 266
Galeano, Oscar Danilo, 266

Galtieri, President Leopoldo, 298,
    299
Gandhi, Indira, 151
Garay, Amado Antonio, 272
Gateshead-on-Tyne, 31-33
Gayn, Mark, 196
Germany, 306-307, 317-19, 324
Ghadaffi, Colonel Muhammar,
    189
Ghotbzadeh, Sadegh, 147, 239
Gmünd (Austria), 96, 98
Gomulka, Wladyslav, 86
Gonzalez, Felipe, 290
Good Soldier Švejk, The, xiv
Gorbachev, Mikhail, xii, 11, 101,
    150, 151
Great Britain, xii, 11-12
Great Wall of China, 204-205
Greene, Graham, 160
Grenada (West Indies), 188
Grey, Anthony, 194
Guarjila (El Salvador), 133-41
Guevara, Nacha, 301

Haggart, Ron, 121, 124
Haig, General Alexander, 12
Hájek, Jiří, 104-107, 313
Hanna (cousin), 54-55
Harvey (Associated Press, Prague),
    91
Hašek, Jaroslav, xiv
Havel, Václav, 105-106, 113, 309,
    313-16, 320-22
Hébert, Gerard, 158-78
Helena (girlfriend, Prague), 96-99
Henlein, Konrad, 11-12
Herald, L' (Paris), 129
Himmler, Heinrich, 53
Hinton Hall, 34
Hitler, Adolf, viii-ix, 2, 5-7, 14, 16,
    57, 322
Hlinka, Andrej, 6
Hlinka Guard, 6
Hlohovec (Slovakia), 44-45, 72-73

Ho Chi Minh, 181-83
Ho Chi Minh City *see* Saigon
Honduras, 134-35, 265
Hong Kong, 153, 194-96, 202-204, 214-17, 323
Hong Kong Foreign Correspondents' Club, 194
Hosking, Brian, 158, 166-67, 170, 174, 211
Hsinhua (New China News Agency), 195-96
Huey helicopter, 157-58
Hungary, 307
Husák, Gustav, 107, 111
Hussein, Imam, 235
Hussein, Saddam, 246
Hutchinson, Helen, 122

Indochina, 171
International Herald Tribune (Paris), 92, 126, 129-30
Iran, 155-56, 189, 227-53
Iranian TV, 147, 245
Iraq, 230, 236, 246
Islas Malvinas *see* Falkland Islands

Jakeš, Miloš, 111, 309-310, 315-16
Jaleh Square (Teheran), 228, 230
Japan, 306
Jaruzelski, General Wojciech, 107-108
Jazz, 108
Jazz Section, 105, 108-110
Jazzpetit, 108
Jennings, Peter, 245
John Paul II, Pope, xii, 47-50, 151
Johnson, President Lyndon Baines, 177
Juneau (Alaska), 117

Kafka, Franz, xv
Karel, Dr., 78

Karnow, Stan, 183
Kennedy, President John F., 188-89
Kennedy, Senator Ted, 147
Ketichikan (British Columbia), 117
Khan, President Yahya, 25
Khomeini, Ayatollah, 151, 156, 187, 189, 229-31, 234-52
Kissinger, Henry, 201-202, 205
Kitimat (British Columbia), 117
Kladno (Czechslovakia), 310-12
Klímová, Rita, 106-107
Klondike, 117
Kohl, Helmut, 151
Kolakowski, Leszek, 107
Kolbe, Father Maximilian, 46-49
Komárek, Valtr, 112-13
Konev, Soviet Marshal Ivan, 63
Koppel, Ted, 245
Kowloon, 196-97, 215
Kubišová, Marta, 304-305
Kundera, Milan, 156
Kuron, Jacek, 107
Kwangdong (China), 198

La Prensa (Nicaragua), 268-69
La Recoleta, 287-88
La Rinconada (Nicaragua), 267-68
Lacayo, Antonio, 269
Lacaya family, 269
Lanzmann, Claude, 56
Lebanon, 188-89
Lee Kuan Yew, 215
Lenin, 182
Letná (Prague), 316
Levi, Primo, 48, 58
Li (guide), 206
Libya, 189
Life with a Star, 44
Lindbergh, Charles, 186-87
Little Red Book of the Helmsman's Thoughts, Quotations from Chairman Mao Tse-tung, 199, 213-14

Liu Binyan, 223
Liu Shaochi, President, 208, 220
Llanwrtyd Wells (Wales), 35
Lobositz (Czechoslovakia), 23-24
Loc Ninh (Vietnam), 168
Loew, Rabbi Judah, 326-27
London Daily Express, 39
London Daily Telegraph, 39
London (England), 128-29
Louis, Joe, 5
Lowu Station, 197, 203
Lublin (Poland), ix, 46
Lydia (Associated Press, Prague), 93

M*A*S*H, 190
Macao, 194, 196
Mahmoudabad (Iran), 155-56
Malvinas *see* Falkland Islands
Malý, Václav, 105-107, 113
Managua (Nicaragua), 261-64, 266
Mao Tse-tung, x-xi, 134, 151, 193, 199-202, 207-209, 211, 218-19, 221, 250-51
Marco Polo Club, 195
Marti, Augustin Farabundo, 276
Martinez, General Maximiliano Hernández, 276
Masaryk, Jan, 80
Masaryk, Tomáš, 42, 310
Masaya (Nicaragua), 281, 283
Massu, General Jacques, 168
Matagalpa (Nicaragua), 264
Mawhinney, Barry, 106-107
Max und Moritz, 9
Mencius, 225-26
Menem, Carlos Saul, 300
Metropolitan Cathedral of San Salvador, 255
Michnik, Adam, 107
Mindszenty, Jozsef Cardinal, 88
Minimal + Earth + Concept Art, 109
Mitterand, François, 151, 305
Molina, Colonel Arturo, 257

Moravia, 110
Mowat, Farley, 154
Muller, Filip, 53-57
Mulroney, Brian, 151
Munich, 6-7, 12-14, 16
"Music of the Terezín Ghetto, The", 109
Mussolini, Benito, 290
My Lai (Vietnam), 185

Naipaul, V.S., 301-302
Najaf (Iraq), 230
Najibullah, 11
Napoleon III, 177
NBC (National Broadcasting Company), 196, 202-204
Neauphle-le-Château (France), 235, 238-39
New China News Agency (Hsinhua), 195-96
New York Herald Tribune see International Herald Tribune
New York Times, 129-30
New Yorker, 92
Ngo Dinh Diem, 181-82
Nicaragua, 188, 258-70, 278
Nicholas II, Czar, 224
Nicol, Eric, 121
Niquinohomo (Nicaragua), 259
Nixon, President Richard, 151, 201, 205
Nol, Marshal Lon, 143-44
Noriega, General Manuel, 189
Nüremberg (Germany), 57

OAS (Secret Army Organization), 125
Oatis, William, 89-90
Opletal, Jan, 307-308
Ormesby (England), 33
Ortega, Daniel, 262, 266, 269, 270, 281-85
Ortega, Humberto, 284
Orwell, George, 139

Oswiecim *see* Auschwitz
Owens, Jesse, 5

Pahlavi, Shah Mohammed Reza,
    155-56, 224, 228-34, 237-40
Pakistan, 25-27
Palermo Chico, 288
Panama, 189
Panama City, 289
Pankrác (Prague), 99-100
Paris (France), 124-31, 153
Parrot's Beak (Cambodia), 161
Passage to India, 191
Patton, General George, 62-63
Pavel the Smuggler, 96-97
Peking, 193-94, 199-200, 205, 210,
    214, 217-18, 223-26
Peking International Table Tennis
    Tournament, 196-97
Pepík (nephew of Antonin
    Rakous), 67-70
Perón, Eva Duarte de, 287, 298,
    301
Perón, Isabelita, 289
Perón, Juan, 288-89, 293, 296,
    298, 301
Persian Gulf, 189
Peru, 217
Petržalka (Czechoslovakia), 94
Pham Van Dong, Prime Minister,
    183
Plastic People of the Universe,
    108-109
Port Stanley (Falkland Islands),
    297, 299
Powell, General Colin, 189
Prague, xiii, 17-24, 51-52, 61-70,
    80-82, 87-88, 99-115, 303-305,
    307-309, 312-15, 320, 325-28
    Autumn (1989), 305
    Old Customs House, 59
    Selection, 108-109
    Spring (1968), 82-83, 100, 105,
        107-108, 305, 310, 313
    Uprising, 63, 74

Priestley, J.B., 40-41
Prince George, SS, 116, 119-20
Prince Rupert (British Columbia),
    117
Proof of Identity, 110

Qom (Iran), 230, 242-43
Quiet American, The, 160

Radio-Canada, 165
Rahman, Sheik Mujibur, 25, 27
Raj Quartet, The, 191
Rajk, Laszlo, 86
Rakouš, Major Antonín, 61-70,
    73-75, 77, 80, 82-83
Rakouš, Dalibor, 64, 80-83
Rakouš, Dalibor, Jr., 83
Rakouš, Darča, 64
Rakouš, Manuela, 80-83
Reagan, President Ronald, 134,
    137-38, 150-51, 186, 188-89,
    243, 260, 270
Regalado, Hector Antonio, 272
Reuters, 194
Reynolds, Jack, 196, 202
Rich, John, 196
Roderick, John, 196
Roethke, Theodore, viii
Romero, Archbishop Oscar
    Arnulfo, 256-58, 271-73, 277,
    286
Roosevelt, President Franklin, 268
Ross, Sandy, 122
Rudé Pravo, 77
Runciman, Lord, 11-12
Rushdie, Salman, xiii, 247

Sábato, Ernesto, 298
Sadat, Anwar, 151
Sadr, Abolhassan Bani, 245
Saigon (Vietnam), 140, 157, 159,
    161-62, 164, 176, 179
San Miguel province, 273

San Salvador, 134, 140, 254-57, 262, 279

San Sebastián, 259

Sandino, Augusto, 259

Saraiva, Alvaro, 272

Sartre, Jean-Paul, 126-27

Satanic Verses, The, 247

Saudi Arabia, 251

Schlesinger, Alfredo (Honduran journalist), 275

Schlesinger, Ann (daughter), 131

Schlesinger, Emmanuel (father), 1-5, 9-10, 13, 23-24, 27, 42-45, 54-55, 58-59

Schlesinger, Ernie (brother), 1, 8, 16, 23, 27, 31, 35-42, 50-52, 64, 70-72, 80, 87-88

Schlesinger, Joseph, 210-14, 247

Schlesinger, Léah (daughter), 130-31

Schlesinger, Lilli (mother), 9-10, 24, 42-45, 54-55, 58-59

Schlesinger, Mike (wife), 129-31, 194

Schmeling, Max, 5

Schmidt, Helmut, 151

Scott, Paul, 191

Sears, Val, 121

Sebaco (Nicaragua), 264-65

Silesia, 78

Service, Robert, 117

Seuss, Dr., 8

Shah of Iran *see* Pahlavi, Shah Mohammed Reza

Shanghai (China), 217

Shansi province (China), 210-14

Shariat-Madari, Ayatollah Kazem, 230, 245

Shoa, 56

Shuan Wang Agricultural Commune, 210-14

Sihanouk, Prince Norodom, 143

Singapore, 214, 216

Sitka (British Columbia), 117-18

Skagway (Alaska), 117

Slanský, Rudolf, xi

Slovakia, 320

Snow, Edgar, 201

Somoza, Anastasio, 269

Somoza, Anastasio, Jr., 270

Soviet Union, 306-307

Sowerby (England), 33

Spirit of St. Louis, 187

Srp, Karel, 105-109, 113

Stalin, Joseph, x-xi, 77, 79-80, 86, 93-94, 250

Štěpán, Miroslav, 99-101, 111-13, 316

Stone, Dana, 161

Struwwelpeter, Der, 8

Sunday News of the World (London), 40

Sweden, 323

Swedish Red Cross, 19-20

Syrový, General Jan, 10

Tabas (Iran), 228-29

Taiwan, 214-16

Taylor, Ken, 147, 246

Teatro Colón (Buenos Aires), 291, 297

Teheran (Iran), 15-16, 147, 155-56, 186, 227, 231-35

Teng Bufang, 220, 222

Teng Hsiaoping *see* Deng Xiaoping

Thatcher, Margaret, 151

Theresienstadt (Bohemia), 109-110

Thesis on the National and Colonial Question, 182

Tiananmen Square, xiii, 141, 201, 218-19, 221-26

Time magazine, 92

Tiso, Monsignor Jozef, 16

Toronto Globe and Mail, 194

Toronto Star, 123-24, 131-32, 196

Toronto Telegram, 123

Trudeau, Margaret, 220

Trudeau, Pierre, 151, 220

Tsinghua University, 218

Tu Doc, 177

Turner, John, 121

Tyneside, 40-41

Ubaldini, Saul, 291, 300
Ubyssey, 121-22, 128
United States, 11, 242-44, 260,
  265, 269-72, 280, 323-24
University of British Columbia,
  120-22
UPI (United Press International),
  128-29, 159-60, 175
Úprka, Joza, 70, 73
Usulutan (El Salvador), 257

Vancouver, 116, 119-24
Vancouver News Herald, 122
Vancouver Province, 122-24
Vancouver Sun, 122
Vaněk, Ferdinand, 106
Vatican, 251
Vienna, 94, 98-99
Vietnam, 134, 144, 157-91

Waldheim, Kurt, 58

Walesa, Lech, 107, 313
Walls, Derek, 206
Wang Weilin, 223-26
Warriner, Doreen, 18, 20
Warsaw (Poland), 50
Washington, D.C., 146-47, 153
Weil, Jiří, 44
Wenceslas Square (Prague), 304-
  305, 307-310, 313, 315-17, 321
Westmoreland, General William,
  168, 183
White, Bob (cameraman), 196
White, Robert (U.S. Ambassador),
  272
Whitney, Jock, 129
Wiesel, Ely, 58
Wiesenthal, Simon, 58
Winton, Nicholas, 16-23, 29
Wojtyla, Karol *see* John Paul II
Wong Tai Sin, 215

Yazdi, Ibrahim, 239, 245
Yazid, Caliph, 235, 247
Yenan (China), 211